THE LAST
TORPEDO FLYERS

THE LAST
TORPEDO FLYERS

The True Story of Arthur Aldridge –
Hero of the Skies

Arthur Aldridge
with Mark Ryan

**SIMON &
SCHUSTER**

London · New York · Sydney · Toronto · New Delhi

A CBS COMPANY

First published in Great Britain by Simon & Schuster UK Ltd, 2013
This paperback edition published in 2014
A CBS COMPANY

1 3 5 7 9 10 8 6 4 2

Simon & Schuster UK Ltd
1st Floor
222 Gray's Inn Road
London WC1X 8HB

www.simonandschuster.co.uk

Simon & Schuster Australia, Sydney
Simon & Schuster India, New Delhi

A CIP catalogue record for this book
is available from the British Library.

PB 978-1-47110-276-9
Ebook: 978-1-47110-277-6

Typeset in Bembo by M Rules
Printed and bound by CPI Group (UK) Ltd, Croydon, CR0 4YY

Dedicated to the lost torpedo airmen

What would I say to those who claim we were only one step short of the kamikaze? Looking back I'd say they're absolutely right! To fly a Beaufort low through a barrage of thick flak and continue undaunted towards a giant enemy ship took a man with nerves of steel and great courage. Such a man was Arthur Aldridge. He inspired great confidence in the capable crews of 217 Squadron as he successfully attacked German and Italian shipping. His bravery was twice recognised when he was awarded the Distinguished Flying Cross and Bar. Perhaps an even greater reward in the long run was the knowledge that he'd helped to win the war and therefore enable countless men and women to resume the peaceful way of life he cherished.

Bill Carroll (gunner on Aldridge's crew
during World War Two), June 2012

Only the names of those who had to come off flying due to the strain and horror of war have been changed. None will receive condemnation or judgement here. If the names adopted to protect their identity bear any resemblance to real names of RAF personnel past or present, it is purely coincidental.

Apart from those name changes, every effort has been made to recount accurately the true story of my experiences and those of my gunner, Bill Carroll, during World War Two.

As I write this in the summer of 2012, Bill and I are still alive, having enjoyed seventy years more life than we could reasonably have expected.

Arthur Aldridge, summer 2012

Contents

Prologue

Thin grey slivers on the horizon, they look so harmless, but I know what they are.

'Look ahead!'

If the others haven't spotted them yet, they will now.

Grey turns to silver in the bright sunlight, and we make out the three enemy ships we've been searching for – two merchant vessels and a destroyer. They're hugging the Tunisian coast, just as we thought. They're out to supply Rommel with arms and precious fuel in order to defeat our army in the desert. We're going to do everything we can to stop them.

It's 21 June, 1942, and I'm flying a Bristol Beaufort – one of nine to have taken off from what's left of Malta an hour earlier. Each Beaufort carries a torpedo and we know the lethal routine. Pick a ship and fly towards it at fifty feet above the waves. When we think we're about a thousand yards away, rise to between sixty and eighty feet to drop the torpedo. As the 'torp' swaps air for sea and swims beneath the surface towards the monster's hull, get out of there. Sounds simple enough.

We near the African coast by Cape Bon in perfect visibility, and we know they must be able to see us, too. That means they're going to be ready. The destroyer will do everything it can to protect the merchantmen carrying the war materials. The two vessels, one German and the other Italian, will unleash their own firepower. No time to dwell on such things. This is it.

Squadron Leader Robert Lynn, a big, cheerful Scot from Inverness, is our leader for this strike. We're in three 'vics', a formation each made up of three aircraft, and I'm leading the second vic. Lynn waggles his wings to signal that he's about to attack. Sergeant Bill Carroll, my gunner, has always seen this as a clear and unnecessary invitation to the enemy to start shooting. The Axis ships accept the invitation.

When Lynn's vic of three planes turns in towards the targets, he's already facing heavy 37 mm flak. Behind them I'm turning into position, too, ready to spearhead the second wave. My focus is broken by Bill Carroll's yell from the turret at the back.

'Get up, pilot! Aircraft to starboard! Pull up!'

Instinctively I pull back on the control column and a plane from Lynn's vic invades our space from nowhere. It's suddenly changed course and slides under us, through a narrow space between my Beaufort's tail and the waves below. We very nearly collide. It's all over in an instant. Unbelievable!

I try to grasp what's just happened. The Beaufort appeared from somewhere over on the starboard side, so it must have been flown by Sergeant Smyth, who was just behind the port wingtip of Squadron Leader Lynn. So Lynn must have suddenly changed direction for some reason, and Smyth was forced to veer just as violently. Now there's a domino effect. The other planes in my vic lurch as they're forced to react to my own evasive action.

There's mayhem and we haven't even begun the attack yet.

This isn't going well. While my Beaufort still holds its own in the air, others are in a frantic battle to avoid the sea. Squadron Leader Lynn has taken a shell right up through his seat while turning, and he's been killed instantly. That's been the catalyst for some of the wild flying we've already seen. Sergeant 'Dick' Dickinson, Lynn's navigator, is trying to keep their aircraft in the air; but he has to get Lynn's body out of the way before he can work the controls. Squadron Leader Lynn is a well-built fellow and his body won't be shifted easily. A third crew member tries to help Dickinson, and they're just starting to haul Lynn out of the way when they lose control of the aircraft completely and smack into the drink. An instant before their aircraft hits the sea, the torpedo separates, rebounds off the surface, and smashes through the wing of Smyth's Beaufort, bringing it down as well. The other plane in the vic, piloted by Flying Officer Phillips, is hit by flak and forced into the waves, too. That wipes out the leading trio before they can land a single blow on the enemy.

Now it's our turn to face the storm. All three ships are firing at us, the destroyer the most deadly. I'm going to aim for the supply ship behind it. The wall of black and grey flak is terribly dense, the worst I've ever seen. There's not a word from my crew. As I fly at the wall, I feel something new, a feeling deep in the pit of my stomach, making me queasy. It's fear. And who wouldn't be scared, faced with this flak? There's no let-up, it's truly awful. On we go towards this welcome. I don't have time to realise these are probably the final moments of my life. I feel the horror of it, that's all. That feeling in the bottom of my stomach is telling me that the next few seconds are not going to be very nice.

From Hammond to Hitler

I was staggered by their sheer beauty. Not the distant North Downs with their chalky paths, where I'd happily cycled for miles; or the huge Kent skies bathed in late summer sunlight. These just formed the backdrop to the drama on the grassy stage in front of us. What had me transfixed were the shots I saw pouring from a bat there; cover drives so effortlessly powerful they could only have been the creations of a sporting poet.

This was the second week of September, 1933 – and the leading performer at Cheriton Road, Folkestone, was an English cricketer called Wally Hammond. A few months earlier, following the famous Bodyline Series between England and Australia, Hammond had scored a record 336 not out against the New Zealanders – beating the Australian Donald Bradman's previous landmark by two runs.

Even before I witnessed his magic, I knew Wally was still in good nick. The English summer season was drawing to a close, but Wally was making hay while the sun shone. A week earlier he'd scored 133 against the West Indies. In doing so, he'd passed 3,000 runs for the season and 28,000 in his career in first-class cricket. No wonder another legendary player, the Yorkshire and

England opener Len Hutton, described Hammond as 'the most perfect batsman I've ever seen'.

We might have known Wally would repeat that sort of form for The South against the Marylebone Cricket Club (MCC) – that's what heroes do. Sure enough, I watched mesmerised as Hammond amassed 184 runs – a fantastic ton carved so stylishly that I still remembered it more than three-quarters of a century later.

My mother was sitting there with me at Folkestone and, even though she didn't know anything about cricket, she was impressed by the way Hammond placed his shots. An MCC fielder would be moved to where the last shot had gone, and Hammond would respond by driving his four through the area where the fielder had been only moments earlier!

We didn't cheer – one didn't in those days. But I was a thirteen-year-old in raptures, and I clapped as loudly as I dared. After The South declared on 462–7, a wonderful local bowler called 'Tich' Freeman took 8–22, skittling out the MCC for 55. I couldn't have been happier, and I knew I'd seen something special. Strange to think that five years earlier I wouldn't even have known what cricket was, let alone enjoyed it as much as I did that day in Folkestone.

My life began on 23 August, 1920 – a long time ago, I must admit. Though I'm British and proud of it, I was born in a villa on a picturesque hillside near Florence, Italy. My father, Harold, was a clergyman. He'd been a British Army Chaplain during the First World War and was posted to the front on Italy's border with Austria. The British and Italians had been on the same side back then, before the rise of the dreadful dictator, Benito Mussolini. My father had stayed in Italy after the war, allowing him to maintain some of his family ties. One of his Christian names was

Gualtiero – Italian for Walter. His mother was half-Italian, which makes me an eighth Italian. I always tell my Italian friends that it's my best eighth – '*Il mio ottavo migliore.*' I was named Arthur after a great-uncle and Harold after my father. My mother Melita was British, yet her name means 'Malta'. She was from a naval family and, though I never asked her, I think she must have been born on the island of Malta to be given that name.

I was an only child, which may have made me a little more self-contained than other children but I wasn't lonely because that first spacious home, the Villa Bruno in the village of Girone, always seemed to be full of relatives – and I even spoke Italian with them. The Villa Bruno overlooked a sweeping bend in the River Arno, and I was lucky to spend my early childhood in such a beautiful place. While my first five years were spent there, the next four were passed in the clean, cool air of the French part of Switzerland. We moved to ease the lung trouble my father had developed and it seemed to work. I have memories of beautifully clear Swiss lakes and a new language to learn. French came quite easily to me; when you're very young it isn't hard to pick up a language. One of my biggest passions from that time on was languages – I love speaking different languages and learning all about them.

When we moved to England, I was nine and I picked up a smattering of this third language, and somehow I retained that smattering for the rest of my days! In reality, of course, I'd long been familiar with English, my parents' language, and I was overwhelmingly English by blood. It was just the country I didn't know too well. All that changed when my father was asked to become the vicar of West Malling, a pretty village in his home county of Kent, south-eastern England.

Some people said the First World War had been won on the

playing fields of Eton. I don't know about the Second World War, but sport certainly played a big part in my life and in the lives of many RAF pilots as they were growing up. When I came to England and was enrolled at St Lawrence College in Ramsgate, there were plenty of new sports to come to terms with.

St Lawrence was actually one of the best-known schools in the country for hockey – not that I was any good at it. I preferred rugger, which my father also liked. We were more like pals than father and son. My father was one of the nicest people I've ever met, and we certainly shared a love for sport. During a holiday to the Scilly Isles, for example, we ran all the way back from the bakers flinging a loaf of bread to each other like a rugby ball.

Cricket became king, though. If only I'd had as much talent as I had love for cricket, I might have played for England; but I wasn't much good. One of my best cricketing achievements was to score an unbeaten 11 runs. It doesn't sound much, but my job was to stay in and support the batsman at the other end, so that he didn't run out of partners. He was our star – he made over 50. I just blocked everything and held on. You could say that was an early example of the stubborn fighting spirit I'd need later – or cite that innings as further evidence of my limitations exposed!

During the 1930s, if the Ashes were being played in Australia, my father and I would rush down early in the morning together, turn on the wireless and listen for the latest developments on the other side of the world. We'd hear the voice of Alan Kippax, the Australian opening batsman who was dropped after the First Test of the controversial Bodyline Series of 1932–33.

'He's too bloody fast for me,' Kippax was reported to have said, having been unnerved by some rib-denting deliveries from the famous Nottinghamshire pace bowler, Harold Larwood. Kippax became pretty good on the wireless, though – and he didn't swear once. 'I'm afraid I've got bad news for you in England,' he'd say with thinly disguised satisfaction if our batting had collapsed and it looked as though Australia were winning. I don't know why I remember that in particular, because it was England who won that Bodyline Series, not Australia – much to the fury of those who thought our bowlers were taking more pleasure in hurting the Australians than knocking down their wickets.

Wally Hammond, who'd played his part in the victory Down Under, wasn't the only legend I was lucky enough to observe in person. At the Folkestone Festival the following year, I saw the most famous Australian of them all, Donald Bradman. My father and I watched him make a century for the tourists against an England XI. It was nearly perfect, because almost every shot was struck low through the outfield. The only exception before he reached three figures was a six he dispatched from the bowling of my hero, Hammond; and that was a rare example of Bradman breaking his own rule: 'If you don't hit the ball in the air, you can't get caught,' he always said. Nowadays a lot of batsmen try to hit the ball over the top from the start but Bradman usually waited until he'd carved out a century with controlled mastery, and only then would he cut loose. Tich Freeman came on to bowl at the wrong time in Folkestone that day. A leg-spinner, Freeman wasn't short of quality. He'd taken 304 wickets in a single season back in 1928 – a feat never equalled before or since – and he still made a habit of taking more than 200 wickets each summer. As he began his over, just a few moments after Bradman had made his ton, it became clear the batsman had no respect for these statistics. Bradman went half-way down the wicket and began to hit Freeman's considered deliveries with such disdain, so hard and so far, that neither my father nor I thought he could possibly keep it up. To our astonishment, he did – 4, 6, 6, 4, 6, 4. We'd never seen anyone score 30 runs in an over before, and Bradman had certainly never done this in England. He finished on 149 not out – quite a performance.

Even though the clinical Bradman was immaculate, I still preferred Hammond. His batting was even more stylish, especially his wonderful off-drives. He was famous for them, steering the ball away so nonchalantly off the front foot. He could bowl if it took his fancy, too, and he was such a brilliant slip fielder that people used to say if a bird flew past, he'd be fast enough to grab it with one hand. If I had two boyhood heroes, Hammond was definitely one of them. The other was Beethoven.

I thought Beethoven was the greatest man who ever lived – still do. A combination of colossal genius and good character defines the greatest man, at least in my view. He was undoubtedly a genius and, although his character was a little rough round the edges, his letters show that he gave his money to others, even when he was living in poverty himself. I believe this puts him above any other genius you might care to think of.

The unmistakeable sound of a Mozart piano concerto flowing out of our wireless in West Malling made me fall in love with classical music as a teenager. And, before long, I adored Beethoven, Mozart and Schubert – in that order. It didn't take me long to come to the conclusion that there are no great British composers, so my musical tastes were less than patriotic. And it was worse than that – Beethoven was German and Mozart was Austrian, just like Hitler, the new German leader. Oh dear! The Bosch, the Hun, the awful Germans! They'd committed the most appalling atrocities in Belgium during the First World War, gassing innocent civilians, and that generation weren't even Nazis, the type of Germans who'd begun to cause concern around Europe more recently. It must be the German character, we decided; deep down they just couldn't be very nice people. And yet their country and neighbouring Austria had produced such wonderful composers.

This was confusing to a boy in his late teens, so I was glad to be given the chance to experience Germans and Germany for myself. Perhaps that way I could make sense of it all. My love for languages took me on an exchange trip in 1938. I was going to stay with a couple in Frankfurt, while their son would stay with my parents in Kent. But as my train crossed over into Germany, I suddenly got a terrible feeling of claustrophobia. The railway platforms were filled with Nazis in uniform. You could see swastikas everywhere. The atmosphere was suffocating, restrictive. It felt like walking into a sort of prison; it was painful. This was the complete opposite of the feeling my favourite composers gave me – they made my spirit soar. It was just as well they weren't trying to compose in the 1930s. How could any artistic individual thrive anywhere near Nazi Germany? These Nazis were not the sort of people who'd created my beloved German and Austrian music. They were up to something far more sinister; so unimaginable, as it turned out, that even those most threatened would struggle to grasp what was starting to happen.

'Take a look at this,' said Herr Külenthal, my genial host in Frankfurt. He showed me a letter he'd received, signed by Hitler. Herr Külenthal had retired by now, but he'd been a Rear Admiral in the First World War, so Hitler had written: 'Because of your service in the war, you will be safe. But I cannot vouch for your wife or give her any similar guarantee.'

Herr and Frau Külenthal, you see, were Jewish. The letter

seemed ridiculous to me. This man had served Germany in the Great War, just as Hitler had done. And now his reward was to have his wife threatened because they were Jewish? What on earth did Hitler have in mind for the Jews, anyway? It was hard to fathom.

Even after receiving that letter, the Külenthals still couldn't believe it was Hitler himself who felt that way. They were convinced his cronies must have been behind it all. As we know now, Hitler hated the Jews more than anyone else but, when you were there, it all seemed too extraordinary to be true.

As for me, I just felt a mounting discomfort; and I was fast coming to the conclusion that Germans were people to avoid. Of course I liked the Külenthals; they didn't seem to fit into any of this. Perhaps that was why they were in such danger. Whatever Herr Külenthal thought was coming, he wasn't taking any chances. Whenever we had any conversations about Hitler, he'd take the phone off the hook, as if someone might be listening through the phone when the receiver was down, and somehow overhear our conversation. It seemed rather a desperate measure, bordering on paranoia but, as that old saying goes, just because someone is acting paranoid doesn't mean people aren't out to get them.

They took me into the Hauptfriedhof, the city's main cemetery, so we could walk among its beautiful flowers and trees. Looking back, the irony becomes obvious, for such places would swell with fresh bodies before long. But Herr Külenthal was a man who appreciated the natural beauty of his surroundings and he took me out for even longer walks in the Taunus Mountains above Frankfurt. One good thing about the Germans, they like trees and they preserve their forests. And when we got back from our walks, Frau Külenthal would be waiting to welcome us. I had a wonderful time with this charming couple, who didn't deserve to be threatened or unsettled by their fellow countrymen.

Yet you couldn't stay in Germany even for a few weeks without becoming caught up in the rising tension. We had to go to a parade in honour of a local Nazi while I was there; we had no choice. During the parade, everyone had to give the Hitler salute, stretching their right arm out straight, their hand flat, their fingers stiff and pointing diagonally upwards. Even I gave the salute. I didn't want to. I'd have liked to refuse on principle, based on what I'd seen and heard about the Nazis so far. In fact, I was going to refuse, but then something inside told me that I had to do it, like it or not. I had two German Jews with me, after all, and it would have been irresponsible not to salute. I couldn't risk bringing unwanted attention to my hosts on a selfish point of principle. Some snitch could have spotted my refusal and told any number of Nazi party members mingling with the crowd. So I gave the Nazi salute, and I don't regret it as such but I remembered how wrong it felt to be forced to behave in a way I didn't want to behave.

It wasn't just the Jews and various Germany minority groups who were starting to feel intimidated, though. This National Socialist movement didn't seem to want to confine itself to the borders of its own country. It was 1938 and the writing was on the wall. Could the rest of Europe do anything about the Nazis? The aggressive nature of Germany's foreign policy meant the major European powers couldn't ignore the situation any longer. My parents were worried stiff because they knew I was in Germany, and a high-level conference was about to be held in Munich. No one seemed too sure what position Britain would take, or how Hitler might react if he didn't like it. As it was, there was no need for my parents to worry for the moment. No one was going to stand up to Hitler, and this would later cause misery for millions, the British among them.

In 1938, Europe's major players felt Hitler had to be appeased. If the Nazis weren't handled very carefully, some warned, the consequences could be catastrophic. So the Munich Agreement, signed on the night of 29 September, allowed Hitler to annex the Sudetenland. This was an important strip of land which had belonged to Czechoslovakia and contained many of that country's strategic defences. Czechoslovakia wasn't going to sign away the Sudetenland, but the major powers simply ignored their rights and signed the Munich Agreement anyway. Germany, Italy, Britain and France were all there, sitting around a table and smiling at each other – but crucially the Czechs weren't. With some justification, they called it the Munich Dictat.

Neville Chamberlain returned to England triumphant, waving a piece of paper and announcing that he had secured 'peace in our time'. Anthony Eden had already resigned in protest at Chamberlain's policy of appeasement. Almost a year after the Munich Agreement, on 1 September, 1939, Hitler made a mockery of that scrap of paper and invaded Poland. A couple of days later, back in West Malling, I told my father and mother that I wasn't going to church with them because an important announcement was expected on the wireless. I stayed at home and listened, fearing the worst. Sure enough, it fell to Chamberlain to tell the British people he'd received no undertaking from Herr Hitler to withdraw from Poland. Therefore we were at war with Germany. What a fool he must have felt!

What was this going to mean for my own future? I couldn't help but wonder what on earth would happen to my good friends the Kűlenthals in Germany, too. Would Herr Kűlenthal die trying to save his wife? Would they get out or find a way to survive inside Germany? It would be seven years before I found out.

In the meantime, despite all the difficulties, the trip to Germany had done nothing to dampen my passion for foreign languages, and I'd performed well enough in my school exams to win a place at Oxford University to study French and German. I went up in October 1939 and settled into my college, St Edmund Hall – 'Teddy Hall' as we called it.

Teddy Hall had one of the oldest foundations in Oxford, a small college with a beautiful inner quad, full of very friendly people and wonderful staff. You could punt on the river if you wanted a change of scenery, a pastime which brought me perfect peace. I liked to ease my way out on to the River Cherwell alone. You could take a punt from Magdalene Bridge and glide silently down narrow, tree-lined tributaries, which were sometimes little more than streams draped in the lazy branches of weeping willows. Then you could make your way out on to the wider waterway to enjoy the sun and splendour of it all. And I loved reading all the French and German literature for my course, too. I remember picking up a copy of Molière's *Le Bourgeois Gentilhomme*, and just laughing out loud. 'Wow, this is real comedy, not like the so-called comedies of Shakespeare,' I thought. I was roaring my head off – until I realised I was supposed to be studying quietly in the reading room. Let's face it, Shakespeare's comedies are not very funny at all, apart from *Twelfth Night*. But Molière? I loved him.

What I most enjoyed was just being at Oxford University, surrounded by some of the most interesting and intelligent people in the world, finding my feet away from my parents. I'd just turned nineteen, I was happy, and everything would have been perfect – had Britain not gone to war with Germany. We all knew deep down there'd be dark times ahead. At Oxford we 'freshers' enjoyed the place while we could, but monitored events in the wider world to see how they would unfold.

What Britain needed was strong leadership, and we were lucky. We had a wonderful king on the throne by then. King George VI didn't want to be king. The awful Edward VIII, who was a Nazi sympathiser, let his country down in order to stay with his lover Mrs Simpson, who was also a Nazi sympathiser. They were absolute traitors who cared only about themselves. He was a dead loss even before he abdicated, and she was dreadful. Pro-Nazi, the pair of them, can you imagine?

So George VI had ascended to the throne and won everyone's respect with a wonderful speech that Christmas of 1939, calling on the nation to find strength and have faith at such a testing time. The most memorable line was, 'Put your hand into the hand of God.' It was inspirational, even to someone like me, who wasn't religious. I realised I'd be prepared to die for George VI; 'For King and Country', as we used to say. I wouldn't have died for the other one. If Edward VIII had been on the throne, I'd have fought for country, but not for king. George VI, on the other hand, made it feel good to be British. So I decided that, sooner or later, I would indeed fight.

We were very lucky to have Winston Churchill, too. He was an incredible inspiration to me. He knew Hitler had to be put in his place, and I totally shared his belief that it was about time someone did something about the 'Nazzzis', as Churchill called them, using a soft 'Z'. He didn't pronounce the word like everyone else – 'Natzi'. Churchill's 'Nazzzi' was so much more disdainful. He didn't want to pronounce correctly the name that Hitler's band of thugs had adopted, because he knew Hitler didn't deserve that kind of respect. So Churchill made me want to fight the Nazzzis, too.

I suppose I could have been a spy, with my knowledge of languages, but I didn't think of that. I certainly could have continued with my studies, because there was no pressure on me to volunteer to fight. It was the first week of May, and I hadn't yet completed my first year. Earlier in that spring of 1940 the Germans had invaded Denmark and Norway; and now our neighbours France were about to be overrun. If we didn't do something, Britain would be next to fall; there was no time to waste.

I knew what I had to do and I didn't feel any need to talk it through with my parents. Everything suddenly seemed clear, my mind was made up. It wasn't a difficult decision, except that I ran into some unexpected resistance from the university. The Principal of St Edmund Hall wasn't too pleased when he heard about my plan to volunteer for war. His name was Alfred Brotherston Emden, and his initials formed his nickname – The ABE. He didn't approve of my timing.

'I'm joining the RAF,' I confirmed, when ushered into his spacious office, surrounded by books.

'You should finish your course,' he told me, a little irritated.

'I'll try to finish it afterwards,' I insisted gently.

The ABE seemed appalled because I hadn't even finished my first year. But I wasn't going to sit there and complete a course while the war raged. Deep down The ABE probably understood, because I later heard he'd seen service as an Able Seaman in the First World War. He even ended up becoming head of Oxford University's Naval Division during this war. Perhaps he'd been trying to protect my best interests; but it wasn't going to work.

On 7 May, I went to the local recruiting office in Oxford. No way was I ever going to join the army, not after all the square-bashing they'd made me do in the Combined Cadet Force at St Lawrence College – those dreaded marching drills on the parade ground. Of course, drills were part of early life in other branches of the services, too, as I'd find out, but I'd always associated end-less drills with the army, and wanted to avoid them if I could.

Unfortunately I had to tell a whopping great lie in that Oxford recruiting office, because I'd failed to anticipate the most obvious question imaginable.

'Why do you want to join the RAF?'

'Why, sir?'

'Yes. Why?'

Damn. Why hadn't I thought about 'why'? It was such an obvious question! I couldn't admit that I had no good reason.

'I've always wanted to fly aeroplanes.'

Where did that come from? This was the first time I'd ever thought about flying aeroplanes – the first time it had ever crossed my mind! In fact, just as I'd gone in, I'd seen the navy recruitment officer out of the corner of my eye and wondered whether that might be a very good alternative to the RAF. I'd only thought better of it because I knew I'd probably be sea-sick. And suddenly here I am, telling this RAF officer it's been a life-long ambition to be part of his gang!

Anyhow, I'm slightly ashamed to admit it, but this policy of dishonesty worked, because they agreed to have me. I was nine-teen years and eight months old. And I agreed to be paid a sum of two shillings per day to be an aircraftsman. There was one problem: this was all subject to passing a medical and I thought I might be colour-blind.

I went straight down to Uxbridge for the medical, secretly rather worried. My father was colour-blind, and I was afraid it might be hereditary. That would have ended any hope of becoming a pilot. It felt like they were on to me straight away. They gave me a sheet with all sorts of colours, and there was a figure or letter within all that. If you couldn't see the figure, you were colour-blind. But I could see it, thank God – and that meant I wasn't! Much to my relief, I was able to continue with the process of joining the RAF ... except that there was no more process for the time being; that was it.

Having volunteered and enlisted in early May, I thought I would be called straight up. In fact, I wasn't called up until 1 July – an extraordinary delay given the urgency of Britain's situation. Of course, it was perfect timing from The ABE's point of view, because I was able to go back to Oxford and finish my first year of studies. It was pretty convenient from my point of view, too. If by any chance I survived the entire war, I could come back and finish my degree by starting my second year a little late – as long as Oxford wasn't being run by the Nazzzis.

I was determined to see that it wasn't. By then, though, the war was taking a serious turn. British forces had to be rescued from the beaches of Dunkirk, leaving many comrades, weapons and supplies stranded in France. There was a real threat of invasion, though Churchill wasn't going to stand for that. I remember the speech he made on 4 June, 1940:

We shall fight in France, we shall fight in the seas and the oceans, we shall fight with growing confidence and strength in the air; we shall defend our island whatever the cost may be. We shall fight on the beaches, we shall fight on the landing grounds, we shall fight in the fields and in the streets, we shall fight in the hills; we shall never surrender.

A total inspiration. Fantastic. That speech of his made quite an impact on me.

My university year finished in mid-June, so I went home to West Malling, scanning the skies for the dogfights above Kent as the Luftwaffe tried to establish aerial superiority. That's when I finally told my parents I'd joined up. They took in the news without protest or anger. They could see what was happening in the skies above them as well as anyone else. They understood this was no time for faint hearts. In fact, my father looked quietly pleased when he heard what I'd done.

'If only I can get in the RAF before a bomb drops on me,' I told my mother to lighten the mood. In truth, Churchill had put so much fire in my belly that I was prepared to go out on the road from the coast up to Maidstone, and stop the German tanks with my bare hands, if I had to. Teenage testosterone plus Churchill; that was quite a combination!

It might have taken bare hands, too, after all that equipment was left in Dunkirk. It was horrendous, but also amazing how many little ships rallied, and unbelievable how many soldiers were taken off the beaches and back to safety – including the French, of course. There was no doubt we were going to be up against it, though. And before I was called up, I remember receiving some extra attention from the local tennis crowd at a party they threw. The get-together wasn't in my honour; we were always having tennis parties at West Malling. But they seemed to realise that, by joining the RAF, I'd done something which meant my life would be on the line sooner or later. Not that anyone dwelt on such matters or even put these thoughts into words. We were young and we just wanted to have a good time. These parties were always fun and tennis was a sport I was good at, so I was in demand. But I always made sure I had the same partner, a very nice girl called Sally Gray. I had a very good forehand but my backhand was pathetic by comparison. So, as a right-hander, I made sure Sally was on my left during rallies, and that way she could take my backhands for me, on her forehand. We struck up an excellent understanding, though I never felt romantic towards her. My mother seemed keener on my behalf than I was myself. In fact, I think she wanted me to marry Sally. I was fond of her, she was a very nice girl, but this wasn't the right moment to start a relationship. The war was on, and even Sally joined the WAAF in the end.

I went from Uxbridge to Torquay on 1 July, 1940, where I joined Reserve Number 54 Group. The Sergeant Major in Torquay was a bit of a tyrant and he made us do plenty of square-bashing. He would treat us like scum if we got it wrong; and every so often he'd march up and down the line, staring us in the face. If he caught us looking back, he'd bark at the top of his voice: 'Don't look at me – I'm shy!' Though I'd been put off the idea of joining the army precisely because I anticipated such ritual humiliation, I actually enjoyed the drills – especially the slow-marching. It was rather fun having to stop the swing of your leg as it passed your standing leg, then let it continue again. Still, I wasn't sorry when the square-bashing was over.

Oddly our next stop was Cambridge University. I was billeted at Trinity Hall. 'How strange,' I thought. 'I've given up my course at Oxford to fight a war, and all I've done is go straight from Oxford to Cambridge.' Having taken a look round, I came to a swift conclusion: 'This university's old – I'll give it that much but it isn't a patch on Oxford.' The ABE would probably have liked that. But I didn't like being stuck in Cambridge as the Battle of Britain raged in the skies above my Kent home that July.

The initiation course in Cambridge was long and totally unnecessary. We had to study the history of the RAF and all that sort of nonsense. It was only twenty-two years old, so the history lesson should have been short. It wasn't. 'The Royal Air Force was founded on the first of April, 1918, when it was decided to merge the Royal Naval Air Service and the Royal Flying Corps . . .' That should have been the end of the lesson, shouldn't it?

Why did they think we'd be enthralled by irrelevant tales of how the RAF was structured between the two wars? It was a complete waste of time. All we wanted to do was get up in the sky to defend Britain against Hitler. Yet I don't even remember studying much about the theory of flying. We may have been told what gives lift to an aircraft – how the leading edge of each wing is rounded, the wing itself convex on top but flat underneath. The air passing over the rounded part will go faster than the air going underneath, which gives lift to the wings because there is less pressure above them than below. All very well, but we still didn't seem any closer to getting into the air ourselves.

The class did a lot of talking down on the banks of the River Cam. It was a pleasant enough way to spend the second half of a summer, but it delayed us getting on to a squadron. Even seventy years later, I still can't understand why they weren't in more of a hurry to teach us what we needed to fight the Germans. The Battle of Britain entered a make-or-break phase in late summer, 1940. What was I doing, while the fate of Britain hung in the balance? Nothing very useful.

Then something happened to shift that balance. When we bombed Berlin towards the end of August, I always thought we did so in order to impress the Americans. In fact, it had a much greater psychological effect on Hitler, because the Luftwaffe retaliated by turning their attention to London. In doing so, Commander-in-Chief Hermann Göring made a big mistake, because he eased up on Fighter Command and its air bases. That change in tactics came as a considerable relief to Fighter Command, since its pilots were on the point of complete exhaustion. So Göring unwittingly gave Fighter Command enough time to recover and rebuild – an error which eventually saved Britain.

I never did get the chance to become part of Fighter Command's regeneration, or fly a Spitfire. It was the one great regret of my life. The Spitfire was the most beautiful functional object ever created by humankind. I could look at a Spitfire for hours in silent admiration; it was such a sublime aircraft. How I'd have loved to fly one! We trainees all wanted to be fighter pilots. We didn't care about the dangers; or at least not enough to want to do something else. At the time, our common desire to fly a Spitfire was colossal, even if we invited death by fulfilling our ambition.

The life expectancy of fighter pilots at the height of the Battle of Britain was about two weeks. That's why fighter pilots were allowed to keep their top button undone, we heard. It was a concession from the authorities, a little perk, perhaps even a thank you, in return for facing probable death. A small reward, you might say, but it was something.

In September 1940, as the Battle of Britain reached its climax, I was sent to Watchfield Flying Training School on Oxfordshire's border with Wiltshire. It was a step in the right direction. The Battle of Britain may have been over before I learned to fly, but there would be other terrible moments to endure.

2

Mr Average and Mark Lee

The shouting. That's what I remember most about learning to fly – being shouted at. Constantly. About anything and every-thing.

'Turn! To starboard, man! Top rudder! I said top rudder! Keep the nose up! You're losing altitude! Haven't you even noticed! Right, do me a spin. Easy on the stick! What are you doing? Did I say control column forward? Why have you applied rudder?! Well now you've done it, level out! You came out of that spin too early! Why? What's the matter with you, man!'

It wasn't just me. Our instructor, Flying Officer Holland, shouted at everyone, apparently. But that didn't make it any easier to take.

Watchfield wasn't an enormous air base. Most of the recruits were about my age, nineteen or twenty. No one I knew on the course was married, and that was probably just as well. It had to be easier without a wife and children to worry about. If you had a family, you'd want to get the hell out of the place. Even if you were unmarried but a bit older, it might make you think twice – the first chap I shared a room with was twenty-eight or thirty and he didn't like flying very much.

I flew Avro Cadets during my initial training; they are bi-planes, rather like a Tiger Moth. When my first instructor, Flying Officer Wilson, took me up in the air I felt confident enough, mainly because he was doing the flying. I was there to gain famili-arity with the cockpit lay-out and get some air experience. 'Just take it all in, Aldridge.' Then it was on to Flight Lieutenant Abbot to see the effect of controls: 'See how it works, Aldridge? Joystick gently forward to descend, back again to climb; now you have a go.' Blimey, they're letting me fly a plane! The basic manoeuvres seemed logical enough: minor adjustments, main-tain straight and level flight.

Then came climbing, gliding and stalling. That's where the logic seemed to fly out of the window. I had to climb to a safe height and then deliberately stall. A lot of people think this involves doing something to make the engine cut out, but that's not it. The expression refers to a loss of lift from the wings, which can happen whatever the engine is doing. What you do is throttle back on the engine, allowing the speed to drop to a point where the wings stall and you start plummeting from very high up in the air – that creates a nervous moment or two. You recover by lowering the nose and increasing engine power. When you manage that, relief pours over you. Still alive, we pro-gressed to medium level turns. This was becoming fun. And then I got Holland.

He taught more medium turns, but this time it was accom-panied by his shouting; then on to taking off into wind and landing. Soon we came to spinning. At first, after about the third spin, I panicked and got out early. Holland was apoplectic with rage. Then I became a little braver. Spin to the left, spin to the right – I loved the spinning. To get out of a spin you put your stick forward first, then you apply rudder. What fun! But there was something I liked even more – side-slipping. Bank to starboard, apply top rudder. Down we go diagonally! You lose height without gaining any speed. That feels wonderful.

In spite of the incessant shouting from Holland, I learned to do these things in my Avro Cadet, and even enjoyed what I was doing. That's what made me think I might become good at flying. If you're not good at it, you don't enjoy it, but I was really enjoying it. More spinning followed, and steep turns. I also had to do a thing called rate-four turns, using plenty of top rudder. If you do a very steep turn you tend to lose height, unless you've got lots of top rudder to keep your nose up. I did loops, which were fun. I didn't feel a thrill as such; I don't like that word, because it's a cheap word and suggests wild emotion – the last thing you need when you're training. What I felt was satisfaction – pleasure and satisfaction. It was the sense of being able to handle a machine; the delight of working well with it. Did I feel at one with the aircraft? Of course not. I'm a human being and it's a machine. Forget the clichés.

I didn't have any difficulties, except with Holland. He shouted and shouted, then he shouted some more. It didn't help me learn to fly, I can assure you. But you couldn't tell him to stop. I couldn't have talked to an officer like that, so I just took it. If I said anything in reply to his barking, I still called him 'sir'. With Holland I also learned a gliding approach – also called 'dead stick' – when you make an approach with no engines running and land that way. I'd done about eight hours flying when it was time to go solo.

That first time flying solo in my Avro Cadet, I wasn't nervous at all. I thought: 'Thank God, I've got a bit of peace. I'm on my own.' I was so thankful not to have Holland hollering in my ear that I had a lovely time. In fact, the feeling of flying through the sky on my own was one of the most wonderful sensations of my entire life. It was a pleasure to be able to fly properly, to be in sole control of the aircraft and do what you wanted to do. I felt the rare satisfaction of it all, and savoured the relief of not being shouted at.

Just because you go solo doesn't mean you never take any more instruction, though. So I had to brace myself for more of Holland's wrath. But something very strange happened: once I'd gone solo, he stopped shouting. We did further cross-country flights together and acrobatics, and still he didn't shout. In fact, he never shouted at me again. It was tempting to ask him why he'd shouted so much in the first place, but I never did. He'd stopped and that's all that mattered. Perhaps he thought a pilot had earned his basic respect once he'd gone solo, I don't know. We were great pals after that and, when it came to map reading, he taught me a simple but very important lesson. You read from the map to the ground. You don't look at the ground and find things and then look at the map; you follow it on the map and then look at the ground to see if you can recognise anything. That's the secret.

The Battle of Britain was effectively won on 15 September, when at least fifty German aircraft were shot down. That was the crucial day. Churchill had made another famous speech, his tribute to the RAF. 'Never has so much been owed by so many to so few.' And thanks to the Spitfire and Hurricane pilots, I was able to continue to learn to fly. At about this time I was moved to RAF College Cranwell in Lincolnshire, and I soon realised how lucky I was to be there.

During initial training, there'd been times when we were treated like the lowest of the low. When we reached Cranwell, however, a chap asked me: 'May I carry your bag, sir?' I couldn't believe it! Cranwell was big, the top place for training, the best FTS (Flying Training School) there was and we were treated as potential officers, rather like the army cadets who go to Sandhurst. We had a white flash in the peak of our caps, to show that we were officer cadets, and we were treated with respect.

Some of the people I'd trained with initially didn't end up at Cranwell, and they were less fortunate. Officer cadets weren't treated with the same respect at other training stations, such as Shawbury, for example. If you weren't careful, you'd find your-self belittled as we were by that 'shy' sergeant major on the parade ground in Torquay. Fortunately, Cranwell was different; we were treated like ordinary regulars, training to be pilots – and the food was excellent, too!

Up in the air there were new challenges. Whereas I'd flown biplanes previously, I was now taught how to fly two-engine monoplanes, such as Airspeed Oxfords. I didn't find converting a problem, the principles were the same. I loved flying and that was enough for me. When I was back on the ground I looked forward to the next flight. I didn't feel the need to go out to the local pubs and socialise in any big way; I just stayed on the air-field. I wasn't the only one who liked a quieter life. A fellow cadet called Mark Lee also seemed more self-contained than the rest. He loved poetry and he had a marvellous collection of clas-sical music – not that he could take it all to Cranwell. Given my own love for literature and classical music, I suppose we were bound to get on. When we weren't flying, we would talk about what works of art had captured our imaginations most.

Mark had his own preferences of course, but he could under-stand my passion for Beethoven. The more we got to know each other, the more I liked him. I felt relaxed in his company, you didn't have to try to impress him; and, like me, he didn't feel the need to be too boisterous. The others probably thought we were a bit quiet, but we understood each other just fine. We liked our own company and when it suited us we liked each other's company, too. That's not to say we didn't mix with the others at the appropriate times. Mark was the sort of person who didn't have an enemy in the world – except the Nazis. People liked him and he made friends effortlessly. In fact, someone later said of him that he couldn't help making friends wherever he went, which was a nice way to sum him up.

Mark had been a wonderful cricketer at school in Leicestershire, and an even better hockey player at Cambridge University. He didn't go around boasting about it, though. In fact, I didn't even know until much later, because that's how modest he was. Had Mark wanted to be boastful, he could have pointed to Bryanston, his public school, where he was the first boy to get his colours for cricket, hockey, rugger and athletics. Then he'd won a place to read English at Cambridge University, and was tipped for a Hockey Blue before his student days were interrupted by war.

As had happened in my case, Mark felt that his country needed him more than his university. The RAF beckoned and Cambridge could wait. There were more important things than studies and sport – such as defending the freedom of loved ones, and the way of life we held so dear. We had a bit in common, he and I; and, if necessary, we were ready to sacrifice everything to make sure the right side won the war.

To fight Hitler we had to learn to fly, and now we were well on our way. In fact, I felt the flying course couldn't have been going better – until the day I got a red endorsement in my logbook. I suppose it was deserved, though even seventy years later it still annoys me! I thought I'd done all the necessary pre-flight checks on 12 October, 1940. I'd made sure the Pitot head cover was off, so that we'd be able to measure air speed once we were in the air; I'd checked the controls were working; and I assumed the ground crew had checked everything else worth checking. That was my mistake.

When I took off, I had a co-pupil with me as well as the instructor. If my co-pupil had been flying the plane, he'd have been the one to receive the red endorsement in his log-book. But he wasn't, so the checks were my responsibility. Frost had been left on the leading edges of the wings; the ground crew hadn't remembered to wipe it away, and because we felt dependent on them in so many ways, I'd just assumed they'd be thorough in this area, too. They weren't – proving that we all make mistakes; but the presence of that frost meant the air-flow over the wings was broken and we didn't have the necessary lift when we took off. Within a few seconds we stalled, and the plane plonked itself back on to the airfield with a thud. None of us was injured by the heavy, unexpected landing; but I was to blame. It had never occurred to me to check the wings for frost because the ground crew should have done it for me; but it was the last time I didn't double-check. The buck stopped with me and next time we might not be so lucky.

Luckily the price paid for learning that lesson wasn't as great as it might have been; and we all lived to fight another day. But seventy years later the incriminating evidence is still in my log-book, written almost unintelligibly in bright red ink. The instructor who made the damning entry was Group Captain Lilihead, or at least that's what I think he was called. I can't quite read the signature in my log-book, because his writing was shoddier than my flying. You can just about make out his censorious, spidery scrawl, though:

'Carelessness in failing to comply with instructions in flight order book regarding hoar frost.'

(They'd given us a book so that we could read up on all the instructions in our own time. I'd read it six months earlier, so long before I'd forgotten most of the contents.)

'Needs to exercise more care in airmanship on the ground.'

In that same month of October, Cranwell described my proficiency as a pilot as 'average'. Most people were rated as average; it was the standard assessment. Yet I felt I was actually above average, so it was frustrating that I'd suffered this little set-back, partly due to bad luck. I had to take it on the chin, but I was still determined to see 'above average' written in that log-book one day.

It wasn't going to happen any time soon, though, because my high opinion of my flying took another knock quite quickly. This time I got lost, which wasn't as hard to do as you might think. There were two airfields at Cranwell, separated by a lot of buildings. On one notorious occasion a pilot took off from one Cranwell airfield, landed at the other, and asked where he was – not realising he was still at Cranwell! I didn't quite suffer that degree of humiliation, though what happened to me was embarrassing enough.

We were in a nearby, subsidiary airfield, which was only used for night flying. We did some of that and stayed overnight; and then in the morning my instructor pointed to our Airspeed Oxford and said, 'Take her back to Cranwell on your own – it's only over there.' I took off alone, flew back towards Cranwell as instructed . . . and completely missed the place. There was dense fog; it was one of those days when you could see something directly below you, but nothing in front, behind, or on either side. I certainly couldn't see Cranwell, and I got completely lost as I went round and round in the hope of stumbling upon our base. In those conditions, I could have been about a hundred yards from Cranwell and still not seen it. As it turned out, I was miles away.

Cranwell is in Lincolnshire and at one stage I thought I saw the tall communication masts of Droitwich in Worcestershire. I thought, 'Blimey! This is getting really worrying.' I'd reached a state bordering on panic. All I could do was fly back in what I hoped was the right direction. It was an awful feeling. Eventually I knew I had to land somewhere or my fuel would run out, so I selected a field. There were some wires there, but I managed to miss them. I managed an adequate landing, the field was quite smooth, and fortunately I didn't do any damage to either me or the plane. I found a telephone box and rang up Cranwell, only to discover that I was actually quite near, not that it seemed to matter any more. One of the instructors came and fetched me back in a car. Someone else coaxed the plane into taking off from that field – but I was no longer there to witness it.

No one was angry with me, so I could afford to smile about my little difficulty on that occasion. But a lot of trainee pilots died in accidents during the war. Not as many as pilots on real operations, but a high number all the same. Flying low over land, you could bump into things – telegraph wires and the like. Having begun night flying, I could see how one mistake could be fatal.

I didn't just fly Airspeed Oxfords at Cranwell; there were Ansons to master as well. I found it difficult to land an Anson because of its low stalling speed. Ansons always seemed determined to stay in the air for ever, clinging to flight until the last possible second, when all you wanted them to do was give up and touch down. But overall I felt I'd handled the challenges of learning to fly better than most, and I was becoming a good pilot. 'Good' wasn't a word the RAF was keen to use in my case, though, and when I left Cranwell for the last time to go home that Christmas, one word apparently summed me up, and that word was still 'average'. Overall assessment: 'Average'. Pilot: 'Average'. Navigator: 'Average'.

Instead of giving me the chance to improve as a pilot, at the beginning of 1941 the RAF decided to work on my navigating. 'I'm a pilot, not a navigator,' I thought. Sometimes I couldn't help but think that the more training I did, the less relevant it was. This time just to reach the scene of that training involved great danger. It was the height of the Battle of the Atlantic, which was infested with German U-boats, and yet they wanted us to sail from Oban in Scotland to Canada, to go back to school. Many convoys were sunk trying to cross that same sea, and we could have been, too.

Luckily we were able to run the gauntlet successfully, and I reached my new base – at a place called Charlottetown on Prince Edward Island – in one piece. Charlottetown is regarded as Canada's birthplace. It's where they first discussed the possibility of forming a confederation. I liked the town and surrounding countryside immediately. Situated off Canada's east coast, not that far from Halifax, Prince Edward Island seemed at peace with itself and covered in natural beauty. 'This scenery's magnificent!' I told locals enthusiastically. 'You should be here in the spring!' they replied. I was – and beyond – because the navigation course was so long.

We plotted our courses on charts in our huts, then put those calculations into practice by climbing into planes and telling a pilot where to fly. What they continued to overlook was the fact that I wasn't going to be a navigator when I went to war – I was going to be a pilot. And if my navigator got hit by flak and became incapacitated, do you think I'd have time to fly the plane and do complicated navigational calculations about ground speed and course? Of course not! You can't work out velocities while you're flying an aircraft. Therefore you can't navigate while you're flying. So what was the purpose of all this? We simply didn't know. Back on the ground, we also practised Morse code with an Aldis lamp and on buzzers. I learned to receive six words a minute, each word being five letters. Again, this was a complete waste of time, a skill I never needed in the war, because I had a wireless operator to do the Morse code for me.

Still, they must have had their reasons for teaching us all this stuff. And since we were there, we thought we might as well learn what we could, and enjoy Canada while we were at it. I remember lovely crisp mornings, when you'd go out in a big overcoat and still feel small against the enormity of Canadian nature. Along with some others, Mark Lee and I went out exploring our little part of the vast expanse that is Canada. We forged a strong bond of friendship out there. I enjoyed photography and took pictures of the beautiful landscape, the cloud-shrouded mountains, the snow-laden trees and frozen lakes.

What a contrast we found when we returned exhausted to our barracks. Each room was very basic, with one bed against one wall and another against the wall opposite. I was sharing with a pilot called Norton, who was pleasant enough, though time could pass painfully slowly if you weren't careful. Mark Lee was in another room with a pilot I remember only by his first name, Bill. This chap was always sketching with a pencil. Ask him about drawing technique and he'd talk about his 'common sense' method. Then he'd happily show you simple ways to achieve perspective.

I was passionately fond of art but that didn't mean I was any good at it – despite Bill's best efforts to help me. And music would always remain my greatest passion. I suspect it was the same for Mark, which is probably why he was wearing such a broad grin when he popped his head round our door one day.

'Come into our room, if you like,' Mark said. 'We're putting something on.'

'A sketching master-class from Bill?' I asked.

'No, I've got rather a lovely recording of Rimsky-Korsakov's "Scheherazade",' Mark replied, and waited for our reaction. My face must have lit up as much as Norton's.

'We'll be right there,' we said simultaneously.

I don't know how Mark had got hold of the record, but I knew it was going to be special. The 'Scheherazade' was inspired by the Arabian Nights, and tells the story of a Sultan's wife who tries to improve his mood with her colourful stories. You find the colour in the orchestration, and her spirit, in the melodies. We listened to this rare, tuneful treat in happy silence. 'Scheherazade' reminded us of the beauty human beings were capable of creating. I don't see why anyone should be considered soft, just because they love music or art. Take me as proof that you can love music and art, go to war, do your bit, see terrible things, and still love music and art when you return ... if you return.

We didn't know it yet, but we were going to be put in situations where you could be pretty sure you weren't going to return at all. And on the other side of the Atlantic, the supreme demonstration of what might be required of us in war was about to take place in the port of Brest, in north-western France. Two German battlecruisers called the *Scharnhorst* and the *Gneisenau* had made Brest their base for forays into the Atlantic. Churchill was concerned that Britain's war effort might crumble if we couldn't protect our supply lines from America. He considered this struggle to be one of the most important of the war.

Even before the Kriegsmarine's formidable ships had been spotted at Brest, Churchill had warned gravely: 'If the presence of enemy battle cruisers is confirmed then every effort by the navy and the air force should be made to destroy them and for this purpose serious risks and sacrifices should be made.' At all costs, therefore, the *Gneisenau* and the *Scharnhorst* had to be disabled or destroyed before any more British ships were sunk.

Bomber Command and Coastal Command had both pounded Brest harbour from late March to early April, 1941. Though they didn't hit either ship, an unexploded bomb wedged itself into the dry dock next to the *Gneisenau*, causing a fierce debate among the Germans about how best to protect their prize asset. One mistake while trying to move or defuse the bomb might result in serious damage to the ship. Better, perhaps, to move the ship instead.

So the *Gneisenau* was moved out from dry dock into well-defended water, a quay in the inner harbour, Rade Abri. But it only took the British hours to discover the new position of the *Gneisenau*, thanks to the keen eye of a Spitfire pilot on a photo reconnaissance sortie. There was a clear window of opportunity for British pilots to pierce German defences and use that water to their advantage by dropping torpedoes at the *Gneisenau*. The Bristol Beaufort planes would have to brave the deadly anti-aircraft batteries at Brest for long enough to drop a torpedo. Pilots would have to run a terrible gauntlet from the mouth of the Channel, the Goulet de Brest, all the way into the port.

In the early hours of 6 April, chaos reigned even before the mission began. Of the six Bristol Beaufort aircraft which tried to take off, three found it impossible, due to the sheer weight of their 1,630 lb torpedoes. Of the three that did take off, only one found the target. That plane was piloted by Kenneth Campbell, who was just a few weeks short of his twenty-fourth birthday. We came from similar backgrounds. Whereas I'd been at Oxford, Campbell had studied at Cambridge. Like me, he'd trained at Cranwell. As I'd do later, he saw operational training on Beauforts at Chivenor in Devon, then torpedo training at Abbotsinch, just outside Glasgow. The path he took to war was essentially the path I'd later take, though mercifully I'd never have to go as far down Brest's estuary as he did.

Campbell stayed low as he flew down the estuary into Brest harbour. His arrival provoked a dreadful response from the three flak ships waiting there, and the gun emplacements all around the port. Blanking out the murderous fire, Campbell timed the release of his torpedo to perfection, so that it flew over the outer mole and into the comfort of the inner-harbour water. It swam true and exploded into the starboard side of the *Gneisenau*, blasting a hole nearly forty feet wide below the water line. The ship's starboard propeller was badly damaged.

Sadly Campbell didn't live to see the fruits of his labour. In my opinion, he'd been sent on a suicide mission, and he knew it. The hills behind Brest harbour were too high; he would never have got out, even if he hadn't been shot down. It was a one-way trip they sent him on. I remember staying with friends in Brittany after the war to survey the scene at Brest. There was only one possible conclusion. Campbell had no chance.

He won the Victoria Cross posthumously; and deservedly so. His navigator was only nineteen – a Canadian called James Phillip Scott. The other two crew members were Sergeant Ralph Walter Hillman, a Londoner, and Sergeant William Cecil Mullis, from Somerset. Their bravery was almost frightening, and Campbell had to sacrifice them all to get that ship. Although the *Gneisenau* wasn't fatally holed, she was put out of action for the best part of a year while they repaired her and then prepared her for a break-out. The *Scharnhorst* stayed with her, so for the rest of 1941 the risk to British convoys was substantially reduced. The presence below the waves of Germany's highly successful U-boat submarines hadn't gone away. But just when the battle to keep open the Atlantic supply lines had been right in the balance, Campbell had made a difference. Churchill had called for supreme sacrifice, and he'd been given just that. Many, many more would go the same way as Campbell and his crew.

Twin-engine Beauforts and Fairey Swordfish bi-planes were going to have to drop more torpedoes against impossible odds in similar feats of attempted giant-killing. In fact when word first reached the squadron I'd eventually join – 217 – of this development, one pilot is said to have burst into the officers' mess and announced: 'That madman Campbell has gone into Brest, torpedoed the *Gneisenau* and been blown out of the sky. Now they're going to expect all of us to do the same thing.' That pilot had reason to be worried. But in the spring of 1941, I was still oblivious to the near-suicidal work to which I'd be introduced later that same year. We were miles away in Canada, I was twenty years old, life was for living – and listening to the lively 'Scheherazade' was sheer bliss.

Rink, Bismarck and Beaufort

You know that rather tricky stage in any learning process, when you think you're becoming so good at something that you start to feel gloriously confident, when in fact you're not yet quite good enough to justify that confidence?

The scars still visible on my forehead in old age were sustained at just such a stage during the war, though not while I was learning to be a pilot or even a navigator. When people ask how I got those scars, I have to tell them the slightly embarrassing truth – I was ice-skating.

Not that there's anything wrong with ice-skating, as long as you can do it without almost killing yourself. I'd always wanted to have a go, perhaps to emulate my father in some way. Before he began to suffer with his lung problems, he'd been fit enough to win quite a few trophies for figure-skating. Eventually someone had crashed into him on the ice and knocked him down, and after that he could never quite extend his arm properly. Perhaps I should have taken that as a warning, but I didn't. It was time to find out whether he had passed any kind of ability for the sport down to his son.

The indoor Charlottetown rink I chose had one flaw; the rail didn't go all the way round the ice. On one side there was just a wall, and the ice curled up a bit there. I don't know whether that was supposed to help people like me, but it didn't. I'd reached a level that allowed me to maintain my momentum on the ice. The only problem was that I didn't always have the control or braking ability to deal with that momentum.

You can imagine my joy at the feeling of gliding along; it reminded me of roller-skating, something I'd enjoyed as a child when I lived in the Villa Bruno near Florence. But this time, the joy turned to a grim realisation – I was on a collision course with the wall. Funnily enough, it wasn't the wall I hit my head against, which was some small achievement. No, when I skated up to the wall I managed to fall over and hit my head on the ice. After that I don't remember much, because I was so dazed they took me straight to hospital. The doctors couldn't have liked the look of me, because I was in there for a week with concussion!

The nurses didn't seem to mind me, though – and I certainly didn't mind them. One asked me if I'd like to accompany her to a dance they were about to have. Like an idiot I declined, telling her I didn't feel well enough yet. The real reason was that I didn't know how to dance!

The 'wound' I received ice-skating in Canada left deeper scars than anything I sustained once the real action started. On that basis, you could argue that ice-skating was more dangerous than flying aeroplanes. Yet I hadn't finished what I'd set out to do on skates, and that nagged away at me, so after I came out of hospital, I went straight back on to the ice. It was part of my nature not to want to be beaten by something, even if I'd suffered an early set-back. This time I chose another rink in Charlottetown, one which had a rail all the way round the ice.

It turned out that I didn't need the rail, because a couple of

Canadian girls took me by the hand and guided me around the ice until I was ready to go solo. And when I did, it felt a bit like going solo in a plane! I was able to skate around in the middle of their rink, happy as a lark, without having to edge around the outside uncertainly. It was just ordinary skating, no cups, not like my father, but I was quite good, considering what I'd been through. The real shame was that I'd forgotten about the girls who'd helped me gain such confidence. When I looked around for them they'd gone, along with the opportunity to meet up afterwards.

By late May, I'd been away from Britain, which I'd signed up to protect, for some five months. All that time I could've been on a squadron; though looking back it was probably a good thing that I wasn't. I might not have survived – while I was still stuck on the wrong side of the Atlantic, 217 Squadron was put on stand-by to attack the mighty *Bismarck*, the biggest battleship ever built.

If the *Gneisenau* and *Scharnhorst* were massive, the *Bismarck* and her sister ship the *Tirpitz* were simply colossal. The *Bismarck* had no less than eight 15 inch guns to unleash on their enemy, housed in four twin-gun turrets, two fore and two aft. The gun turrets were so big they even had names: Anton, Bruno, Caesar and Dora. The *Bismarck* had fifty-six other sizeable weapons to help fend off any attack, too. There were twelve 5.9 inch guns, sixteen 4.1 inch guns, another sixteen at 1.5 inches, and then twelve 0.79 inch anti-aircraft guns for good measure.

Mercifully the *Bismarck* hadn't yet had a chance to do Britain much damage, having only recently been built and fitted out with her extraordinary firepower. That was about to change, though. Perhaps her formidable armoury was the reason why the Kriegsmarine commanders thought she would be safe out on the high seas without a full escort. The *Tirpitz* and the *Scharnhorst* were undergoing overhauls or repairs and weren't quite ready for action, while the *Gneisenau* had been neutralised by Campbell for the time being. The *Bismarck* was deemed virtually indestructible and she was ordered out before any of the aforementioned giants were ready to go with her. A huge heavy cruiser called the *Prinz Eugen* was deemed sufficient to keep the *Bismarck* company. While I was skating in Canada, they made their final preparations to sail west, intent on causing as much chaos among the British convoys in the Atlantic as they could. This deployment, code-named Operation Rheinübung, could have spelt the end for many of 217 Squadron's bravest pilots.

Unlike Campbell's 22 Squadron, 217 had no torpedoes at that time – and no fighter escort either. The very idea of putting 217 Squadron's Beauforts up against the *Bismarck* seems absurd looking back; a complete mismatch. Yet desperate measures were called for in war – especially if other British ships and squadrons couldn't stop the *Bismarck* and *Prinz Eugen* first. Even so, it was hard to escape the conclusion that the sacrifice of pilots and Beauforts would be disproportionate to any superficial damage they could do. Pilots were effectively preparing to die for the right to give the *Bismarck* no more than a graze. They could use two 500 lb bombs and four 250 lb, semi-armour-piercing bombs; but these wouldn't be enough to inflict a penetrative blow. The squadron record inadvertently captured the futility of it all:

> The commanding officer has organised a strike of seven air-craft, led by himself, which will attempt to worry the battleship's upper works and more lightly armoured parts. There is little hope with the armament we have of doing any serious damage to the armoured plate of the Bismarck.

There were forty-eight hours of mental torment for the crews that had been put on stand-by to strike. By 24 May, the *Bismarck* and the *Prinz Eugen* had entered the Denmark Strait, where HMS *Hood*, the pride of the British navy, was ready to face them. If the *Hood*, supported by HMS *Prince of Wales*, couldn't stop the Bismarck, it appeared that shipping in the Atlantic would be at the mercy of the German navy, for all the heroics planned by 217's commanding officer.

Over in Canada, we boarded our ship to sail home across that same Atlantic, and thought we were on our way when we started heading east. At that precise moment, however, someone was coming to the conclusion that it was no longer a very good idea to try to cross the Atlantic with a monster such as the *Bismarck* lurking out there somewhere. Our ship started turning north-east, then turned south-west, and then sailed north-east again. We idled up the coast and down again, until we could be given further news of the *Bismarck*'s break-out.

The *Hood* did her best to eliminate the threat and bravely engaged the *Bismarck*. Tragically the *Hood* was sunk, and all but three of her crew of 1,419 were lost. That was just awful – a terrible disaster. In the heat of battle, however, the *Prince of Wales* had scored three hits on the *Bismarck*. Taking a closer look, the *Prinz Eugen* confirmed that an ominous oil slick could be seen behind the *Bismarck*, signalling damage to a fuel tank.

Admiral Günther Lütjens, in command of the *Bismarck*, had wanted to wait until either the *Tirpitz* or *Scharnhorst* was ready to take part in the operation. Now his concerns had proved all too valid, and the British smelt blood. Some of the ships closer to my side of the Atlantic joined the chase, including HMS *Rodney*, which had been escorting HMS *Britannia* towards a refit at the Boston Navy Yard. HMS *Revenge* and *Ramillies* were ordered into the hunt for the *Bismarck*, too.

In all, six battleships and battle cruisers, two aircraft carriers, thirteen cruisers and twenty-one destroyers were now focused on one mission: find the *Bismarck* and deal her a fatal blow. No wonder the safe passage of a bunch of trainee pilots who'd just completed their navigation course on Prince Edward Island was pushed down the list of priorities. We were effectively treading water until the outcome of the hunt became clear.

A fresh shoot-out took place between the *Prince of Wales* and the *Bismarck*. Neither ship landed a blow, but the *Prinz Eugen* escaped during the exchange, sensing the key to survival was to dash for the sanctuary of a friendly port. By 25 May, the *Bismarck* was heading back towards St Nazaire in France; but HMS *Victorious* came sufficiently close for Fairey Swordfish torpedo bombers to be launched from her deck. Of nine torpedoes dropped, one struck the *Bismarck* amidships, causing minor damage. Meanwhile the net was tightening.

When the *Bismarck* received fresh orders to head for Brest, these were intercepted by the British code-breakers at Bletchley Park, and the navy positioned her ships accordingly. On the evening of 26 May, fifteen Swordfish left the HMS *Ark Royal* armed with more torpedoes. Spotting their approach, the *Bismarck* began to turn sharply in an attempt at evasive action. But a torpedo damaged the *Bismarck*'s rudder assembly, leaving the rudder jammed and the ship locked in a twelve degree turn to port. This circling became the *Bismarck*'s death dance, as British ships closed in for the kill.

Lütjens sent a message to his superiors, full of defiance and loyalty to Hitler's evil regime: 'Ship unmanoeuvrable. We will fight to the last shell. Long live the Führer.'

On 27 May, HMS *King George V* and the *Rodney* led the execution. Lütjens was probably killed along with hundreds of his crew members by a single, devastating shell from *Rodney*. HMS *Norfolk* and HMS *Dorsetshire* had arrived on the scene to deliver the *coup de grâce*; and the *Bismarck* was sunk after the *Dorsetshire* fired torpedoes into her port and starboard sides.

Despite the huge loss of life from the sinking of the *Hood*, ropes were lowered from the *Dorsetshire* and a destroyer called HMS *Maori* to pick up any survivors from the *Bismarck* who could make it across. The Germans might have received more assistance, had a suspected U-boat sighting not ended the rescue operation abruptly. Most of the *Bismarck*'s stricken crew had to be left where they were, in order to protect British lives. Of the 2,200 men who had set sail on the *Bismarck*, only 114 survived.

The news was relayed to the anxious crews of 217 Squadron as swiftly as possible; the monster had been slain and our airmen could sleep at last, knowing they had at least lived to fight another day. And over in Canada we could breathe a sigh of relief, too, because we could sail for home without quite such a strong chance of being sunk. Once again, we avoided the U-boats and crossed the Atlantic without further incident. When we finally reached Liverpool, we knew it wouldn't be long before we went to war. But what type of plane would we be flying?

The answer was the Bristol Beaufort Mark I. I don't know why they put me on Beauforts but any lingering hopes I might have had of becoming a fighter pilot were effectively dashed that summer. While I'd have loved to be in Fighter Command, I'd at least avoided Bomber Command, where I'd have been required to kill civilians. You can argue that much of the bombing of

German cities was justified; and I'm not criticising my RAF colleagues, brave men who simply did what they were told to do. If I'd been issued with the same orders I'd have had to carry them out, too, I suppose. Yet it was still a relief to me that I wasn't sent down that route.

I was to be part of Coastal Command, which actually took its orders from the navy. In reality I'd been chosen to do something just as dangerous as most of the challenges faced by Fighter and Bomber Commands during the darkest hours of World War Two. By learning to fly Beauforts, we were unwittingly accepting some unpleasant consequences of our own. It effectively meant we would soon have to fly straight at enemy ships – with a high chance of being shot down – in order to give our bombs or torpedo a reasonable chance of hitting home. Either we'd be killed, or some of the enemy seamen would be killed by us – assuming we managed to sink something. But first we had to get through more training.

It was high summer when I reached Chivenor, Number 5 Operational Training Unit (OTU), the birth place of the Shipping Interception Unit. We were to spend June and July at Chivenor, a pleasant enough place about five miles from Barnstaple. Here I'd learn to fly the twin-engine aircraft Campbell had used on his suicide mission.

At no point was it explained to us how very dangerous our operational role was going to be. This was war, everything was dangerous, we'd volunteered to join the RAF and now we just wanted to get on with it. There was no question of transferring away from this specific and near-suicidal work; no chance to take a different direction within the RAF. From the moment you joined up, you just went where you were posted, and you did as you were told. There was no choice.

We were informed that Beauforts were very difficult to fly and, sure enough, the first thing we saw when we reached Chivenor was the sight of a stricken Beaufort, which had recently crashed off the runway and ended up on its side on the grass. This wreck was our introduction to the aircraft; and we wondered what could have happened. It had probably swung off the runway as it landed. No wonder the idea of getting to grips with the plane preoccupied us more than the way we might be expected to use it against the enemy later.

The Beaufort was a tough little plane, and it could take some punishment. However, its twin Taurus engines left it slightly underpowered, and therefore difficult to fly if one engine was knocked out. Suffer an engine failure on take-off and it was curtains, though we didn't even like to think about that.

My instructor at Chivenor was Squadron Leader Anstead, a man I quickly came to admire, and on 26 June, 1941, he let me fly a Beaufort for the first time. Until then, what lay inside that brown-and-green camouflage and blue-grey under-belly had remained something of a mystery. Anstead had quickly shown me the ropes, with a view to me taking over as soon as possible, and now this was to be my turn. The objective was to acquire the skills to go solo. When I'd proved myself that way, I could have three crew members.

For now it was just me, the instructor, and the detailed routine. Wearing our leather Irvin jackets and flying helmets, we approached our Beaufort for the first lesson with me as pilot. She wasn't a beautiful aircraft, this Beaufort; she was laid out unusually, almost as though she had two facades at the front. She had a huge Perspex nose, designed to house the navigator. The pilot's cockpit was positioned above and behind that nose, though he, too, was surrounded by Perspex windows.

When I reached my aircraft, the first thing I had to do was check the Pitot head, which is where the air comes in to feed the air speed indicator (ASI). The Pitot head is situated on the front of the aircraft, under the nose. The ground crew put a little bit of cloth over it to protect it. I had to remember to take that bit of cloth off, because if I didn't, I'd have no air speed reading, nothing to be calibrated on to the instruments. Without air speed, no pilot really knows what he is doing, and the risk of stalling increases dramatically. So I took the Pitot head cover off. Good; the first vital job was done.

Then there was the red tape. Each pilot had to sign something called the 'Form 700' before he could take an aircraft up. The ground crew brought us the relevant form, their signatures already visible, from fitter to rigger. The rigger was in charge of the wings and tail, the fitter in charge of the engine. How well they did their job could decide whether you lived or died. This was wartime, men were being asked to learn things quickly at an OTU. These aircraft were being badly treated almost every day by pilots who had no choice or knew no better. Throw a Beaufort around the sky and its Taurus engines might become a little temperamental. I don't know how many cylinders each Taurus had, but they all had a spark plug and everything was tested regularly. Every fifty hours they went for an inspection. Every hundred hours they went for another, more rigorous inspection. After two or three hundred hours, they went for a major inspection. On that one, the maintenance people virtually took the aircraft to bits and put it back together again. We were taught to respect our ground crew and do what they required of us.

I clambered on to the port wing and dropped into the cock-pit, going down through the top hatch and straight into the pilot's seat. Once in, you put your headphones on and switched on the intercom, so that when the time came to have a crew, I could communicate with them. For now it was just Anstead who confirmed: 'Intercom OK.'

I started doing my cockpit check – testing the flaps, throttles, fine pitch, that sort of thing. It was important to make sure the hydraulic system was working, too, so that I could operate the undercarriage and bomb doors while in flight.

My joystick was in front of me, though its cross-frame design actually created two handles on the same feature, one for each hand, with everything firmly fixed to the central column. It was a bit like a rectangular version of a steering wheel, except that I could push forward or pull back, depending on whether I wanted to go down or up. When it was time to take to the air, the pressure I exerted on that control column would determine where I went. If ever I had to drop a torpedo or bomb, there was a button on that control column. The pressure I exerted on that button and the accuracy of my timing might determine whether men below lived or died.

First I started to work all the controls, to check they were functioning properly. On the back of the wings you had the ailerons. I moved the control column to the left and right to check those. The ailerons wiggled up and down on command, so I knew all was well. I checked the tailplane, flipping the tabs up and down by moving the control column back and forth. I worked the rudder with my feet and that felt fine, too. When the time came to have a gunner, he'd be able to watch it move this way and that, then confirm from the back: 'Rudder OK.' The navigator and wireless operator would help me establish that everything else was OK, too.

For now it felt good to be working alone – or at least under

Anstead's tuition. As pilot all this would be my responsibility, even when I did have a crew. So I completed the cockpit check very thoroughly before take-off. I had my window open now, talking to the mechanics on the ground, down on my left-hand side. 'Carburettor to cold, gills fully open.' The mechanic put his thumbs up. I leaned my head out of the window and shouted, 'Prepare to start!' The ground crew had a starting battery and plugged it in. They primed the induction system while they were underneath the two engines. They used the electronic starter to rotate each propeller twice, and switched on the starting magnetos.

I waited for the ground crew to get clear of the propellers, and then I yelled out the magic word: 'Contact!' Switching on the main magnetos, I pressed the port starter button and then the starboard one. First I heard a splutter from each engine, then that promising hum as they began to tick over together properly. What a lovely sound! I had the brakes on, so I could rev up to full throttle to test each engine. The throttles were to the right of the control column. I revved up my engines to the full amount with the chocks – blocks of wood – still in place in front of the wheels. I ran the engines like that to check for fine pitch. 'Pitch fully fine,' I shouted down to the mechanic. Then I signalled 'chocks away' to the ground crew, starting with my arms crossed at face height, before uncrossing to stretch them out on either side, the palms of my hands opened outwards.

If I'd had a gunner at the back, the mechanic might have shown him the chocks to prove they'd been pulled away. But I knew they'd gone, and now I could get the Beaufort moving. By opening the port engine to go right and the starboard engine to go left, I lined up the Beaufort on the runway so that

I was taking off into wind. Always turn into wind for take-off, otherwise the design of the wings can't come into play. To take to the air, I wanted my flaps down at an angle of about thirty degrees, because that increases lift.

I was in position, I was ready. Anstead gave me a nod. I opened both throttles simultaneously, pushing them forward with my right hand while keeping my left hand on the control column. The engines roared into life, I felt their power in my back, and we were away. I was getting slight lateral swings while racing down the runway, but told myself not to worry. That's quite normal; you just use the rudder to correct them, and that's what I did, while keeping the Beaufort moving dead ahead. We must have done 600 yards or so by now. We were nearing a runway speed of 80 knots, which was just what I needed for take-off. Here we go ... 700 yards ... it was now or never ... I eased back on the control column and felt that subtle, special sensation – I'd taken to the air!

My right hand stayed on the throttles; it was big enough to cope with both, so my left could raise the undercarriage lever. We were clear of Chivenor before we knew it, and soon we were close to completing our little climb to 700 feet in the sunshine. I pushed gently down on the control column to bring the tail up, raised the flaps and checked we had reached our cruising speed of 140 knots. I'd be flying at fifty feet all the way when the real action started, so we weren't encouraged to climb too high. But I'd done it, we were up, and all was well.

I checked my blind-flying panel, including the oil and cylinder pressures: 'Always trust your instruments,' Anstead constantly told me. When you're inexperienced, you can be tempted to go with your instinct and ignore your instruments. You might be convinced they're wrong, but if you allow that belief to persist, then pretty soon you'll be dead. No such inner conflict on this day, though. We could see for miles – across the green fields and all the way to a shimmering blue sea.

It was time to adjust the cooling gills. 'Don't enjoy the view too much, concentrate, now,' I reminded myself. 'I like flying this Beaufort! She's supposed to be difficult, but she's really being very good to me.'

We swept out over the sea together, with a glorious feeling of freedom. And as I flew her back in over north Devon, I spotted some intimate-looking coves on the coast, with pretty little ports nearby: Woody Bay, Lynton, Lynmouth. 'If I survive this war I'm going to visit them,' I promised myself. 'This is beautiful!'

But all too soon it was time to land. And I didn't want to spoil it all by getting that final phase wrong. I eased her into the approach, full flaps down, undercarriage down, speed coming back to 80 knots. I touched her down smoothly enough to sense that Anstead was quietly impressed. 'I'm a good pilot,' I reassured myself. 'I'm going to be better than average.'

4

Asp and Bill

Only one of my initial Beaufort crew lasted almost the entire war with me; and that man was Vince Aspinall, my navigator. We never did find out his precise age, we think he was around thirty. He was a handsome chap with a strong chin and deep-set eyes, his dark features caught somewhere between roguishness and sensitivity.

One of the reasons 'Asp' and I got on so well was that he was almost as passionate about music as I was. We could discuss the great composers or debate any subject we chose, because Asp had an opinion on everything. Although he had spent much of his peacetime life in the sedentary world of accountancy, he also wrote the occasional column for the *Manchester Guardian*. He knew a bit about the world.

Aspinall liked his 'little brown jug', as we used to say. It meant he liked a beer – and he could sink quite a few. I was never a drinker, so I rarely if ever witnessed this phenomenon but the boys in the Sergeants' Mess always said that the more Aspinall drank, the gloomier he became. That's why his nickname was 'Happy'. Don't get me wrong, though – he was always sober on operations; and a jolly good navigator he was, too.

Asp was a Catholic and very insistent on going to church. If you let him, he'd even take Mass. I don't remember any of the others in my crew going to church very much, and I certainly didn't; but no matter how much Aspinall had to drink on a Saturday night, he'd always be there on a Sunday, ever-dependable, playing whatever role in the service that was asked of him.

And he was just as dependable as a navigator, which could be a tricky business. For example, navigators had to take into account the magnetic pull on the compass caused by the metal in the Beaufort. If your course should have read 249 degrees, it might read 247 instead. The bomb load increased this magnetic effect and we had to make adjustments accordingly, based on readings we'd taken on a test day.

I'd have to swing the aircraft in different directions on the ground and note down whatever reading the compass was show-ing in the aircraft. Then someone in a field somewhere, far away enough to be free from the interference of all the metal, took the reading for whatever your direction really was, north, south, east or west. You compared the two and the difference – or 'devia-tion' – went on a card. It was up to Aspinall to put the card in the cockpit with the relevant figures.

Whether you had to add one or two degrees due to the metal in the aircraft would depend on the reading you'd received. It all sounds complicated, but Vince had what he needed to do this calculation in a few minutes. He would then give me the course by handing me a chit of paper, so that I could set my gyro a couple of degrees out if necessary. Asp had a gyro as well, and if he felt I was even a fraction of a degree off course once we were in the air, his job was to tell me as quickly as possible.

Work closely like that with someone and you soon form a

bond, because you have to trust and help each other all the time. Add the mutual love of music and we were destined to become good pals.

To my shame, perhaps, the rest of my original crew at Chivenor didn't stay very vividly in my memory. However, I'm reliably informed by the surviving NCOs who remembered him, that Pocock, my first gunner, was as grumpy as his sour-faced expression suggests in a surviving photograph from our Chivenor days. No one got to know him very well because he wasn't one for conversation – he wasn't 'one of the lads', which counted for a lot in the Sergeants' Mess.

My first wireless operator was Sergeant Thompson, a mild-mannered chap, while a certain Sergeant Warwick made the occasional appearance in his absence. Partly because the worst action hadn't yet started for us, none of these wireless operators or air gunners (WOP/AGs) made a long-lasting impression on me. You always remember more clearly who was at your side in the toughest situations.

Chivenor wasn't as big as Cranwell, so although it was still an RAF conveyor belt for training new crews, it was slightly more intimate. Our 'Flight' of twenty-eight men, for example, was made up of seven crews. It was called 7-A Beaufort Squad. Our Chivenor superiors had a photograph taken of us quite early on; you'll find it in the picture section of this book. You can see me in the middle of the back row, with my hair trying to break out of my cap because I've let it grow too long. I don't remember how it came to be that long without anyone telling me to get it cut. Even seventy years later, my good friend Bill Carroll was still teasing me about it, and referring to me as 'the bloke at the back who needs his bloody hair cut'.

Bill's in the same picture, a cheerful-looking chap sitting third from the right on the front row. Look carefully and you'll see a twinkle in his eye, just a hint that he knows a bit more about life than his boyish face is prepared to let on. He eventually became my gunner, and helped me and other pilots to stay in the air on more than one occasion. He helped me again when it was time to write this book, offering his own vivid recollections of how we lived, fought and in many cases died, from the perspective of someone based in the Sergeants' Mess.

While we were remembering the order of events, and disagreeing as only good friends can, Bill worked out a rather disturbing statistic about that photograph. Of the twenty-eight young men in the picture, twenty were killed in the war, one was shot down and became a prisoner of war, four more sustained wounds of some kind from enemy fire or crashing, and two were branded LMF – 'Lack of Moral Fibre'. This was a horrible military term which was supposed to denote cowardice.

That only left Bill Carroll to come through the war entirely unscathed, unless you count the times I managed to shake and bruise him by throwing my Beaufort around in unexpected ways. The fresh-faced young Carroll in that photograph looks happy to take whatever life is going to throw at him – and it threw plenty. Yet you might detect from his expression that the prospect of war isn't worrying him too much.

Bill, it soon turned out, was well equipped to handle any situation. He hailed from the tough streets of Bermondsey, in the south-east of London, a very different background to mine:

'I was a young working class bloke. Arthur and my first pilot Tommy Carson were university people; so there's a difference to start with. People like me weren't used to that kind of person and they weren't used to me.

'I think we used to make Arthur's life hell; first Aspinall, as a member of his original crew, and then later me, too. Aspinall and I were different breeds to Arthur. Arty had lived all his life in comfort; his father was a clergyman. Then he runs into characters like us! But we got along famously. And that says something for both of us, given the sort of life I'd been used to in London.

'I was lucky when I was growing up, because I could get into trouble in Bermondsey or Peckham and then say, "Have you met my big brother?" My elder brother Peter was very athletic. I could also run, which came in handy a few times.

'My father died in 1935, and I was a teenager at technical college learning about tool making when a man called H.P. Smith, who'd been a fighter pilot in the First World War, helped find me a job as an apprentice engineer. The boss at this company was a royalist and when he heard the new King George VI was to open an extension at the nearby Tate Gallery, he gave people time off to go.

'I positioned myself on the stairs going up to the first floor along with another apprentice. As he passed, the king stopped and shook hands with us in front of all these people. When he heard about that, our boss couldn't have been more pleased.

'My best friend was a bloke called Alan Johnson. As kids we used to go scrumping together – stealing apples. One morning I found Alan had signed up for the Royal Air Force without telling me. "You rotten bugger, you were supposed to wait for me," I said. He replied, "OK, put your coat on. I'll show you where I joined up."

'You could say I joined for patriotic reasons, because an engineer was in a restricted occupation – I'd never have had to join. Alan and I tried to get on the same crew; but he kept getting into trouble and was posted to Canada. Eventually he became a Squadron Leader, and a heck of a good pilot.

'Meanwhile, I was left with about twenty others who took the oath and heard a Group Captain tell us that in nine months we'd be sergeants in the Royal Air Force. To be a sergeant was really something, he added. We fell for it.

'I was sent to Blackpool to train as a WOP/AG – a wireless operator and air gunner. Then at a place called Yatesbury, I paired up with a West Country lad called Jack Featherstone, ready to be put on a crew together at some stage. First we had to do some more training at Watton in Norfolk. Some people in the air force are horrid, and a sergeant at Watton was one of those people.

'He said: "OK, you future WOP/AGs, I want you to go and clean that turret in that Bleinheim over there." Some poor sod had been hit by a cannon shell or two, and there was blood and guts all over the place. He thought it was a big joke, this sergeant. Anyway, Jack wasn't very happy; but I cleaned the thing up.

'We were soon sent to a gunnery school in Dumfries, the home of Robbie Burns, before coming all the way down to Chivenor. That's where I first saw Arthur Aldridge. His hair was too long, so I crewed up with another pilot. Seriously, though, I don't know how he got away with that hair at Chivenor. But I certainly wasn't going to say anything to him about it.

'Pilots were regarded as a cut above, if you'll excuse the pun. They were mostly university-educated, as I said. They were from a different social background, and if you were going to be cheeky to a pilot officer, you had to know he'd take it in the right way. I wasn't sure about Arthur at that stage.'

The formation of crews was a lottery from the start. As a sergeant, your fate might depend on whom you 'crewed up' with,

as Bill puts it. Your fate might also depend on how forgivingly
the Beaufort behaved under the crude guidance of a new pilot.
In the summer of 1941, none of us knew the odds were going
to be as bad as they turned out for the Beaufort boys. How could
we have known there was going to be an eighty per cent casualty rate for a full operational tour in a Beaufort, compared to
sixty-six per cent in Bomber Command? How could we have
foreseen that four of the chaps photographed that day on 7-A
Beaufort Squad wouldn't even make it out of Chivenor alive? As
a pilot, I did know that I had to master every aspect of the plane
thoroughly, because at some point in the future, perhaps sooner
rather than later, my life and the lives of others might depend on
how well I continued to learn my lessons.

Bill struck lucky with his first crew. He was approached by
Tommy Carson, the tall and extremely likeable pilot who'd been
in Canada with us. As you'd expect from a former Cambridge
University student and lawyer, Tommy had a dry wit; and Bill
was never short of a sense of humour either, so it was going to
be an interesting combination:

'Tommy Carson came up to me and Jack Featherstone, and he
said, "Are you guys looking for a driver?"

'We said, "Yes."

'The first time I flew with Carson at Chivenor, he made a
bumpy landing. But when we all got out, he pretended it hadn't
happened.

'"How did you like the landing?" he asked us as we all stood
on the tarmac by the plane.

'"Well, that was a hell of a bounce," I told him truthfully.
"Must have been about twenty feet!"

'He feigned astonishment and said: "What?"

'"Well, OK . . . maybe eighteen and a half feet," I added.

'He smiled and told me, "You and I are going to get along well."

'Carson didn't want to be regarded as superior to his crew in any way. So he told us: "I'm not 'Sir' or 'Pilot', I'm 'Tommy'." He used to get in trouble with his CO for that. In fact, a notice soon went up in the Sergeants' Mess: "Non-Commissioned Officers will address their pilot as 'Sir'."'

Bill and Tommy were destined to remain firm friends for as long as the war allowed. And when he wasn't flying with Carson, Carroll was clearly the life and soul of the Sergeants' Mess wherever we went, something I didn't get to see as I was only allowed to go in the Officers' Mess. Looking back it was quite wrong that officer pilots were separated from their crew in this way. We were risking our lives together, after all. Yet once we had left the aircraft, I rarely saw my crew. They went to the Sergeants' Mess, and I went to the Officers' Mess. It was ridiculous, the segregation; but that's the way it was. Vince Aspinall should have been an officer, and so should the others in my crew. But I didn't encourage my crew to call me Arthur, or 'Artie', which is what Bill called me after the war. During the war, they called me 'Pilot' and nothing else – to my face, anyway!

I was one of the quieter ones at Chivenor; and in my spare time I sometimes went bathing at nearby Croyde Bay. Meanwhile, Carroll was usually at the heart of any evenings out with the drinking crew:

'When we were stationed at Chivenor, Barnstaple was where we always wanted to go in our spare time. It had a few pubs and some night life, so we would get the bus from Chivenor into Barnstaple at about 5pm. What they didn't tell us was this: the bus turned straight round and that was it – you were stranded there in Barnstaple for the night.

'Another gunner called Maurice "Moggie" Mayne and I found a solution to that. There was a big railway siding in Barnstaple, ten tracks with trains staying overnight. We did some reconnaissance and found they left the first-class carriages open on one train in particular. So instead of walking five miles back at night, we'd go down to the sidings and kip there.

'One time my roommate Jack Featherstone came out for a drink with us. Jack was a wonderful lad, a little older than most of us, even though his thin face somehow made him look younger. He may have done a couple of extra years' living, but he definitely hadn't done much drinking. After not much more than half a pint of beer he was drunk and asked Moggie and me exactly where this secret place was where he could sleep in town.

'Once we'd told him, Jack went down to the railway sidings by himself. The rest of us opted to walk the five miles back to the base that night. The next morning, Jack didn't show up on the first bus. We were in breakfast, wondering where he was, when over the PA system I heard the words: "Sergeant Carroll, you have a phone call." I thought, "What have I done now?" I got to the phone and it was Jack.

'I said, "Jack, where the hell are you calling from?"

'He said, "I'm in Bristol."

'I realised right away what must have happened but I couldn't resist asking, "What are you doing there, Jack?"

'He replied, "I went to the first-class carriages like you told me to . . . and I woke up in Bristol."

'"Jack," I told him, "you went to the wrong first-class carriages!" I had to laugh at that point.

'"I'm going to come and sort you and Moggie Mayne out when I get back," Featherstone said – though he saw the funny side later.

'I can't explain the comradeship that was developing – it was fantastic. All the WOP/AGs had been together since October 1940 in places like Blackpool and Yatesbury. To me, the people were more interesting than the prospect of war, so it didn't necessarily dawn on me what kind of ordeals we would go through in time.'

And a sense of comradeship was developing between me and my fellow music-lover Vince, as well. After all, the navigator could save a pilot's life just as easily as a pilot could save the navigator's. When we went to war for real, the same would be true for the gunner and wireless operator. What we went through together over time created a common bond among different types of men.

5

Crashes and Torpedoes

We pilots were learning all the tricks of the trade, or so we thought. For example, since you could start your night flying tuition at dusk, the joke was, 'Get as much night flying in as you can before it gets dark!'

My instructor was a legendary Beaufort pilot called Norman Hearn-Phillips — except that he didn't do much instructing. In fact, he never said anything. He was the complete opposite to Holland. Hearn-Phillips just sat there in silence. And then, when he thought the time was right, I went solo at night, too.

The task was simple: I had to take off, come back around and land again — 'circuits and bumps' they called it. I had a bit of a shock the first time. I'd let it get dark for my night flying — always a mistake. I took off and turned to port to go downwind, so that I could find the flare-path for landing. I couldn't see it. There was a moment of panic; it's pitch-black and there's nowhere to land! Eventually I spotted the flare-path and, of course, it had been there all the time. I landed quite happily and did it again.

That certainly wasn't the first piece of confusion Chivenor had seen at night. Word got round of an extraordinary incident not long before we'd arrived. The control tower had given what they'd thought was a Beaufort the green light to land, only to find a Junkers 88 coming to a halt on the runway. The German pilot had lost his bearings and thought he'd reached the north of France. Before he could take off again, the Chivenor staff realised their mistake, stormed the plane and took the crew into custody. It hadn't been a bad night's work, as it turned out, because they'd been gifted all that German technology, fully intact; we can only assume they learned a good deal.

By now we thought we'd learned plenty, too. We were growing in confidence as a group of cadets; we'd begun to feel we were ready for action. Then at the start of August things began to go wrong. Two Beaufort airmen I didn't know were killed in a crash, while another crew could have caused more casualties when they accidentally released their bombs.

On 9 August, tragedy struck at Chivenor itself, or at least just outside the perimeter. No one who witnessed the incident would ever forget those dreadful seconds. Bill Carroll was among those who stood helplessly transfixed as they watched from the ground:

'Each crew had about two hours in a Beaufort, and then another crew took over almost as soon as the previous lot had landed. I think we were due to take off two hours after this happened, but you had to be ready and I was walking across to the end of the runway to join my crew.

'I knew the crew whose turn it was to take off. One member of that crew, Sergeant Fell, had just had his wife come to visit him with their first baby. Another, Sergeant Wesley, was a really tough young man who did so much body-building that he had muscles coming out of everywhere – even behind his ears.

'I was on the walkway between the buildings and the runway when I glanced over to see this aircraft take off and go into low cloud. The next thing I heard was this horrible, horrible noise. The pilot must have had trouble and the damn thing had obviously stalled, so he was goosing the engines to try and pull her out of it. He was trying to come out of a death dive and there was this horrible screaming of the engines.

'The river was quite close to the end of the runway there. This noise was coming through the clouds, it was really terrifying, a horrible screaming and then there was a colossal bang. I think I was only two hundred yards away from the crash, and the whole lot went in the river. And, of course, all four men were killed. If you imagine going in at that speed ... they didn't find very much of any of them. They were all good blokes. I'd had tea with Fell only the day before.'

The Chivenor record book stuck to the simple facts:

August 9.
P/O S.H. Last met with a fatal accident when his Beaufort L9953 got out of control in a cloud and dived vertically from 500 feet into the River Taw half a mile south of Chivenor Aerodrome at 10.15 hrs. The following members of his crew died in this accident: P/O V.J. Hall, 115840 Sgt D.H. Wesley, 1311089 Sgt W. Fell.

Wing Commander Samuel McCaughey Boal, a genial Irishman known simply as Paddy, was the officer in charge at Chivenor. He'd been rested and given the post to allow him to recharge his batteries after a tour of operations. For a short time the following year, Boal was destined to lead our squadron but in the immediate aftermath of the crash at Chivenor, it was his grim responsibility to write to the families of those who had lost their lives, or to speak to any who were in the vicinity of the base.

Bill Carroll's popularity made him potentially useful at a difficult time like this:

'It was about 4.30pm when someone comes up to me and says: "The Squadron Leader wants to see you, Bill." I thought, "Oh no, what have I been up to now? Hasn't this day been bad enough?" So Paddy Boal is in his office and sees me hovering outside.

'"Come in," he says. He's sitting there with his dark, slicked hair and central parting, and he has a pad in front of him. He's scribbling. He's mumbling something. And then he looks across at me and says, "Well, I suppose if you knew him pretty well, you know her pretty well, too. You'd better introduce me, if you don't mind."

'"Excuse me, sir, what is it you want me to do?" I asked.

'And by the time it had dawned on me, he'd replied: "I want you to come and introduce me to Sergeant Fell's wife."

'I said: "Sir – she went back yesterday with the baby."

'"Oh," Boal said, letting out a sigh. You could see the relief on the man's face. And then he said, "I'll get the adjutant to write to her."'

Though I hadn't known Pilot Officer Last, we all felt a sense of shock. And we never did understand quite what happened in that cloud to cause the accident. Even before this tragedy, I never got into cloud if I could help it – once you're there, you don't know where you are. Always stay out of the clouds unless taking evasive action – that would remain my golden rule. It is generally possible to stay below the cloud, whatever the weather.

This crew was one of many to lose their lives before they could be let loose upon the Germans, and a detailed analysis of Beaufort losses later revealed that a tremendous number happened during training at OTUs. This seems to support the theory that the Beaufort was a difficult aircraft to fly, particularly for newly trained pilots. However, considerable losses occurred during training on other aircraft, too, so it doesn't necessarily follow that the Beaufort was any more difficult to fly than the others. All we knew at Chivenor was, if we hadn't known it before, training could be extremely dangerous.

We had to put the accident behind us, though, hold our collective nerve and keep learning. There was a week to go on our course at Chivenor. No room for mistakes now, errors could be fatal; we'd seen that for ourselves. One of the last skills to master was formation flying. This was potentially even more perilous, with one pilot's lapse in concentration liable to take another pilot down with him. Yet I realised immediately that I loved formation flying. I tucked myself in behind the leader, and really found it fun. Thankfully there were no collisions and no more tragedies during my stay at Chivenor, and in mid-August I left North Devon and headed up to Scotland.

I was following in the footsteps – or should that be slipstream – of the Victoria Cross winner, Kenneth Campbell, by taking a torpedo course at a place called Abbotsinch, just outside Glasgow. Mark Lee and Tommy Carson were among the pilots who came, too, along with their crews. It meant Bill Carroll, Vince Aspinall and the rest of the fun-loving sergeants were about to be let loose on a new playground north of the border, though for Asp it was familiar territory, as he'd trained to be a navigator at Prestwick in Ayrshire.

Abbotsinch, near Paisley, is now Glasgow airport. Even back then it had been a civilian airport before the RAF took it over; there were hangars wherever you looked. It was a really nice station, though the sergeants seemed to be more interested in what lay beyond its perimeter. Bill reckoned the ratio of girls to boys in Paisley was about ten to one, though surely he must have been exaggerating? He also claimed that if you left Abbotsinch to go into Paisley, there were young ladies waiting to accost you by the guardroom. 'Are you doing anything tonight?' they'd apparently ask. If there were such girls gathered there on occasion, I never saw any. I had no such luck!

None of us could be distracted for too long, though, because even learning to drop dummy torpedoes was going to be a tricky business. We were going to fly out over the Firth of Clyde, and when we reached a small, uninhabited island called Lady Isle, we were to look for a lighthouse. Then we had to come in low, as though we were attacking it. The idea was to drop our dummy torpedoes, which were about fifteen feet long, eighteen inches in diameter and weighing around 1,500 lb, into the water so that they ran towards the lighthouse. There was a hut next to the lighthouse, full of cameras and other scientific equipment. We'd also carry cameras on board our Beauforts, and take pictures at the precise moment we dropped our torpedo. From all the data and photographs, they could determine how successful our torpedo might have been if it had contained an explosive warhead. As it was, the dummy missiles were stopped by nets, and motor boats with divers rushed in to retrieve them before they disappeared for ever.

It all sounded rather fun. But stories soon reached us of a horrific incident which had happened just a few weeks earlier, during the previous course.

The Abbotsinch record book explained:

30/6/41
Beaufort Aircraft No W 6539 crashed between Beith and Howwod [sic], near Loch Winnoch at 17.49 hours. Aircraft Burnt Out. Sergeant Murdoch, H. No 645615 W/Op/AG

very seriously injured, in hospital. Pilot Officer Williams, JKD
No J4689 killed. Pilot Officer Anne, R. No 60338 killed.
Sergeant Stanley, A.W. No 926597 W/Op/AG killed.

To those who heard about the tragedy before we were sent on
our first dummy torpedo run, this was a timely reminder of what
could go wrong. Still, I was confident of my ability by now, and
ready to skim the waves if that's what it took to register a theo-
retical hit on the target.

We took off and set a course for Lady Isle. Even though I
don't like the word 'thrill', this feeling of almost caressing the
water below while remaining in swift flight just above it, did
come close to thrilling me. And when you have already done so
much low-level flying over land, it seems simpler to fly low-level
over the sea. Flying at fifty feet above land or water is a sheer
pleasure.

This time there was a specific point to our low-level flying –
there would be a climax. Success or failure was going to be
down to me, the pilot who dropped the torpedo. It had to be
me, because only I could time the torpedo's release in relation
to the Beaufort's height, speed and direction. In the second it
might take to convey the order to Aspinall, for example, the
moment would be gone. That's why the button was on the control column, ready to be pressed at precisely the right moment.
On a real operation, the execution would depend on my judgement, as well. And you couldn't help but ask yourself: 'What
devastation will I cause, if by applying simple pressure on this
button I ever release a truly explosive torpedo? Will I have to do
that?'.

We reached Lady Isle. I spotted the lighthouse and the shed
next to it. I was cruising at 140 knots and held the plane level at

just fifty feet. I was closer than a thousand yards now. 'Line her up nicely, that's it. Nine hundred yards …' I rose slightly, to a height of between sixty and eighty feet, and now I was ready. I felt the button under my thumb. I just had to press it. Eight hundred yards. Perfect. 'Torpedo dropped!' I said, trying to suppress my excitement. One little press and it had gone. What followed depended on what the scientists had designed.

Connected to the torpedo were two cables that ran to a drum in the bomb bay. The drum tipped over as soon as the torpedo dropped. The cable connected to the torpedo's tail remained attached to the drum for a fraction longer than the one connected to the main section of the torpedo. This ensured that the torpedo began its flight towards the water pointing slightly downwards, at an angle of seventeen degrees from horizontal. The impetus given to the torpedo by the fast-moving aircraft, combined with its aerodynamic features, sent it flying through the air for 250 yards before it hit the water.

There was a small bar sticking out of the torpedo, which was connected to the tail. When the torpedo met the water and the bar was ripped away, the tail automatically dropped off, its purpose served. Now the torpedo could swim on its own in the water, with the help of four wooden fins which stabilised it. Fan blades in the nose of the torpedo were designed to arm and cock a real warhead automatically after a certain distance, leaving the detonators to ignite the explosive on impact. Propellers had to power the torpedo through the water for 350 yards at 40 knots, before it was ready to blow. So, in total, the torpedo needed 250 yards airtime and 350 yards in the water, rendering any release closer than 600 yards to the target pointless.

In reality, the intense flak we were going to be facing on operations made it highly unlikely that we would ever be tempted to go closer to the enemy ships before dropping our torpedo anyway. Eight hundred yards would be quite close enough, thank you; eight hundred yards was the perfect distance, smack in the middle of that window of opportunity, between a thousand and six hundred yards.

In the slow seconds it took for the torpedo to find its target, enemy ships were going to blast away for all they were worth. As with the heroic Campbell in Brest harbour, death might find the Beaufort crew before their torpedo found the enemy. Beaufort airmen had to brace themselves, knowing full well that in these few, specific, excruciating moments they would either be killed or know they'd survived to fight another day. That knowledge brought with it a critical test of nerve, one that could never be reproduced on a torpedo range.

Campbell was probably still having fun when he came through Abbotsinch. He must have seen the motor boats come in, as I saw them now; converging as soon as the dummy torpedo had expended its energy. He must have wondered how he'd done, as I wondered. Judging by the way the dummy torpedo had run, and the angle I'd achieved for release, I felt this first effort had gone well.

Sure enough, photos later confirmed that I'd approached the 'target' side on, at the ninety-degree angle my superiors demanded. Success! Or so I thought. In fact, there was a difference between what the instructors considered to be the correct angle for a torpedo-attack on a ship, and what the correct angle actually was. I didn't know this yet. All that mattered to me for now was that I hadn't had any trouble hitting the target. Then again, the target wasn't moving. Perhaps the training course would provide us with moving targets towards the end.

*

On the last day of August, we did have a ship to aim at. Sadly it wasn't moving any more. I did a dummy torpedo drop and camera run on HMS *Mullahn*, a ship so dilapidated, it had been designated for use as target practice. Unfortunately we never did aim at a moving ship during training, either up in Scotland or anywhere else. I don't think we ever aimed at any sort of moving target. To say that the training was faulty was something of an understatement, though it didn't trouble us at the time.

How could anyone have guessed at that stage that we were being taught the wrong lesson? We should have been taught to drop torpedoes at forty-five degrees and just in front of a moving target, whereas in fact we were taught to come in at ninety degrees to the ship's beam. These people were meant to be the experts, we were new to it all; so we questioned nothing. It didn't make me nervous to think that we were being trained to drop torpedoes by flying low at enemy ships. I didn't lose any sleep worrying that real enemy ships might turn out to be better equipped to defend themselves and more elusive than the old carcass we were targeting. I don't know why it didn't make me nervous, it just didn't. Torpedo target practice was actually very pleasurable.

While we were at Abbotsinch, the British tested a weapon they called a Toraplane. It was a torpedo with wings and a tail plane; a missile designed to glide. The brain-child of Sir Charles Dennistoun Burney and Nevile Shute, the Toraplane had been in development for a year or more by the time we laid eyes on it. This glider-torpedo was almost eighteen-feet long with a tail-span of about six feet. Hanging down below the Toraplane was an arm, and when that hit the water ahead of the torpedo, the wings dropped off and the torpedo continued. In principle, therefore, it wasn't so very different from the ordinary torpedo; except that the Toraplane was supposed to enable us to fly towards the target at 2,000 feet instead of fifty.

Once dropped from up on high, the Toraplane was supposed to do the rest of the hard work by itself. This would, of course, have eliminated the most dangerous part of the job for us – the head-long charge, flying low at the enemy ship. The Toraplane would probably have saved an awful lot of lives had it been truly reliable. Unfortunately, it wasn't.

They'd played around with blast-start release systems, the tail plane booms and release bars, ballistic heads to steepen trajectory; you name it, they'd tinkered with it. There had been a Toraplane Mk 1 and a Toraplane Mk 2, with interchangeable designs in wood or metal … but still something wasn't quite right. Sometimes it hit the target, sometimes it didn't. Too often some kind of distortion occurred; and without consistent accuracy, the Toraplane couldn't be given the green light for use in the war. They kept trying to get it right – and that's where we came in.

Tommy Carson, Bill Carroll's pilot, was one of those detailed to drop the latest Toraplane as part of a demonstration for an American colonel who was visiting Abbotsinch. If this particular Toraplane showed signs of working, the colonel was apparently going to take one back to the States with him. The Americans still weren't in the war in August and September 1941, though they were definitely thinking about it.

The workings of the Toraplane and the results of the demonstration were supposed to be top secret; so it didn't go down too well when Tommy made the mistake of leaving the radio on when he was explaining the weapon to Bill and the rest of his crew on the intercom. Carson's indiscretion could be heard by some of those who had gathered for the demonstration below; and when he returned to base, the Squadron Leader was not a happy man. The results of the demonstration didn't seem to cheer anyone up, either. Yet again the Toraplane had failed to convince, and tests would have to be ongoing.

My own involvement with Toraplane tests in mid-September gave a further indication that the authorities weren't prepared to give up easily on this weapon, having put so much time, energy and money into the project. On 15 September, we flew in formation to execute a 'dummy Toradrop' on another stationary ship. If they couldn't get one of these things to work properly when it was released alone, maybe some success stories would emerge if you dropped a few of them simultaneously. This flimsy logic was soon exposed.

I was involved twice more in 'Tora sighting' in those final training days before joining a squadron. That meant lining up the plane to release the weapon at just the right height and moment, then following its progress down through the air. Unfortunately for the war effort, however, we had no more dealings with the Toraplane after that. Our efforts probably represented no more than a few frustrating steps on the road to an inescapable conclusion. The powers that be started to lose faith in the project, we certainly never used it in action, and the Toraplane was finally abandoned the following year.

Shortly before I left Abbotsinch, I blotted my copy book, or at least that's what the official account would have you believe. On 7 September, 1941, the Abbotsinch record book claimed that Beaufort N1103 – the plane I was flying – 'crashed on landing'. Let's just say the writer of that account must have had a keen sense of the melodramatic. He went on to say:

Aircraft damaged. (P/O Aldridge, 929571 Astinal [sic], V, both uninjured – 993168 Sgt Thompson, C.M. and 922862 Sgt Pocock D.W. both slightly injured).

What actually happened was I slightly overshot the runway, because I couldn't get the aircraft wheels to touch down in time. The Beaufort went gliding on like an Anson. Maybe the WOP/AGs were thrown about a bit, but there were no injuries as far as I remember. It was a poor do, I must say; but in the end I just came to a halt on the grass. The report was exaggerated, the aircraft wasn't damaged, and I went straight back up again in the same plane, this time with an instructor, to see if I could do it properly. The main thing is that no one was seriously injured, and we went about our business as usual.

It didn't leave me any less keen to swap training for real action, though. For some time I'd felt ready to fight the Germans with whatever weapons I was given – bombs, torpedoes or bare hands. Finally it was time to leave Scotland and move to England's south coast, which was the front line in the defence of the country. I'd made it through my long year of training! I still remember the feeling of satisfaction.

Thompson and Pocock seemed less satisfied with the prospect of staying in Britain, as they'd have to do, at least for now, if they remained on my crew. A circular came round, inviting crews to volunteer for Egypt, because they were sending more squadrons there. I was more interested in doing my bit to defend Britain herself; while Pocock and Thompson wanted a change of scenery and applied for North Africa. From that moment on, those two crew members were destined to go one way, while Vince Aspinall and I went the other. Doubtless they were brave men, but more than that I cannot say. Sadly I'm told their plane crashed in North Africa and they were quite seriously injured. If they survived, they were two of the luckier ones from our class in North Devon – that's how alarming the casualty rate became.

Despite a few scrapes along the way, I'd just about mastered the Beaufort, and I was ready to use her against Hitler. The total time I'd spent in a Beaufort when I finished my training was 82 hours 30 minutes by day and 6 hours 25 minutes by night. My efficiency was regarded as, wait for it, average.

It seemed I'd never be regarded as anything but average, even though I'd spent 35 hours and 55 minutes flying solo in a Beaufort. At least the time had come to prove myself in war, instead of constantly trying to please my instructors.

6

Woe to the Unwary,
Welcome to Alan

On 18 September, 1941, I joined 217 Squadron, taking my navigator Vince Aspinall with me. The squadron was based at St Eval in Cornwall; and when Tommy Carson brought his crew down, it didn't take Bill Carroll long to discover the delights of nearby Newquay:

'I was walking along the cliffs between St Eval and Newquay when a friend called Eddie Beesley made the mistake of telling me he had twenty-one quid in his pocket. He was going to take the night train and buy an engagement ring for his girl in London.

'Well, there were so many pubs in Newquay that he never left for London. And, as far as I know, he never bought this girl an engagement ring either. At least he survived the war, which pleased the Wing Commanders, because he became their peace-time bookie!

'It wasn't just the pubs I enjoyed down in Cornwall, because there were some lovely bays near St Eval. There was a rock pool in one, which someone had cemented in; so that at high tide the water would be left in there. It was quite deep and you could really enjoy a swim in there.'

If I didn't share Bill Carroll's taste for beer, I did share his enjoyment of the local scenery. The Cornish coast was spectacularly rugged. At St Eval I'd go for walks on the cliffs, which were really dramatic because they were so very high above the waves crashing below. I could hear those waves but didn't actually see them, because I wasn't stupid enough to start peering over the edge. It was stirring enough just to be walking alone along the top of those cliffs, and they offered me a further reminder of how beautiful Britain was; a place to be protected at all costs from the evil of Hitler.

As officers we were stationed in the Watergate Hotel – and at times it almost felt like we were on holiday. Not that it was going to turn out anything like a holiday for any of us. We'd know the reality of war soon enough.

The motto of 217 Squadron was 'Woe to the Unwary', meaning, of course, woe to your enemy. The joke was that it really applied to us. Woe to the unwary pilot, flying a Beaufort! The emblem on the 217 Squadron badge included a shark. I never did learn the exact significance of the shark, though I assumed we were meant to be the predators, searching the seas for prey.

Joining a squadron felt new and exciting. I was blissfully ignorant then that losses in Beauforts averaged about one in three on each op, and that most of my friends and comrades would be dead inside a year. Nor did I realise that the twenty per cent survival rate within the squadron might have been even worse had the previous chief, Group Captain Bolland, not shown some heroic insubordination just a few months earlier.

Back in March, Bolland had been asked to send his Beauforts into Brest in broad daylight to attack a heavy cruiser called the *Admiral Hipper*. He'd responded by declaring all his planes unserviceable – meaning unfit to fly. This prompted a furious reaction from his Commander-in-Chief, and after a heated telephone conversation Bolland was forced to make three Beauforts available for the mission. He continued to insist that a daylight raid on heavily fortified Brest was tantamount to suicide, totally futile and doomed to failure. Sure enough, none of his crews returned, and he stormed into the offices of his superiors in Plymouth to confront the Air Officer Commanding (AOC) and the Admiral. Bolland's account of the subsequent exchange is priceless:

'I told them as clearly as I could that the order to send young men to their deaths on useless missions was not on and I did not think they could possibly understand what the defences at Brest were like. Perhaps it would be better if I could discuss this with someone on their staff who had fought in the war? It was a useless visit which cost me my command, but no further daylight attacks were made on Brest by 217 Squadron, and I feel I might have saved many lives ... The next day I handed over my Squadron to Wing Commander Bower.'

Bower was the man in charge when I reached the Squadron; but when I see Bolland in the next world I'll thank him, because my life was probably one of the many he helped save. He felt a tremendous sense of responsibility, on a scale I'd never experience.

What I did know, though, was that it was my responsibility to keep my crew alive. Apart from my navigator, my crew had changed as we prepared for war. I was glad Aspinall had come down to St Eval with me, because the chemistry between pilots and navigators was important. The man who filled one of the vacancies left by Pocock and Thompson was someone I would grow to love like a brother – I didn't choose my new radio man, Alan Still, but if I could have done so, I would have. I soon came to realise that Alan was the nicest man I'd ever met, and the nicest

I'd ever be likely to meet. Softly spoken and hailing from the North-east, Alan just had a way with people. He was thoughtful and kind, but funny, too. He had a big chin and a big smile, which he wore just as often as a man in our situation could. Neither of us were big drinkers, which probably only enhanced our friendship over the years. I can't tell you why I liked Alan so much, he just had an innate goodness about him. He wasn't too imposing or opinionated; he didn't seem to have an ego at all. He was simply a kind, amusing person – excellent company.

Alan Still had joined the Royal Air Force in 1939 – long before I did. He, too, had hoped to become a pilot. But Alan was a big fellow and his head was a little strange. When you looked at him, you'd notice that his eyes were not quite aligned; the left eye was higher than the right. That may have been why he wasn't cut out to become a pilot. Instead, they trained him as a wireless operator at Hamble, near Southampton, and then as a gunner elsewhere.

Bill Carroll remembers him fondly, too:

'Alan was a wonderful bloke. He wasn't as outgoing as Aspinall and me, but he was one of the very best. Trouble was, if he was sitting in a living room shooting at his TV he would miss it – and I'm not joking. He passed his gunnery course at Stormy Down in Glamorgan – but no one knows how.'

No one ever knew where bullets went if Alan fired them. For some unknown reason, however, he'd try to get in the turret on occasion, hoping to be the gunner he'd supposedly been trained to be. But when it was time for serious action, I'd have to order him out. Alan was best suited to the wireless, and that's where he spent nearly all of his war, while he was still able to fight.

Fortunately, my new gunner, Flight Sergeant Grimmer, knew what he was doing with a Browning. I think he must have been a regular air force man, though he was so quiet I never found out for sure. As a WOP/AG, he must have been in the RAF for a long time to become a Flight Sergeant. He'd probably even had a Vickers in the turret when he started out, which had been replaced by the Browning long before we flew Beauforts.

Grimmer, a handsome chap with neat ginger hair and moustache, kept himself to himself rather more than the others. Apparently his wife was pregnant, and that might explain why he was rarely if ever in the Sergeants' Mess. So even if we'd been in the same mess, it would have been practically impossible to get to know him. Because he was so self-contained, he didn't make a big impression on me. I do know he never let me down, though.

So this was my crew for now: Asp was down in the nose, navigating diligently as we continued to wonder how old he really was; Alan was half-way along in the wireless compartment, wishing he was a pilot or a gunner; and Grimmer was behind him in the turret, ready to do his duty but probably wishing he was back home with his pregnant wife.

Bill Carroll always delighted in telling me that no one looked upon my crew as the number one crew until he joined it later. And, even then, he claimed, we only became the number one crew after a lot of experience. I'll take his word for it, though we already felt like a team before Bill came on board, and we had to act as one. That teamwork started before take-off.

The pilot and his crew synchronised watches in the Ops Room before we got on the plane. Now that we were on stand-by to go on real 'strikes', the pilot and navigator synchronised watches with an intelligence officer before we took off. The Intelligence Office was situated next to the Ops Room, which was convenient.

Once we reached the aircraft, my crew climbed in through the port waist hatch, putting a foot on a protruding support and using a grab-rail to haul themselves up. The ground crew pulled two locking pins out of the undercarriage – otherwise I wouldn't have been able to get the undercarriage up when we were airborne. The ground crew went round to Grimmer and gave the pins to him.

There was no point in taking off if I didn't know where I was going. Once I received the location of a possible target, Aspinall had to do some quick calculations. Asp had a plastic-topped disc as part of his equipment. He could enter our course on there with his pencil, turn the disc and read off the necessary adjustments as they came up. By entering the relevant information, we came up with the true course.

Before take-off, Alan Still checked that all his radio equipment was working. He had a lot of information in a book, but there was no substitute for a practical test. He switched on the radio, focusing on the receiver first, then the transmitter. He turned his transmitter on using the Type A starter, because the voltage in the transmitter was far higher than it was in the receiver. On an op he couldn't do a radio check with the ground station, he'd just have to satisfy himself that all was well.

Meanwhile the gunner at the back had also been busy, ensuring that the hydraulics would allow him to rotate his guns and their platform in the turret. You ran checks on everything. I'd ask: 'Radio working? Turret working?' Once I'd had confirmation, we were ready to go and do some damage to the Germans.

Seven complete crews, Mark Lee's and Tommy Carson's among them, made the same important step up to operational readiness. We were among the first torpedo-trained crews to join

217, though other squadrons had begun dropping torps earlier in the year.

We'd have to wait if we were going to use the skills we'd learned at Abbotsinch, though. Bombs and mines were still the weapons favoured by 217, and so it would remain for the rest of 1941. Our lives were therefore about to be risked in the dropping of devices for which we'd not been specifically trained – not that it bothered us much.

My first op that September was gentle enough – a patrol out into the Western Approaches to look for enemy submarines. It felt more like a training run, because nothing actually happened. We didn't see anything, except another aircraft on the way back. Then on 26 September, I was sent on my first shipping strike, down to the Bay of Biscay. A Hudson had spotted what the pilot thought was an enemy merchant vessel there for the taking. Pilot Officer Opperman, a nineteen-year-old from the Isle of Wight, was flying that day, along with Wing Commander Bower, who led our little formation. When we reached the Bay of Biscay, we couldn't find anything worth dropping any bombs on, though. We began to head for home. We lost sight of each other in storms and poor visibility. Without radio contact, Bower could no longer do anything for his inexperienced pilots; and we couldn't do anything for each other either. It was each man for himself.

The 217 Squadron operational record book explains how the tragedy unfolded, though for some reason it omits one member of Opperman's four-man crew:

The weather became bad and the formation was compelled to separate. W/Cdr Bower landed at Chivenor. P/O Aldridge

struggled through to land at base, but P/O Opperman and his
crew, Sgt Carter and Sgt Ryder failed to return. Reports came
in that they had struck the County Quarry, Tregouning [sic]
Hill, Breage, and the plane blown to pieces.

Poor Opperman. His death left the rest of us in the Officers'
Mess feeling numb. Yet the human cost of this tragedy was felt
more keenly by Bill Carroll than me, due to the role he was
given in its aftermath:

'Tubby Carter, one of the men who died, was a Londoner
whose house wasn't that far from mine, so I took his gear back
to his family. They'd already been given the sad news through the
usual RAF channels, though I suppose it was only natural that
part of them didn't want to believe it.

'So I knock on the door, his wife opens it, takes one look at
me – I was in uniform and the same height as her husband – and
she faints on the spot. Her father wanted to take a swing at me
for turning up like that, but I was only there out of courtesy.

'The other sergeant lost in the crash, Ryder, was a Dr
Barnardo's boy. He'd never had any family and he could take
things the wrong way. At Abbotsinch, for example, there'd been
a party and some idiot had been going around cutting people's
ties off as a joke. Most people thought it was funny, but when the
culprit tried to cut off Ryder's tie, he nearly got his thumb bitten
off. Let's just say Ryder had developed a different sense of
humour to the rest of us. Now the poor lad was gone, just like
Carter.'

On 14 October, 1941, I flew a night mission along with Mark
Lee. We went to lay mines outside the port of Lorient. If a big
German ship tried to come in or out, there'd be a nice little

surprise waiting for her – or at least that was the idea. We didn't call it mine-laying, though. Our superiors had come up with a different expression to describe what happened when we swooped down to fifty feet to plant mines in enemy shipping lanes. We called this activity 'gardening'. That was the official term and we were 'gardeners', planting the mines. So in my log-book I recorded the op as 'Gardening at Lorient'.

On this occasion, unfortunately, we didn't find Lorient or do any gardening – at least Mark and I didn't. The third pilot, called Philip Hanson-Lester – a born show-off and peacetime music-hall performer – managed to do the job perfectly, of course. The 217 operational records state:

> Sergeant Hanson-Lester had successful trip, planted in ship-ping channel, and gave information of lights observed.

Meanwhile Mark 'was unable to locate his target in the intense darkness and returned with his load'. No shame in that, because it would have been pointless and perhaps even potentially dangerous to our own shipping just to dump the mine for the sake of it.

Mark still did better than me. The truth was that I missed Lorient completely, an error which could have proven fatal. One or two degrees deviation from the correct course at an oblique angle sends you miles further down France's west coast.

It wasn't Asp's fault. We'd only been one or two degrees out – and the wind speed and direction across the Channel could have caused that. Still, I'll never forget the moment I voiced my concerns, while flying at about a thousand feet in a cloudless, moonlit night sky. The shiny mouth of a river below set off alarm bells instantly.

'The big river below us now, Asp.'

'What about it?' he asked.

Aspinall probably didn't know the geography of France quite as well as I did – and now I was sure. 'It's the River Gironde,' I told him, mildly horrified. 'Bordeaux! We've flown all the way down to Bordeaux! Blimey!'

I tried not to panic, but we were so far south that I was immediately worried about my fuel consumption. We could forget all about dropping the mine now. From this moment, getting home in one piece was my only objective. I decided to take a calculated risk, and warned my crew.

'We're turning back – but we're not going to fly all the way around Brittany. We've got to think about our fuel consumption, so we're going to cut across France. We'll just have to risk the night fighters.'

'OK, pilot,' my crew members replied uncomplainingly.

Each of us knew that a Beaufort was no match for enemy fighters. Beauforts could occasionally come to each other's rescue when under attack. But if you were all alone against an aircraft with vastly superior speed and manoeuvrability, you knew your time had come. If they found us, there'd be no way to evade them in a cumbersome Beaufort. We'd be shot out of the sky for sure. Yet the alternative carried an even greater risk – fly round and run out of fuel, ditch in the sea somewhere and there'd be little chance of survival and rescue.

'This is the first and last time I'm going to fly over enemy territory like this,' I thought. As the neutral sea below was replaced by occupied land and we scanned the night sky, not a word was spoken. There was little choice but to climb to two thousand feet and hope to avoid detection by the German forces below.

As we braved Brittany, all eyes searched for the moonlit silhouette of an enemy predator. For endless, nervous minutes, which seemed like hours, we peered into the darkness, until we saw what we'd all been waiting for – the coast again. Without hesitation, I flew for the fresh comfort of open sea. We'd got away with it! We were leaving the Cherbourg Peninsula behind, each one of us experiencing a relief which bordered on elation ... until I realised we didn't even have enough fuel to reach our base in St Eval.

'We're not going to make it, Asp, where can I land?'

'Predannack, on the Lizard Peninsula,' he replied.

It was right there on the first sliver of English land we'd see, and it would have to do. I aimed for the airfield, and stayed beneath the clouds which were trying to obscure the moon. I could see the outline of the English coast, but suddenly something strange and almost ghostly glistened just a few feet below me in what remained of the moonlight. It gave me the fright of my life; then I realised what it was – a great big barrage balloon. But realising that didn't make me any less scared.

There was no time to react. It flashed below me and there was no collision. Blimey! If I'd been just a few feet lower, I'd have crashed into the balloon and its cable! That would have been it. I still had the mine in the bomb bay as I looked for Predannack Down and a flare-path to guide me to safety.

I'd never landed at this tiny base before, and I couldn't see it! 'Keep calm,' I told myself, though it was easier said than done. At last I spotted the flare-path, illuminated by a Chance Light, the floodlight which shines its beam on the whole runway. How had I missed it? No matter, I had to hold my nerve and come in as tight as I could. There was no time or fuel to do a circuit or think about how to bring us down in one piece. Instinct played a big part my approach. I felt the pressure that comes with the knowledge that the lives of your crew are on the line, too. I seemed to be getting it right, though. 'Please, no more nasty surprises.' I felt the wheels touch down and I managed to stay in control. When at last we'd come to a halt in one piece, there was profound and silent relief among the four of us.

With a little extra fuel, I took off and completed the short flight to St Eval in the morning, wondering what the reaction would be back at base. Mercifully there was no reprimand, and no one teased me about what had happened. Mark Lee wasn't about to make me feel any worse; he probably realised what I'd been through, having failed to find the target himself. At least we'd lived to fight another day. We couldn't expect to be so lucky next time, though. We knew we'd have to learn quickly and adapt to all these new situations. The war wasn't going to get any easier; not for a long time.

My future gunner, Bill Carroll, found himself in an even deeper crisis over northern France that autumn, along with his young friend Jack Featherstone, who'd managed to make it back from Bristol by now. They were still part of Tommy Carson's crew, along with a navigator called Owen. As his name suggested, Warrant Officer Owen was a Welshman. He had four or five children and he was in his early forties. Owen was about as senior as you could get as an NCO, indicating that he'd been in the RAF since Pontius was a pilot. You had to serve about twenty years to become a Warrant Officer in the peacetime RAF, so he'd certainly made a career out of it.

One night Carson, Owen, Bill and Jack headed for Lorient, with orders to try out a very dangerous mine-laying technique: 'We flew all the way over at 60 feet and finally climbed to two thousand feet to drop the mine by parachute. The problem was this: even though it was dark out there, the chute was white, and it showed up in the sky. So we got caught in the searchlights – Jerry was terrific with those searchlights off Lorient. If you got caught like that, it became so bright inside the plane that you could read the Lord's Prayer off the top of a pin.

'Inevitably the flak came up, with Warrant Officer Owen down in the front. He started screaming with terror, and then he screamed some more. He was an RAF career man; but in those twenty years, he'd never seen this type of thing. There was tracer, too. At night it comes at you in all colours ... blues, reds, whites – beautiful and deadly. The navigator kept screaming; he was scared stiff. He started yelling at Tommy Carson to come back round, he'd had a complete breakdown on the spot. So Tommy did a stall-turn and flew back over the sea. After he'd pulled down close to the waves, he said to Owen: "Give me a course to steer." Nothing came back. In fact, Owen never said another word. He just froze. He wouldn't give Tommy the course for home, even though he was supposed to be the navigator. Mentally, he'd had it.

'We tried to head for home as best we could, and that's when we got this WT [Wireless Transmitter] failure. So Jack Featherstone and I tried to get a QDM, a magnetic course back to base, on the radio. But the radio wouldn't work and we didn't find out why until the next day. You have a transmitter and a receiver. And when you switch from the transmitter to the receiver, there's a big voltage jump. What we didn't know was that the screws were loose on the contact. Anyway, we switched to the civilian chaps – radio hams – on 3480. They were sitting there doing nothing all night and they were glad to get the business. They must have heard us because right away they challenged us, to make sure we weren't Germans. We had the challenge numbers for the day, and we did the challenge correctly. Then we asked them for a QDM; but by that point they couldn't detect us because of the vibrations.

'We tried to find the problem. Tommy Carson saw that Jack and I had the transmitter almost in bits, trying to change the channel. You have to take the damned thing out, and they've got coils in the back and you even have to move a lever. It was getting pretty tense because we didn't know where we were flying. I got back in the turret to try to see something that would tell us where we were. It was pitch-black at night, our first op; but I spotted something and said: "Tommy, there's a group of islands over here!"

'So he circled around and we realised they were the Scilly Isles. That's when we knew where the hell we were, and we also realised we'd been about to head up towards Ireland. So finally Tommy was able to do a quick right turn and work his way up the coast to St Eval. We came in and landed, and the navigator disappeared – we never saw him again. I don't know what happened to him, the poor guy; we really felt sorry for him. He was a nice guy but the man had to come off flying, he was going to be LMF [Lack of Moral Fibre].'

After that navigator lost his nerve in the searchlights, it was a miracle they managed to get home. Perhaps the pilot's navigational course in Canada had been more useful to Carson than to me – though Bill had been the one to spot the Scilly Isles.

Owen wasn't the last to lose his nerve. It happened to pilots, too. In fact, it happened to thousands of airmen in any given year of the war. Each man has his breaking point, and one man's breaking point might come sooner than another's. Perhaps I was helped in holding my nerve by the fact that I loved flying so much – I don't know. I certainly don't seek to judge others, and there will be no condemnation of LMF cases in this book. It happened, and therefore it should be aired without shame, and everyone given the respect they are due. Each man climbed into his plane wanting to be brave after all.

7

They're Trying to Kill Us

When we were told to drop mines outside the French port of Brest, we were automatically reminded of what had happened in the harbour there earlier in the year. Campbell's gallantry, a supreme example of self-sacrifice, had left its mark. Partly thanks to him, the German battlecruiser *Gneisenau* was still stuck at Brest with its sister ship the *Scharnhorst*, instead of causing destruction to our shipping lanes out in the Atlantic.

These ships had demonstrated their frightening combined power off Norway in June 1940, when they had sunk the aircraft carrier HMS *Glorious* and two accompanying destroyers, HMS *Ardent* and HMS *Acasta*. Although the *Scharnhorst* had been damaged in that fight, and by subsequent bombing raids at La Pallice, the necessary repairs had since been carried out; and it wasn't hard to imagine what mayhem these deadly German sisters might cause if they were allowed out on the high seas together again.

Both the *Gneisenau* and the *Scharnhost* would be ready to go back to sea before long. The *Prinz Eugen* was also in Brest harbour, having sought refuge there soon after leaving the doomed *Bismarck*. It was inconceivable that the trio would simply sit there for the rest of the war; so time was clearly running out if we wanted to hit these ships while we knew exactly where they were.

It was always possible that our commanders would order us to carry out a strike similar to the one which saw Campbell die so heroically. I wouldn't say the prospect of having to go up against these giants of the Kriegsmarine in a suicide mission cast a dark shadow over the squadron; but it was a challenge we suspected we'd have to face in some shape or form, sooner or later. For the moment, our job was to block or at least hamper the German ships' possible exit by laying mines.

It was still October when we were given the order to fly all the way to Brest at about fifty feet above the sea, so Jerry wouldn't detect us by radar. Campbell had gone the full fifteen nautical miles down the estuary to Brest itself. My job was to plonk down a jolly old mine in the estuary entrance, and then wait for observers to confirm we'd done the job properly. A squadron officer called Roy Nesbit was in charge of overall navigation. It was his job to look at the charts, listen to our accounts of any given gardening trip, and check we'd dropped our mines in the right place. My crew and I would have two other Beauforts for company, We tried not to think too much about what it might be like outside Brest, or reflect upon the fact that we were going to be facing our most dangerous sortie so far. The route was designed to help us avoid enemy night-fighters. It meant going around the Cherbourg peninsula and past the island of Ushant at the mouth of the Brest Estuary.

Unfortunately, I was the only pilot who made it to the target area. One Beaufort began to experience engine trouble and had to go back. The other pilot lost visual contact with us in the gloom – we still didn't have any radio contact – and couldn't find the Brest Estuary alone. So three became one and it was all down to me, along with my crew, to complete the mission.

Since we knew what fearsome defences awaited anyone daring to fly up that river, it really shouldn't have come as a surprise to discover defensive gun positions where the river met the sea, too. It was dark by the time I entered the approaches to Brest Estuary, and came within range of both promontories. I'd kept low but the Germans had seen me anyway – and they opened up on me from both sides.

Silver flashes of zipping tracer, dark puffs of flak, people trying to kill me for the first time. The flak wasn't too thick, but it was coming at me from two different directions – and that made it twice as frightening. Somehow I'd braced myself for flak coming up at me once I started ops. But this wasn't coming up at me at all – it really was coming in laterally. That reminded me how low we were, and we were going to fly at their level and stay at their mercy for a while longer.

I tried to ignore the efforts of the German gunners as best I could. It wasn't easy, you have to shut out the obvious danger and focus on the job. But we were still under fire as I dropped my mine in the approaches to Brest. Luckily for me, Jerry didn't manage to catch me in their cross-fire. Looking back, they didn't even come very close; but while we were being shot at, we didn't know how rapidly their accuracy might improve. So it was a great relief to turn away and realise when we were out of their range that we'd come away unscathed. Yet I was left exhausted by the experience – I remember feeling so tired on the way back to Cornwall that I switched on my 'George' – my automatic pilot – for a while.

My trusty wireless operator Alan Still sent out the correct IFF (Identification Friend or Foe) signal for the day as we approached home, a procedure as comforting as the familiar bacon and eggs we were given on our return. To smell those was to know you'd survived to enjoy life's simple pleasures for a little longer. And at that point you could afford to reflect on your good fortune.

At least we hadn't been told to climb to 2,000 feet to drop our mine by parachute, with the increased risk of being trapped in searchlights. Perhaps by the time I flew to Brest, our superiors had realised it wasn't a very good idea to do that. As far as I was concerned, low-level was best, despite the danger I'd just been in. My opinion didn't change, and was only reinforced, when subsequent reconnaissance revealed I'd dropped the mine in the right place. That showed I'd been able to focus on my job in difficult conditions. My mother didn't view my contact with the enemy quite so positively. When I went home for a couple of days' leave and told her the Germans had opened fire on me, she was indignant. She thought it was a cheek! Then, as it dawned on her that the Germans really had been trying to kill me, she became furious. 'How dare they?!' That's what she said, over and over again. 'How dare they?!' As far as she was concerned, this war had suddenly become personal, and she wasn't going to stand for any German trying to harm her boy.

You never knew what was coming next, and on Sunday, 26 October, 1941, some of the boys were handed an unusual op. The mission was for six Beauforts to bomb the docks at Nantes and, perhaps more interestingly, to drop leaflets over the city. The Germans had occupied Nantes more than a year earlier, and the French resistance had just assassinated the top local Nazi, Feldkommandant Karl Hotz. Hitler had ordered immediate retaliation, with fifty innocent civilians to be taken and executed.

Tragically this order was carried out and the Germans were due to execute another fifty at any time.

Even the Americans, who hadn't yet entered the war, were in uproar about these acts of brutality from the occupying forces. Franklin D. Roosevelt, the US president, had protested officially, warning: 'Frightfulness can never bring peace to Europe. It only sows the seeds of hatred which will one day bring fearful retribution.' Churchill issued a similar statement: 'These cold-blooded executions of innocent people will only recoil upon the savages who order and execute them!'

The leaflets given to 217 Squadron were designed not only to raise the morale of the French people who opposed the Nazis, but also to warn the Germans and local collaborators that such war crimes would not be tolerated by the Free World. Through the delivery of this unusual airmail, we could show that we weren't like the people we were fighting.

To my frustration, however, I wasn't sent on the operation. I knew about the leaflet-dropping before it happened, and was rather disappointed that I wasn't going. I wish I'd gone myself and I don't know why I wasn't sent; it was a great pity. Apart from the good I hoped it might do, I thought it would be rather fun to scatter propaganda over France. Tommy Carson was picked to lead the mission, so inevitably Bill Carroll was there, too:

'This was our third trip without Owen. For the first few flights he was replaced by a Canadian called Johnny Foster, who was extremely good. Then Foster was put on Mark Lee's crew, so Carson recruited Mickey McGrath as navigator. Mickey was very effervescent, a rugby star who played wing-threequarter for a really good team. He was a great bloke and he had good schooling.

'Anyway, we'd been to Nantes before, to bomb three ships in the harbour, a trip I'd never forget because I'd made the mistake of wearing nothing warmer than my flying suit at 12,000 feet, and it was freezing up there. But for the leaflet drop we flew at a low level all the way over, and I saw the islands off the French coast that tell you you're nearing the Loire and Nantes. When the locals saw us fly over, young kids flashed a "vic" – a V for victory. When we went low over those French islands off the coast, it became clear that they didn't have any Krauts on them, because the local people opened their doors and waved at us. It was unbelievable, I'm telling you. The Loire was such a deep waterway that I think ships of up to 10,000 tons could get up that river.

'We went about fifteen miles up-river to the city of Nantes, still flying at deck level. That's the way you should fly and the way I enjoy! We dropped our bombs on the docks and climbed east to about five thousand feet, turned back over the city and got ready to throw the leaflets out. There was an elastic band at one end of the thick pile, so that when you threw them out by shoving them down the flare chute they would scatter in all directions.

'I reckon the people of Nantes were happy to read them, even if the Germans weren't. They weren't very welcome down there, those Krauts; but we were!

'Roosevelt had given a speech saying that he was going to hold Hitler completely responsible for the death of the people who were being executed. As far as I know the Nazis did what they wanted anyway; they shot the other fifty people, and perhaps they'd already done so by the time we flew over. But this wouldn't be the last time the Americans and British showed a united front against the Nazis.'

Though the leaflets didn't have the immediate effect the Allies had hoped for, it seems that Lieutenant General Otto von Stülpnagel, the German military commander for France, halted executions locally in the longer run. Eventually he had to be replaced for speaking out against such atrocities; and he committed suicide in 1948 while being tried for war crimes.

Who knows, perhaps von Stülpnagel read those leaflets back in October 1941 and listened to the message they contained. Not Hitler, of course. By executing those prisoners, he showed once again that he was evil personified. As Churchill put it at the time: 'Retribution for these crimes must henceforth take its place among the major purposes of the war.' Brutal events like this reminded us what we were fighting, and what Hitler might do if he ever made it across the water to Britain.

We were determined to undermine the Germans in any way we could; but there were also times when our role as part of Coastal Command meant it fell upon us to help our own people in difficulty out on the water. My log-book entry for 22 November, 1941, reads simply: 'Sea rescue – contacted submarine.' The 217 operational records explain what it was all about:

> Pilot Officer Aldridge, who was Air Sea Rescue pilot, was sent out to find a friendly submarine which had lost contact with its escorting trawlers. Both trawlers and submarine were contacted, our A/C [aircraft] directed both until they were seen to exchange signals with one another.

It wasn't much, but it was more satisfying than searching for – and completely missing – an enemy port or ship!

In early December, after a few months of ops, some members

of 217 Squadron were sent on leave. They weren't going to be allowed to forget the war, though. The Japanese chose 7 December to bomb Pearl Harbor in Hawaii, though they must have known their treachery would have far-reaching consequences. Even the average Brit in the street knew it.

Bill Carroll was on leave, and this is his recollection:

'I went home to see my mother in Beckenham – we'd moved there from Bermondsey after my father died – and she said: "You don't have to worry now, Bill, the Yanks are coming into the war." I'd brought home Johnny Foster, the Canadian who had done a stint as navigator in our plane after Owen cracked up over France.

'Foster was a character. There was a space on the official forms where servicemen were asked to state what they used to do before the war. You filled them out when you went station to station. In this space, Foster used to write "Conman". After he visited my house, I decided this must really have been pretty much what Foster was before the war. It didn't stop me from liking the lad, though.

'Almost the first thing he said when he met my mother was, "Oh, Mrs Carroll, do you know your butcher very well?"

'"Of course," said mum.

'"Well, would you mind if I walk up there with you now?" asked Johnny, sweetly.

'"But it's the afternoon," she said. "I usually go shopping in the morning."

'"Well, can I talk you into going up to see the butcher anyway?" Johnny persisted, using all his charm. My mother wasn't very happy but she agreed to go with him and they walked into the butcher's together. Johnny picked out the best piece of steak in the whole place and put all his leave rations on it.

'When they got home, Johnny asked: "Can you cook that for us, Mrs Carroll?" She used to be able to fry a very good steak, my mum, but Johnny was so cheeky that he even oversaw everything. "Just turn it one more time, please, Mrs Carroll," he said cheerfully, looking over her shoulder at the piece of meat.

'When the steak was to his liking, he had her put it on a plate and he ate it. As soon as he'd finished, he turned to me and said, "OK, pal, I'll see you back at camp!" And off he went!

'Apparently Johnny went up to London's bright lights, got into some kind of card game, and must have met an even better conman; because he lost all the money he had set aside for his leave and had to return to base early. It was a real shame, because that leave was going to be the last chance for some fun he would ever have.

'As for me, I called up my fellow gunner from 217 Squadron Moggie Mayne, who lived over in Peckham, and we went down to my favourite pub, met some girls we knew, and had a great time. Sixty years later we're still disputing who locked the other man's girlfriend in the toilet for a joke.'

On 9 December, 1941, it wasn't cold for the time of year. After some drizzle early morning, it started to brighten up a little. Even so, a high cloud cover continued to frustrate the sun above Manston, a grassy airfield not that far from my home in Kent. Manston became our base when we were sent east for operations further up the Channel and beyond.

We had a chance to put the disappointment of the previous day's failed search for a lost RAF crew behind us. The order had been simple enough: 'Pilot Officer Aldridge and Flight Sergeant Stewart to search for a missing Hampden, believed to be down in the sea.' We'd looked long and hard, covering a specific area as instructed in 'creeping line ahead'. We couldn't find anything. Two more pilots from 217 Squadron, Sergeants Morgan and Banning, had searched another area later in the day, but again nothing was found. What we were looking for on this day, though, we were going to find.

We'd already been in the Operations Room together, Mark Lee and I. Surrounded by maps on walls, we'd been told there was a German convoy somewhere off the Hook of Holland. Just three Beauforts were to be sent out to intercept it; each of us ready to drop four 500 lb bombs on the ships if we could. There was no special significance to this convoy, except, of course, that it was carrying materials for the German war effort, and there-fore needed to be sunk.

We were to have no fighter escort, no diversionary tactics – it was just us against the ships. We were going to skim the waves on a low, predictable bombing run, and the enemy cannons were going to try to shoot us down.

Mark and I were to be led by Flight Lieutenant 'Ginger' Finch, a fearless South African. In the Officers' Mess he'd often let it be known that he was out to win a Victoria Cross – the highest honour for bravery. Another pilot's response was proba-bly more representative of the general mood: 'I don't want to get the VC,' he said. 'VCs tend to be awarded posthumously.'

In the Ops Room we'd been given the order of attack. Finch, unsurprisingly, was to go in first; Mark would attack second and I'd be third. This was to be our first big anti-shipping strike and the first time we'd dropped any bombs. The training had been torpedoes and on all previous ops we'd been dropping mines. The feeling was very different this time because a different level of aggression was expected of us. Even so, each man was focused on what he had to do, as always.

Mark and I didn't exchange words before we climbed into our respective Beauforts via the port wing and a hatch above the pilot's seat. He was with his crew; I was with mine. We prepared for the strike in our own ways. We were in our Irvin jackets and 'Mae Wests' – our life vests, named after the busty American film star. We'd have to inflate those life jackets ourselves if we ditched – as long as we still could.

Flight Lieutenant Finch was first up into the air at 15.40, flying Beaufort 'F'. A minute later, I followed him up in my trusty Beaufort 'B'. Mark was last into the air in Beaufort 'K', his take-off timed at 15.42. We didn't climb very much. We went out over the sea at no more than fifty feet above the waves to avoid detection by German radar. We were in a 'vic' – V-shaped formation – with Finch the spearhead. We kept our speed at a steady 140 knots, which was expected to put us face to face with the enemy within an hour.

Despite knowing how close this confrontation was, I felt strangely calm. Deep down I was resigned to my fate, whatever that might be, and I wasn't getting too worked up at all. It was my nature to stay calm, and I just hoped that would help get me through when it mattered. I had to stay alert at the same time, though, I knew that much.

Though our senses were sharpened, our concentration total, the flight across the choppy sea to the target was uneventful. We still had to avoid going so low that we hit one of those waves, all the time knowing that we would soon face people who would want to kill us. We knew we'd have to react quickly the moment we saw the enemy, to take advantage of the element of surprise we hoped to have retained.

Just under an hour later (16.39hrs), we spotted the German convoy pretty much where our intelligence officer had said it would be – just off the Dutch coast near Den Helder. There were eight ships, including one monster which looked about 12,000 tons. We all knew to go for the biggest vessel, so that's the one we singled out. There was no RT (radio traffic) between planes, there were no call signs, no 'tally-ho!' battle cry between the pilots before we went in. For us, it wasn't like the exchanges you heard between the Spitfire boys in the war films. This was reality. There were no last words.

Finch led us astern of the convoy as though the enemy had not been sighted, and turned to attack from the land side. It worked! The tactic caught the escort ships by surprise because they were grouped on the seaward side, so initially they couldn't do much about the attack. Finch went in low, using rudder movement to veer this way and that. He was already anticipating the heavy flak that was bound to come his way sooner or later. The tactic was called 'skidding', something more commonly done after an attack than before.

The German guns didn't get Finch; he flew in at below mast height and dead amidships, rising only slightly to dump his deadly load on the target. He timed it just right and three of his four bombs burst near the base of the funnel position. There was supposed to be an eleven-second delay before any explosion, to enable him to fly clear. Instead the blast was almost immediate, so it looked as though at least one of his bombs had gone into the boilers. Finch must have been badly shaken by the upward blast; you could see his plane shudder with it. The Beaufort was a steady, stable lump of a plane, but he needed all his skill and determination to maintain control and fly back out to safety.

Now it was Mark's turn; but the Germans were ready for him. I saw the deadly flak creeping towards him. You could see it, but you couldn't hear it; not with the headphones on. Mark could see it, but he couldn't do anything about it. He was hit in his port engine. He veered to the left, lost control and quickly became engulfed in flames. It was a terrible sight. My best friend. Mark's Beaufort didn't explode into pieces; but I knew in that moment he was losing his life. I saw him bang into the sea, still short of the target ship and across to the left. Shot down right before my eyes. It was over.

I had to carry on. There was nothing else to do, I was number three and it was my turn to attack. Tracer was coming at me; trying to send me crashing down in flames like Mark. This wasn't about revenge. I was too numbed by what I'd seen to feel anything like that. It was my turn, that's all. I flew very low to avoid the tracer flak, right down near the waves. It was the only way to get beneath those tracer bullets, which were skimming the upper surface of my wings. I tried to fly even lower than before – at 'zero feet', they called it. Good. The German gunners couldn't depress their guns this far down. They couldn't get me. But I was flying right at the ship, well below mast height. I had to pull up now to drop my bombs, or else I'd just slap straight into the bows. I reared up over the bows and dumped my load with the press of a button. The bombs hit home, I was sure they did, but I hoped they wouldn't explode until I was clear.

I felt a judder, and something told me I'd reared up a fraction too late. I'd run into something on the ship, but I was still flying. What was going on? Soon I'd be slapping into the sea. I'd be joining Mark any moment. Strange, it wasn't happening; not yet. There was chaos as the flak grew thicker all around me. Somehow my Beaufort had absorbed the shock of whatever impact she'd suffered. We weren't hit again, I was managing to skid, and I was getting clear. My crew saw the ship well ablaze behind us. It turned out to be an auxiliary vessel called the SS *Madrid*. Pretty soon she was down in the bows. The flak kept coming, but that ship wasn't going anywhere – except down.

The judder, though. I couldn't get away from that. My Beaufort was handling slightly differently. Something was wrong. I looked to the left and that was when I finally realised. The tip of my port wing wasn't there any more. It had been sliced off, probably by a bracing wire on the ship's mast, acting like a cheese-cutter. How much had gone? Eighteen inches? Two feet? You needed two wings to fly a plane. Two wings, both intact ... Didn't you?

I'd come up a fraction too late and this was the price I'd paid. A few feet further along the wing, and I'd have crashed immediately. I couldn't believe it hadn't happened already. I'd heard of Beauforts returning to base riddled with bullets, even with holes blasted in the tailplane; but with part of the wing sliced off? There was no guarantee my sturdy Beaufort 'B' would stay in the air for much longer. Night was closing in now, and we were a long way from home.

At first, though, all I could think about was how to evade the flak, which was thickening as the crew on the SS *Madrid* sought further revenge. I skidded, shoving the plane left and right, staying as low as I dared with a damaged plane, dodging the shells and waves. Beaufort 'B' was an obedient beast, and continued to follow instructions despite the amputation. Soon we were clear; we'd escaped Mark Lee's fate and we climbed away from the dreadful scene. Yet for all we knew we were heading for a slower death, which would come in the sea if my Beaufort disintegrated any more. I didn't know how stable the rest of the structure was. How were we still in the air? I scarcely dared to feel lucky, because any more wing loss and we'd crash. We were still in danger and it was my fault. If I'd pulled up a fraction earlier we'd have been fine, and so would my wing.

The sky was turning dark as we headed for home; and it felt a long way back to Manston from the coast of Holland. The rest of the crew didn't say much, which was hardly surprising. They knew I'd just lost a close pal, and they'd lost friends among his crew. I didn't feel like talking, but I asked Asp for my course and dutifully he obliged. As we tried to limp home, he confirmed at various intervals that we were still on the right track. Otherwise we were left to our private thoughts, wondering whether the structure of the plane would hold up, or trying to take in what had just happened. What use were words? Nothing we could say altered the fact that we were missing a wing-tip – or that Mark Lee was dead. We'd all seen it, so there was no point in going over it. We'd have to do that in the debriefing . . . if we made it home. For now, there was just a stunned silence.

Beaufort 'B' was stubborn, and so was I. Together we managed to find a way to stay in the air until we could see the English coast through the gloom. We may not have had two full wings to fly on – and it felt like part of me had been left back there in the North Sea with my friend, too – but it looked as though we might still have enough of a plane to get home.

The light was fading fast, and the next few minutes would determine our fate. By the time I spotted Manston and I was ready for the approach, it was completely dark and I'd switched on my navigation lights – only to realise that I no longer had two. One had disappeared with the wing-tip, so we must have looked a strange and confusing sight as we approached the airfield. From the ground, they could only see one light in the sky. If they couldn't understand what was coming towards them, there was nothing I could do about it. I had my own problems to deal with. Would the undercarriage come down? I pushed on the lever and hoped for the best. Yes, the wheels were coming down, and we were almost there. Flaps fully down, that's it. Speed down to 80 knots. I held her steady, discouraging any thought she might have of tilting to the left due to the lack of a complete port wing. Remarkably, the missing tip wasn't making much difference at all. Somehow Beaufort 'B' had adapted!

We grazed the grassy runway, found a way to stay down, and slowly came to a halt. Only now, when we were still, did we fully realise what we'd just been through. Perhaps we saw it in the faces of the ground crew as they approached and peered at the plane through the murk. They couldn't believe what they saw, and I felt responsible.

'I'm sorry about this, but I'm afraid I've lost my wing-tip,' I said, rather stating the obvious. Extra work for them, unfortunately, and one never liked to be responsible for that.

'That's all right, sir, we'll try to get that fixed for you,' they assured me, not wanting to ask too much about what might have happened. They were very good about it.

Before they went to work on those repairs the next day, someone took of photo of what was left of that port wing, to prove what a mess it was. I don't know how I managed to fly with that lot flapping around, though fortunately I couldn't see the true extent of the damage at the time.

Someone said they could mend the plane by attaching a new segment of wing. And they did a good job, too, because I was back in Beaufort 'B' within about a week. The ground crew were wonderful – they were unsung heroes throughout the war.

Planes or their bits and pieces could be replaced but friends couldn't, and the enormity of what had happened wasn't lost on me. The operational record is poignant in its simplicity:

F/Lt Finch: Up 15.40 Down 17.56. P/O Aldridge: Up 15.41
Down 18.02. P/O Lee Up 15.42.

In reality Mark was down at about 16.40, his life over. After the
debrief I went off and wrote a letter of condolence to his parents,
Captain Frederick Lee and his wife Constance Mary. I'd never
met them and don't even remember how I got their address, but
they lived in a place called Low Ash, near Kibworth in Leicestershire. The letter was short, to the point and from the heart. I
said he was a good friend of mine, explained what had happened
in essence, without giving all the painful details, and offered them
my deepest sympathy. He was their only son, although he did
have a sister called Vivienne, who was in the WAAF.

As I wrote, the Germans were pulling Mark's body out of the
sea, and they did at least afford him the respect he deserved from
that point on. He was buried at Ameland (Nes) General
Cemetery, Friesland, Holland. His grave is to be found at plot
reference D, Row 15, Grave 4. It is the final resting place of a
fine human being. He was the first of many close friends of mine
who would lose their lives during the war. The expression we all
used to describe this type of thing didn't begin to describe how
I felt. 'Mark Lee's gone for a Burton,' we all said. The expression
came from an ale advert. They showed an empty chair; empty
because its owner had gone for a pint of his favourite Burton
beer. The phrase stuck in the RAF, such a casual way to describe
people who didn't come back. There wasn't time to be too sen-
timental, because it was happening so frequently. The expression
helped us to cope, I suppose, without thinking too deeply or
emotionally about the people involved. They had 'gone for a
Burton'. If my turn came, that's what they would say about me.
'Aldridge has gone for a Burton.'

Tommy Carson was the one who went to collect up Mark's things to send to his parents. Perhaps I was writing or just didn't feel up to it. But when Carson got there, Wing Commander Bower was already there, going through Mark Lee's music. He'd had part of his wonderful collection of classical records sent to him since our return from Canada, or else he'd brought them back from leave. This collection, which illustrated Mark's impeccable taste and sensitivity, was something deeply personal. And there was the Wing Commander, picking through it at will. Tommy was only a Pilot Officer, very inferior in rank, but that didn't stop him from giving the Wing Commander a piece of his mind. And he prevented him from taking anything. For his part, Bower must have accepted he had been in the wrong; he backed down, spared himself a backlash, and later went on to become an Air Commodore.

Mark Lee's loss was the one I felt most keenly, though of course it wasn't just Mark who died. Bill Carroll knew Mark's crew members best:

'You've already heard about Johnny Foster. My mother and I hadn't been angry about what he'd done for more than a few moments; we just had to laugh and marvel at his powers of persuasion. Poor old Johnny.

'Harry Carter and John Chadaway were the other sergeants to die with Mark. Harry was a married man and a master plumber. He was about thirty and he had four or five young children. He and his wife had some kind of row, and that's why he'd joined the bloody air force. His wife had come up to see him when we were at Abbotsinch. Harry went to Paisley railway station to pick her up, had a few drinks while he was waiting, lay down on the seat at Paisley and missed her. He got shot down and now his widow had to face bringing up four or five kids on her own. That was the trouble when a plane went down with its crew.

'Chadaway – he'd never been with a woman, never had a piece of tail in his life. Once we'd taken him to a dance in the Marine commandos' base on the next island from Thorney Island. We were trying to instruct him; we picked a girl out for him, and made sure he gave her lots of booze. The silly bugger spends a fortune on whisky for her. He's filling her with drink and then he decides it's time to go for a pee. Time is running short because pretty soon we'll all have to get back on the truck. She's disappeared, and when John comes back, we all start looking for her. Where did we find her? She's outside on the back of the truck with a Warrant Officer, who's a signals guy or something. Moggie Mayne is there and he strikes a match; and all you can see is this white thigh. Chadaway? He died a virgin.'

Each airman was an individual with his own story, sometimes of a life unfulfilled or a falling-out unresolved. Their lives and deaths were just as important as those of the pilots, of course; and their families were left to deal with the consequences, both emotionally and practically.

The Operational Records of 217 couldn't afford to be too emotional. In fact, if there is any emotion to be detected from the official account of what happened that day, it is one of satisfaction with the overall outcome. The entry for 9 December, 1941, reads:

Three A/C led by F/Lt Finch carried out a very successful raid on enemy shipping. The other members of the team were P/O Lee and P/O Aldridge ... P/O Lee came in second but was seen by P/O Aldridge to have his port engine on fire and to strike the sea ahead of the target ship ... P/O Aldridge went in at zero feet and while scoring more direct hits missed disaster by inches and good airmanship. His wing tip fouled a stay on the ship and left bits and pieces behind. F/Lt Finch and P/O Aldridge were awarded the DFC. Congratulations!

The squadron had to have an overview and regarded casualties as an inevitable price for 'success'. All I can say is that on the evening of 9 December, I didn't feel like being congratulated.

8

Medals and Feathers

When they awarded me the DFC, the authorities chose not to award Mark Lee one posthumously. Mark had given his life and shown as much bravery as I had, or indeed Finch; so personally I think they should have given him a DFC, too. Sadly, our superiors didn't see it that way. In fact, it had been made perfectly clear that pilots who lost their lives in action were not to be awarded a DFC. Those in authority believed the alternative would have opened the floodgates. Given the opportunity, every commanding officer of a pilot who lost his life would have felt compelled to put the dead man in for a posthumous DFC. They would have felt an emotional pressure to do so, whatever the circumstances of that death, in order to ease the grief of the pilot's family. It was therefore deemed wiser to spare those in command of the squadrons from what might have become a relentless, automatic application for a posthumous award. You could see their argument. Yet it seemed less than fair that Mark should die so bravely at just twenty-one years of age and not have that bravery marked in a fitting way.

His local paper, the *Kibworth News*, recorded his passing with great warmth and dignity. It wrote:

Mark has joined our Roll of Honour. We will try to live up
to the tradition he has established and to his glorious memory.

The tribute concluded with the following lines of poetry:

I hold
That it becomes no man to nurse despair,
But in the teeth of clenched antagonisms
To follow up the worthiest till he die.

Life went on, and I tried not to feel too sad about Mark's passing. Yet I could never hear the tuneful 'Scheherazade' from that
moment on, without thinking about my unassuming and tal-
ented best friend.

The ship Finch and I had destroyed, the SS *Madrid*, weighed
a little less than we had first estimated. Her true tonnage was
8,741. Built in Hamburg in 1922, the *Madrid* had been a pas-
senger ship in peacetime, and had acted as an auxiliary ship and
dormitory for submarine crews in wartime. Our strike cost
twelve lives, I later learned. I never found out whether that list
of fatalities included Mark Lee and his crew, though I somehow
suspect it didn't. Most of the German crew, which apparently
numbered eighty-six in total, managed to get clear before she
sank. I had no particular feelings about the human cost of the
raid on the German side.

There was precious little time to grieve for Mark, even if that
had been the way people did things in the squadron. Three days
later I was ordered out again on a similar mission. This time I
flew in Beaufort 'H', my trusty 'B' having been sent for repairs.
But this time we didn't find our target.

Two days later I was back in my mended Beaufort 'B', and was sent to St Eval on stand-by for yet another shipping strike. Within hours news came through of a confirmed sighting of two enemy convoys, close to each other and seemingly there for the taking. Minutes later I was leaving the familiar outline of the Cornish coast behind, along with two fellow pilots and friends, Robert Seddon and Alan Etheridge. Flying out around north-western France and enemy-occupied territory, I knew this was going to be another very dangerous day, much more demanding than any 'gardening' expedition I'd done in those waters during the autumn.

Less than a week earlier, I'd been reminded through bitter personal experience that friends who set out on strikes together don't always make it back together. I didn't sit there in the cockpit worrying that it might happen again; you couldn't function if you did that. Besides, it wasn't in my nature to dwell on any worst-case scenario; I just got on with it. But there was no escaping what I knew deep down: this was going to be no ordinary strike – if such a thing even existed. Although my favourite plane felt reassuringly familiar, the load in the bomb-bay was different. The doors weren't fully closed on this particular day, because they couldn't fully close. For the first time, I was going to attempt what I'd actually been trained to do up at Abbotsinch the previous summer. I was carrying a torpedo. But instead of aiming at a lighthouse on a Scottish island, I was going to try to destroy a moving enemy merchant ship.

Unfortunately, we must have been spotted quite early, judging by the flak which welcomed us. And in those moments after we found our quarry, it became clear that Beaufort 'B' and I were developing a nasty habit of getting into trouble together. Seddon had gone in first and enjoyed some success, because dark smoke was already pouring from the leading ship. But, by the time it was my turn to go in, a flak ship had positioned itself bang in front of the target, and was trying to make a target of us. This made aiming a bit awkward, to say the least. Training at Abbotsinch hadn't prepared us for such moments. Our instructors in Scotland had never arranged any kind of distraction for us, let alone physically blocked our line of attack. As for being fired at just as we were about to release the torpedo, no training could replicate that. I was no stranger to flak or its deadly effects; but being surrounded while trying to judge precisely the right angle and distance at which to press the button was tricky. I didn't duck the challenge and I dropped my torp just when I thought I should. But I wasn't going to hang around to see what happened next. Did I do any damage to the German convoy? Who knows? Others may have had more success than me that day; but at least the flak ship didn't bring me down. And this time all three pilots from 217 Squadron were able to return home together safely. The record shows:

> Two convoys sighted: one of eight merchant vessels and one of nine merchant vessels. Seddon attacked and torpedo was seen to score. Clouds of grey smoke, and ship thought to be on fire and sinking ... J/217 (Etheridge) and B/217 (Aldridge) dropped torpedo but results were not observed as evasive action was taken from flak ...

So I lived to receive my DFC, news of which was telephoned through to the West Malling post office in Kent, where my father and mother got to hear about it. I don't know why my superiors did that and I was rather surprised to hear they had. I suppose my parents were proud; a nice Christmas present for them, perhaps. I don't know, because I didn't telephone them personally to tell them about my medal. I knew my parents were proud of me during the war, and they didn't need to say anything about my medal for me to know that.

Back at Thorney Island, another of our coastal bases, this time in Hampshire, my colleagues threw a big party for me in the Officers' Mess. All the sergeants came in, which was quite rare in itself, because that wasn't usually allowed, so my crew were there to celebrate the DFC with me. It was all rather nice because this was just before Christmas and therefore a good time for a celebration. I should have bought drinks for Alan Still, Vince Aspinall and Flight Sergeant Grimmer when they came in. In fact, I should have bought everyone a drink! I was bought a couple of beers, which I could hardly decline; but returning the compliment and getting drunk weren't high on my list of priorities that evening.

There was a very nice WAAF working in the Officers' Mess; she might have been a waitress, and I quite liked her. I know she was stationed at Thorney, because I had often seen her around the place. That evening I went out to the cinema with her. How I managed it, I don't know; we didn't do it to celebrate my medal. I wanted to take her out to the cinema just because she was nice and she was pretty, too. I can't remember what the film was or even the girl's name after all these years but I do remember that, as far as I was concerned, the date was better than the party they were throwing for me in the Officers' Mess. That's no disrespect to my crew members or the RAF, merely a reflection of the fact that I definitely preferred to be in the quiet company of an attractive woman than in the thick of a boozy party. And, after everything that had happened a few days earlier, I think I just wanted to get away from the RAF environment for a few hours.

In stark contrast, the other recipient of the DFC from our strike on the *Madrid* liked nothing more than a boozy party. And if Bill Carroll's account of Flight Lieutenant Finch's celebration is anything to go by, there must have been quite a few sore heads the following morning:

'Our crew was posted to Manston and we found Flight Lieutenant Finch there, practically in charge of the place. That's when the news that Finch had won a DFC, along with Arthur Aldridge, came through. Finch loved his booze. I think Tommy Carson was the only other commissioned officer with him, and they decided to celebrate. They had a Shooting Brake, one of those big old estate cars sometimes used for hunting expeditions, so Tommy called me and our navigator, Mickey McGrath, and he said: "We're going out for a party." Finch insisted on ordering all the drinks. He chose Blue Niles for us all. It was awful stuff – gin and crème de menthe. That was what we drank all night. He'd been in the desert, he said, that's why he loved to drink, and that's why he loved that drink. My goodness, he could drink those Blue Niles! I wasn't used to gin and crème de menthe, I was a beer drinker.

'"Come on, drink up, it's Christmas, remember?" he said.

'"I'm OK with this one, thanks," I replied.

'"I'm paying," he insisted. "And you're drinking."

'So I drank Blue Niles with him; and for a young twenty-year-old used to drinking beer, that really put the hair on your chest. He was a jolly boy, Finch. Mad bugger, but a good guy. And that wasn't the only big night out while we were on Finch's patch.

'The next time, eight of us were crammed into the Shooting Brake, and Finch was sitting in the front with this little French guy. There was a lot of snow and ice at Manston that year. "Get out and see where we are, we're bloody well lost," Finch tells the Frenchman. But he hadn't even stopped the car when he shoved this guy out in the snow to look at a sign.

'We went and got tanked up that night and a few other nights. You'd never have got Artie doing that – but that's the kind of guy Finch was.'

Finch and I really were very different people. The trouble with Finch was this: he was so overbearing that he was one of the few people I actually disliked in my entire war in the RAF. And when someone comes close to killing you quite unnecessarily, as Finch did a fortnight later, it hardly endears that person to you.

In the meantime, I didn't get a chance to go home to spend Christmas with my parents because by Christmas Eve I was back in St Eval. On 28 December, though, I was promoted from Pilot Officer Aldridge to Flying Officer Aldridge, and, a few days later, I was finally given some leave. I went home to see my parents in West Malling, recharged my batteries, slept and ate well, and tried to imagine what the rest of the squadron was doing in my absence. In one case, at least, that would have been impossible. As was so often the case, Bill Carroll was in the right place at the right time to witness the scene:

'British convoys would go up the English Channel flying balloons, because Jerry used to come in and bomb the hell out of them. The only British convoy out at the time was supposed to be up on the coast of Essex, but it was actually flying balloons near Dover at about five thousand feet. Fortunately we picked up on this as we came back from a strike somewhere, and we went all the way around the convoy – and the balloons – to land at Manston safely. But some bloody admiral guides in a pilot from our squadron named McGregor right over Dover, and he picks up one of these flying balloons. The first thing he does is to go out to sea again, and ram the throttles open to stay in the air. If he's going to go down, he definitely prefers the idea of going down into water than dirt.

'Well, on a Beaufort you're only supposed to be able to use the throttles like that for about ten minutes before the bloody thing blows up. He was screwing around out there in the English Channel, but he takes the opportunity to pull this big toggle in front of him, which is the jettison plug, to get rid of his bomb load. This will give him two advantages in what is now a fight for his life: if that extreme use of his engines does spark some kind of fire, or if he crashes, there'll be no bombs in the bay waiting to explode; secondly, while he's still in the air, he'll be free of some of the weight that's trying to pull him down to his death.

'Pretty soon Manston is on the radio, working out a way to keep McGregor alive a little longer. They give him directions to come in, but he's got fifteen hundred feet of cable dragging behind him. So they bring him in over Ramsgate towards Manston. At least it's a grass field there, so he doesn't need a runway.

'By this time it's almost dark and the rest of us have landed and we're all standing there watching this aircraft come around. All we can hear is bang, crash, wallop – it's the sound of all the chimneys in Ramsgate falling off their roofs with this bloody cable hitting them. But against the odds, McGregor comes, lands and just about pulls up dead with all this stuff behind him. Everyone rushes out to the plane, Tommy Carson included. Even the Wing Commanders and fighter pilots are out to see this spectacle.

'The mechanics come and tow the plane to a decent spot in the muddy field, and we follow it there. The Group Captain is there, with everyone else gathered around the aircraft. The armament guy checks the cockpit, sees the toggle switch had been pulled, and he opens the bomb doors in front of all of us. Four 500 lb bombs drop out. McGregor had pulled the jettison and he figured the bombs had gone down into the Channel in an area of sea where British ships weren't waiting to be blown up; so they should have been resting at the bottom of the Channel by now, but what he hadn't done was open the bomb doors to let them leave the bay.

'So now four 500 lb bombs have suddenly come tumbling out. Well, Jesse Owens couldn't have out-sprinted us all as we ran towards the back of the aircraft to get out of the way. But we forgot that fifteen hundred feet of cable was waiting for us there. Everyone tripped over it and fell flat on their faces, all the highest ranking officers in the mud, too. Well, I tell you it was one of the funniest things I've ever seen, and the reason I could still laugh about it seventy years later was that the bombs didn't explode.

'The ground crew got the shears and gave everyone a foot of the cable as a souvenir. Then everyone went into the mess and got roaring drunk. The gunner on McGregor's aircraft got absolutely blotto, as you can imagine. Couldn't believe he was still alive, but he was already worried about something else. He was in the bunk next to Jack Featherstone and me, and all night long he was asking: "Where's my bloody piece of wire?" The damned cable they'd given him – that's what he cared about. It was hilarious.'

Even though I hadn't been there, I didn't want to miss out on the banter entirely. 'Any fool can fly into a barrage balloon,' I told McGregor when I came back from leave the very next day. (I should have known, because I'd very nearly done exactly the same thing on the way back from Bordeaux.)

'True,' he replied, 'any fool can fly into one. But it takes a good pilot to fly out of one and take the cable home with him.'

How he managed to do so without being dragged down, I shall never quite understand. McGregor never tired of telling us that it required a good pilot to be able to pull that much cable. He created chaos all over Kent; hit all sorts of chimney pots, though I don't know how close he came to knocking my parents' chimney off our roof at West Malling. He was telling us how well he had done for quite a while after that, it was the talk of the squadron, and we all had a great laugh about it.

I was the next pilot to come close to losing his life at the hands of his own side. I recorded the incident in my log-book as a routine air test. It became anything but. Ginger Finch insisted on taking me up to show me how to 'feather the prop' above Thorney Island.

Feathering the prop is a flying term, describing what you can do if one engine fails while you're flying. You reduce drag on the dead engine by turning the blades of the redundant propeller sideways into the airflow, parallel to it, thus eliminating air resistance as much as possible. To recreate this scenario in training and prove you can handle it, you switch off one engine and fly on the other. It's a risk created with the single push of a button; but a Beaufort doesn't always take well to it. I could have done this myself if I'd wanted to take the risk; but Finch insisted on showing me, even though he wasn't even an instructor.

He took me up to 10,000 feet, switched the engine off and couldn't switch it on again. He got into a complete muddle and couldn't control the aircraft or right it again. I thought, 'This is it – he's out of control.' We started hurtling down from 10,000 feet in an uncontrollable dive. Nine thousand, eight thousand, seven thousand ... He doesn't even look close to finding an answer. Six thousand, five thousand, four thousand … For God's sake, man, get a grip of your aircraft. I didn't say it, because there was nothing I could do. Three thousand, two thousand … 'My end has come,' I thought. 'And I'm not even fighting the enemy; I'm just losing my life to a show-off.' We were below 2,000 feet now, the ground was rushing up at us, and I prepared for the impact. Not that I would know much about it … I hoped. Just before we met oblivion, Finch managed to pull out of the dive. But could he get her level in time? He did it with a few feet to spare. It was terrifying, but against all odds we landed safely.

I was angry beyond description. We'd survived, but the fact remained that he'd almost killed me. He didn't apologise, and that was no surprise to me, because it wasn't his style. He didn't even buy me one of his precious Blue Niles. After what he'd put us through, I might even have drunk it! I didn't like Finch. I couldn't like everyone, and here was a man I didn't like at all.

Bill offered a possible explanation for what happened:

'The Mark I Beauforts we were flying in England in 1941 had Taurus engines, which was a Bristol-built engine. You couldn't feather the props on it, not completely. But then they started fitting some of the Beauforts up with a Pratt & Whitney engine, which was an American engine. Although Arthur's Beaufort didn't get one of these new engines, some in the squadron did. The Pratt & Whitney engines were more powerful so you could go on one engine.'

Who knows whether Finch had somehow confused the engines, or if he just had a death wish? Finch wasn't going to be with us much longer. Something truly horrendous was just around the corner.

9

The Channel Dash

On 2 February, 1942, the Admiralty issued an appreciation of the probable departure of the giant German ships, the *Gneisenau*, *Scharnhorst* and *Prinz Eugen*, from their haven in north-western France: 'The Brest ships cannot be fully efficient yet, but where they have led a charmed life, the Germans must be anxious to get them away to a safer harbour . . .'

A further clue to Britain's high state of alert came in 217 Squadron's operational record book for 4 February:

Flap on this afternoon. Some eight aircraft standing by. Probably our old friends coming out of Brest.

The French resistance were able to send messages to warn that the German fleet was making ready for departure, and aerial reconnaissance confirmed as much. They might try to head for their own harbours, or they might even try to break out into the Atlantic, to have another go at our convoys there.

Either way, Churchill wasn't in any mood to let them get away. At 217 Squadron, I remember, we knew what was going to happen. We'd practised formation flying with torpedoes before, and I'd already tried to hit an enemy ship with one; but from now our planes were permanently fitted with torpedoes and we never went back to bombs or mines.

The torpedoes had to be lifted up into the bomb bay, protruding as usual so that the doors couldn't close. Though you could land safely enough with the torpedo still there, we were more sure than ever that those 'fish' would be going for a swim, whatever the human cost. I suspected many of us wouldn't survive the battle that was coming. No airman could assume he was going to come back; not once we were thrown against those colossal ships. So I took the opportunity to call my parents, though of course I couldn't tell them what was imminent. It wasn't even a question of telling them I loved them – we never really talked like that; it went without saying. I just wanted to have a last chat with them, because I knew the break-out, when it happened, was going to be a bit tricky. It might be the last time I'd ever speak to them. It was mother who answered the phone. I was glad to have a last talk with her, though I didn't get to speak to my father, for some reason. It was just one of those ordinary little chats. A little bit of normality before something very abnormal; small talk before something very big indeed.

'Yes, I'm OK, how are you and father? Bit chilly, isn't it? Not exactly tennis weather. Oh, you've seen Sally, have you? Yes, send her my regards. Perhaps we'll team up in the summer for a spot of tennis if I have some leave. See you soon. Tell father I called. Look after yourselves.'

The other chaps on the squadron probably made similar phone calls. Grimmer, our gunner, knew his wife was about to have their baby, so it couldn't have been easy for him. Such moments must have been harder for crew who had more to lose, and suspected they were indeed going to lose everything. As for me, I had no wife or children, not even a steady girlfriend, so life was a little more straightforward. I had my parents but I wasn't responsible for them. I was their only child, and I didn't suppose it was going to be easy for them if I were to be killed; but they'd cope. As a vicar, my father had his faith in God. I had no strong feelings about religion in those days. I was brought up a Christian, went to church, took it all automatically, but I didn't think about God during the war. I never went to church at all during World War Two, not if I could help it. People later suggested to me that the war might have been quite a good time to pray, just in case God really does exist and I was about to meet him! But still I didn't – and God is not what I encountered during the war. My parents, they were the true Christians. I knew they'd be praying for me but I had a more fatalistic attitude to life.

Not that I was superstitious, as some were. Bill Carroll, for example, carried a lucky charm:

'When we took off I always used to blow a kiss to England – "see ya later". And I always used to carry with me a piece of black rock with a little hole in the middle, shaped like a cone. I'd found it between Deal and Hastings on the southern English coast when I was four. I'd been walking there with my father, a Cockney who'd been gassed in the First World War. He bought me a ring to put that little stone on, and he said to me: "Bill, this is a good luck charm – never take it out of your pocket."I flew with it everywhere. Later a geologist and a historian told me that my piece of stone came from a certain part of France and could only have been dropped by a French archer in 1066, because the archer had used the conical centre of this really hard rock to sharpen his arrows. That was in my trouser pocket everywhere I went, every strike we did.'

Unwittingly, Bill was carrying something belonging to the

last winners of a famous battle on our shores. And since he was the only one from that photo at Chivenor to come through the war entirely unscathed, maybe there was something in it after all. Me? I didn't carry anything like that; and I tried not to think about what might be coming. It was just a case of what will be, will be. As we waited at Thorney Island, time could go slowly. I hardly had any books with me to read, and most of the time I had no means of listening to my beloved classical music. How I missed it.

Often it was a question of just sitting in the crew rooms on stand-by, doing nothing. Games were out for me, I don't know why. I played chess before the war and after the war but not during the war. I wasn't a crossword fiend either. So thank heaven for one of the greatest comedy shows ever broadcast. Sometimes the radio would be on in the crew rooms and I would listen to the *ITMA* programmes – 'It's That Man Again'. The title came from the newspaper headlines which appeared every time Hitler took over some new territory that didn't belong to him.

Tommy Handley and Ted Kavanagh were *ITMA*'s creators. We'd be waiting in the crew room on stand-by and you couldn't help but laugh at some of the sketches set in the seaside resort of 'Foaming-at-the-Mouth'. There were characters such as Funf, a German spy who spoke with an exaggerated accent. Those with telephones in England had already started mimicking him by calling one another with the opening line: 'Ziss iss Funf speakink.' There was another character called Mrs Mopp, the office cleaner, whose catchphrase was, 'Can I do you now, sir?' We'd be listening to the radio and splitting our sides, and then suddenly we'd have to go and risk our lives trying to bomb or torpedo someone. You'd take what amusement you could get from the radio, though, because it might be your last laugh, quite literally. Otherwise we had the simple comfort of chatting to each other about this or that, keeping the tone light, knowing we were all in the same situation.

Unfortunately, as we prepared for the German break-out, which we knew was coming, the squadron was dealt a body blow. Squadron Leader Larkin, a New Zealander who had only taken over from the outgoing commanding officer, Wing Commander Bower, in January, was lost to us. He failed to return from his very first operational trip, on 8 February. Later that month it emerged that he and his crew had been picked up by the enemy uninjured. They didn't know how lucky they were to be out of the firing line just before some of the worst events of the entire war. Or perhaps they did. Cynics on the squadron darkly intimated that Larkin had gone into the drink deliberately, to avoid what was to come.

When Squadron Leader Taylor, DFC, AFC, arrived to take over Larkin's duties on 9 February, he immediately cancelled all leave for Beaufort squadrons. There was sufficient activity in Brest harbour by now to suggest the break-out was very close. Cancellation of leave quickly turned into permanent stand-by, and some of the crew weren't best pleased. Young men wanted one last chance to have some fun, including Bill Carroll:

'We were twenty, a happy bunch – at least some of us, like Moggie Mayne and me. The war didn't bother us too much. Forget this business about being brave. We were young and stupid. "We didn't give a damn and we loved our fellow man." The guys were unbelievable – I'm so glad I was one of them.

'Thorney Island was a nice station and the WAAFs would put on a dance, just like that. Suddenly the bosses were saying the NCOs weren't allowed out of camp, weren't allowed to drink, and we were supposed to stay in the mess, even when the girls were putting on a dance.

'About half a dozen of us wandered over to the WAAFs dance and had a couple of beers. Well, we hadn't left camp, had we? Problem was, Tommy Carson's crew was the duty crew – and I was on that crew. You do four days on, and two days off. This was one of our four days on.

'Some silly sod sent the message back to Squadron Leader Taylor that we were over at the dance. Someone got on the PA system and told everybody: "The duty crews of 217 will return to their own messes." Well, we didn't like that because the dance was just getting going. Then the Controller took it up a notch and called us out on a trial run. We had to rush to our aircraft after a few beers!

'Tommy Carson said to me: "Bill, you sit in the turret and don't you open your mouth to anyone, especially if you've been drinking."

'"Me, drinking?" I said innocently.

'"Just sit in the turret," said Tommy, not fooled for an instant.

'We didn't take off, thankfully.'

Then it happened. The date is etched on my memory – 12 February, 1942. The *Scharnhorst*, *Gneisenau* and *Prinz Eugen* broke out of Brest harbour and tried to head up the English Channel as fast as they could in an attempt to return to their home German ports of Wilhelmshaven and Brunsbüttel. This gamble became known as the Channel Dash.

A stupid Spitfire pilot was patrolling and spotted the German ships on the move in the early hours; he maintained radio silence. Usually you're supposed to keep radio silence, but he should have realised this was the one time not to! The official 217 record lamented:

Terrific flap today. Scharnhorst, Gneisenau and Prinz Eugen are out of Brest and heading up towards the North Sea. How they managed to get as far as this without detection is one more mystery of this war . . .

The German ships were round and into the English Channel before anyone knew it.

It wasn't just the fault of the Spitfire pilot, because there were other factors. A patrolling Hudson went back before the next Hudson arrived, so there was a gap in the surveillance on Brest Harbour from the air. The Germans didn't know that, they just got lucky. I don't doubt they planned to use the murky weather to their advantage, though – and it worked a treat. But that Spitfire pilot could have blown their cover if he'd given us all an early warning.

I should thank him really. If he'd broken radio silence I might not have survived, because I'd have been able to attack twice from Thorney Island, or perhaps even from St Eval. The ships would have been within range to do one early strike and then another later on. Then we might even have been asked to go out and face them a third or fourth time from Manston. You had their fighters to contend with, too, because the ships were within fighter range of the French coast. The idea of surviving two attacks seemed rather optimistic, though some pilots did so once the mayhem started. But I wouldn't have survived three or four sorties. No way.

The events of the day are painful to examine, because the whole show was so chaotic and poorly handled. It was 9 a.m. before another Spitfire pilot, a Wing Commander, radioed in three giant ships and fifty or sixty others, all on the move. At that point, our superiors knew what was going on – they just didn't bother to tell the pilots who were going to have to do the job. Initially, we weren't even told the truth about what we were going to be targeting, or indeed where. They told us the targets were three merchantmen, and we were to fly from Thorney Island to Manston in Kent, and then strike from there. Three merchantmen! It was ludicrous, but that's what they said in the name of security! Unfortunately, we had been given the wrong position as well as the wrong targets. Bill Carroll remembers the confusion well:

'It was about 10.30am when we heard over the PA system: "Will the duty crews of 217 squadron report to the Ops Room." When you heard that, you felt a flutter. Jack Featherstone and I went to pick up our parachutes and other equipment; and then we went to the Ops Room where we met the rest of our crew, Tommy Carson and Mickey McGrath. Tommy had been bumped up to Flight Lieutenant and he was the blue-eyed boy around there at the time. We all heard the briefing and were told of a large convoy, doing about 7 or 8 knots, going up through the Channel. We went to the aircraft, only to be told not to take off. Then, lo and behold, we were taken back to the mess and given an early lunch.

'It was about 11 a.m. by now, and the guy that's sat in front of us at the table was a little Scotsman on Flight Lieutenant Finch's crew. His name was Sergeant McNeil, and the last time I'd spent any time with him had been on Christmas Day at Manston. As was traditional, the officers had taken their sergeants to their mess to ply them with drink and McNeil had been laughing his head off when he saw me. "Bill, you're a crazy bastard," he'd said by way of a greeting. "You and Aspinall come in and get bloody drunk every night and then you just go to bed and sleep it off. What you should do is get drunk in the day time and then you can have fun all day!" About ten minutes later he'd been snoring, his face in the soup.

'Now McNeil wasn't laughing or snoring, he was just very quiet. He knew that something was going to happen to him; he was sitting right in front of me and I felt sorry for him. As Finch's gunner, he knew what Finch was like. Apparently Finch had told somebody: "I'm going to hit whatever is out there straight down the funnel." He probably died trying, and took McNeil with him. They never came back – they bought it.'

That was just one example of the high human cost of what was about to unfold. As they sent out men like Bill and me, our superiors must have known the casualties would be significant. It has to be said they didn't all lead from the front. Squadron Leader Taylor was the chap who sent the men of 217 Squadron out on what became known as the Channel Dash. I thought: 'Why don't you come out yourself?' He'd won a DFC and he seemed a good chap, so I was surprised he didn't come out himself. I didn't know him that well, though. And there was certainly no time to have a debate about it as we headed back to our planes. Six Beauforts took off from Thorney Island, but in all the chaos we lost formation above Manston where hundreds of planes were circling, mostly Spitfires.

You had to wait your turn to join the orbit – and this time a pilot called Reggie Bell and I were last to join. By the time we did, we'd lost touch with the rest. We circled for quite a while before we finally gave up hope of finding the other Beauforts and landed at Manston to receive what we hoped would be our first clear orders of the day. I stayed with my plane and sent a member of my crew to find out precisely what was going on. Only then were we given the correct position of the ships, and their true identity. Of course, many of us had known or at least suspected what they really were, and what the strike was all about. Why all this mystery? We just didn't understand; the security was ludicrous.

When we received confirmation of what we were up against, and what it would mean for many of us, the news had an interesting impact. My friend Alan Etheridge, who was going to be on the trip, apparently went green when he heard. Others knew their fate was sealed. The commander of six Fairey Swordfish biplanes, Lieutenant Commander Eugene Esmonde, went white as a sheet. He knew it was going to be a one-way trip.

English born with Irish blood, Esmonde had only just received the Distinguished Service Order for leading an attack against the mighty *Bismarck* the previous May. Even the bravest of men feel the shock when their fate has been sealed. As Esmonde took off with his squadron, never to return, the Group Captain saluted.

Esmonde's courage did not fail him. The citation for the posthumous Victoria Cross he was awarded tells us what happened:

On the morning of Thursday, 12th Feb, 1942, Lieutenant-Commander Esmonde, in command of a Squadron of the Fleet Air Arm, was told that the German Battle Cruisers SCHARNHORST and GNEISENAU and the Cruiser PRINZ EUGEN, strongly escorted by some thirty surface craft, were entering the Straits of Dover, and that his Squadron must attack before they reached the sand-banks North East of Calais.

Lieutenant-Commander Esmonde knew well that his enterprise was desperate. Soon after noon he and his squadron of six Swordfish set course for the Enemy and after ten

minutes flight were attacked by a strong force of Enemy fighters. Touch was lost with his fighter escort; and in the action
which followed, all his aircraft were damaged. He flew on,
cool and resolute, serenely challenging hopeless odds, to
encounter the deadly fire of the Battle Cruisers and their
Escort, which shattered the port wing of his aircraft.
Undismayed, he led his Squadron on, straight through this
inferno of fire, in steady flight towards their target. Almost at
once he was shot down; but his squadron went on to launch
a gallant attack, in which at least one torpedo is believed to
have struck the German Battle Cruisers, and from which not
one of the six aircraft returned.

His high courage and splendid resolution will live in the
traditions of the Royal Navy, and remain for many generations
a fine and stirring memory.

In fact no torpedo had hit home. On the *Scharnhorst*, Captain
Hoffmann was almost aghast at what he saw. He wrote: 'Poor fellows, they are so very slow, it is nothing but suicide for them to
fly against these big ships.'

Thirteen of the eighteen Swordfish airmen lost their lives.
Soon it would be my turn to go out, though I couldn't expect
much company. Most of my squadron hadn't landed at Manston,
even though they'd reached the skies above it. They'd flown
straight out searching for German ships instead. Sadly, they'd
been given false positions and no protection from our fighters.
Bill Carroll was in Tommy Carson's Beaufort:

'Tommy Carson was leading three aircraft. I know Pilot
Officer Stewart was one of them because he'd been a sergeant in
our mess and he'd just got his commission. He was senior in the
sense that he'd been on the squadron before Tommy or Arthur,

though he'd been an officer much less time. The other pilot in our vic was Mark Banning, the brilliant Canadian flyer.

'The idea was to circle Manston and pick up a fighter escort. It was a bad day but the fighters were there. Tommy Carson and I both said we'd never seen so many Spitfires in our lives as we did when we circled Manston. All of a sudden, these Spitfires took off – they were up through the clouds and gone, almost before we realised. We had no communication with them; we had VHF radio sets like the fighter boys by this time but with A, B and C channels only.

'We chased after the fighter boys, but there was no way a Beaufort could keep up with a Spitfire. Then, one at a time, Stewart and Banning left us in their Beauforts, too. Poor old Tommy – this was pretty much his first time as a leader, and it wasn't going well. He was losing everybody and he knew he was going to be in trouble for it. We felt sorry for him, he was really worried.

'We'd been given a position of the "slow-moving" convoy, which should have been up off the Dutch Coast somewhere. In fact, the convoy wasn't slow-moving at all, otherwise it wouldn't have been anywhere near Holland. It had already managed to dash through the English Channel and beyond the Straits of Dover while our commanders dithered. The German warships were through us, then up, round and heading for home before most of us could have a really good go at them. As for Jack Featherstone and me, we didn't even know they were warships. Mickey McGrath gave Tommy the course for what some bright spark had calculated as the latest point of interception, and we flew off, alone now, heading for Holland. We found the coast, Jack's eyes were glued to the ASV [Anti-surface Vessel] radar; but we didn't pick up a sign of those ships.

'"When I get back I'm really for it," Tommy said. We were all worried, out there all on our own. Carson was a good guy but he was muttering under his breath: "I'm going to get shit from the Wing Commander when I get back. I'll be up for Court Martial." He was very upset.

'"Tommy, it's not your fault," I said. And it wasn't. This was chaos and each man was trying his hardest to make a difference in impossible circumstances. We were all pretty much of the same mind in our plane – before the day was out, we were going to find those ships, if it was the last thing we did. If we'd known exactly what we were up against, we'd probably have had another thought: this might well be the last thing we do.'

10

Our Turn

Asp, Alan, Sergeant Grimmer and I prepared to take off in our little Beaufort. We had no right to believe we would ever come home again. But we all knew this was an important moment in the defence of Britain, perhaps even for the outcome of the war. However thick the flak we were going to face, I was determined to try to plough through and make our torpedo count.

I was confident that the pilot in the other Beaufort, Sergeant Reginald Bell, would feel the same way. Ask anyone who'd ever flown with him, and they'd tell you Reggie Bell had never been short of nerve. Here he was, flying right beside me, and I was pleased about that; two might be more effective than one, though we could have done with a few more.

If we wanted to turn ourselves into a truly effective attacking force, we should have had much more support: more Beauforts, a fighter escort, some coordination between the two. Maybe our superiors reasoned that in such terrible visibility, we might be lucky enough to find and surprise the ships if we spread our numbers thinly over a wide area. Yet the whole thing seemed badly organised; and to me it already felt like a mistake to go out to face the German giants in ones and twos. The planners had originally hoped to form us up in vics of three under fighter escort; but now just the two of us were going to take off to meet our fate. And our superiors were letting this happen. There would be no Spitfire escort for Sergeant Bell and me. It wasn't my place to question anything; and it wouldn't have made the slightest bit of difference in all this chaos if I had. We just had to get on with it.

We took off into the mist and soon we could hardly see anything, because mist turned to thick murk. The Germans had chosen their weather very well to make this break-out. At least the worsening weather had also made fighter interception more difficult. There was cloud as well as murk, but Bell and I flew just below the cloud to give ourselves some sort of chance of seeing what was in front of us. It was second nature after our Abbotsinch training. Fly in at fifty feet and rise to seventy or eighty feet, then drop the torpedo. But even down at fifty feet the murk enveloped us that day, threatening to disorientate us. Surely finding ships, even big battle cruisers, would prove impossible?

We didn't know it, but we'd been lucky with our timing. Pilot Officer Stewart, who'd left Tommy Carson above Manston, had teamed up with a Beaufort flown by Sergeant Rout over the Channel. Ahead of us, Stewart and Rout had found the German convoy just before we reached the area, and had drawn the enemy fighters in the process. Within seconds, Stewart in particular would have reason to be thankful that his gunner, Sergeant Henry Parry, was as accurate as he was defiant.

The squadron records later gave a good indication of Rout and Stewart's ordeal, and their determination to return to the airfield against the odds:

Sgt Rout and crew landed at Manston, with Sgt Rout wounded in the hand by a shell fragment, his WOP/AG with a bullet in his arm and leg, and his rear gunner wounded in the eye by Perspex splinters and a number of holes in his aeroplane.

P/O Stewart and crew were set on by fighters as they went in to attack but Sgt Parry fought back with his two G.O.s and Stewart made his attack when he was set upon by fighters. Again Sgt Parry fought them off, claiming one down and one damaged.

The fighters were busy, though we saw nothing of this, only murk. Then Alan Still, my wireless operator, piped up. 'I've got three big blips, pilot,' he said excitedly. He was on the ASV and it was about 15.40hrs. 'Three blips!' he had time to repeat, before it happened.

We came out of the murk and suddenly I saw a ship so colossal that it towered above us, its upper structures seeming to stretch into the clouds. Even though it was still over a thousand yards away, I felt shock at this monster's proximity. Was this the *Gneisenau* bang in front of me, or the *Scharnhorst*? What did it matter? Somehow Bell and I had already pierced the protective screen created by the accompanying destroyers. We had no idea how we'd achieved this. Without that little clearing in the mist, we might have flown straight into the ship's hull.

We had only seconds to react. Holding our nerve, we went in together. I lined up my little Beaufort and took aim. I knew I had quite a good angle, but I also knew it wasn't perfect. This is the dilemma that flashed through my mind:

'Should I try to adjust my position? Can I move round a bit? I'm within the destroyer's screen; I'm quite near this beast. I haven't been shot down, this may be my last chance, and I'm more or less on the beam. If I dither I may be shot down, and that will be the end of me. I will never be able to drop any more torpedoes; whereas if I drop this one right now, it may still hit home, because I'm on the beam. I'm in a possible position for success. Even if I miss, at least I have a chance of getting clear, so that I can drop some more torpedoes in the future. Let's get this torpedo away!'

There were less than five seconds between seeing the giant ship, having fragments of these thoughts flash through my mind, and releasing the torpedo.

'Torpedo gone!'

I'd dropped it from the angle I'd already achieved, I didn't push my luck. This had still been a copybook attack, at the correct angle according to our training, even if it hadn't felt right somehow. A copy-book attack, as I was taught in training, was executed at a range of between a thousand and six hundred yards on the beam. But this ship was so big. Did I think I was nearer than I really was? Who knows? It was done now.

As far as I knew, Sergeant Bell had done exactly the same thing at the same time as me. But even in this moment, I knew, I felt instinctively that I should have moved into an even better position. It's easy to start agonising over something like that, even seventy years later.

'Torp running strongly,' Sergeant Grimmer noted encouragingly from the back.

No time to see if it hit home. I turned away and disappeared back into the comfort of the murk. The bad weather had saved me, because by the time the German gunners could depress their cannons and aim their firepower towards me, I'd gone. So had Sergeant Bell, whose torpedo was also seen to run strongly. Neither of our crews could follow their torpedo all the way to its destination. I was climbing now, heading for the safety of the cloud, and I didn't see Sergeant Bell's Beaufort after that. As far as I was concerned, we'd worked well together to give our torpedoes a chance. Now that we were trying to get clear and head for home, we didn't need to fly in formation.

Whatever shells came down at that point, and whatever their unseen source, Bell's plane must have been much closer to them than mine. I heard later that he began screaming with terror when his Beaufort was thrown upwards, and only quick work by his navigator John Sinclair helped them to make it home at all.

When I climbed up to about a thousand feet and disappeared into the cover of the clouds, I thought Sergeant Bell had done the same thing, and I knew nothing of what had been going on inside his Beaufort. What unnerved such an experienced man? Was it the temporary relief, the feeling that he was clear of danger, followed by the sudden, unexpected onslaught of shells exploding beneath his plane that made Bell crack? I have no idea. I was just mightily relieved to be alive. I flew back to base and as soon as I stepped down from my Beaufort, Flight Lieutenant Percival – who seemed to be trying to coordinate this show instead of Squadron Leader Taylor – approached me.

'Prepare to go out again, Aldridge.'

Those words hit me like bullets. 'Blimey, not again,' I thought. 'I've survived once, I won't survive twice.' I wilted visibly at the news. Percival saw my face drop; I knew that he'd seen it. He looked me in the eye and said, 'It's very important. You've got to take off again.'

So why on earth wasn't he flying? He was telling me I'd got to go twice, because this was so important. Why wasn't Percival going out, then? Everyone should have been involved in this one, shouldn't they? Someone had to organise things, but Squadron

Leader Taylor was there for that. So why the hell wasn't Percival going out? Whatever happened to leading from the front?

Percival wasn't without compassion, though. He came up to me a few minutes later, and for some reason he was looking relieved.

'Your plane is U.S.,' he said.

Unserviceable? Why? There didn't seem to be anything wrong with it when I'd landed. I didn't know what the problem was; but Percival was visibly relieved at not having to send me off to face the German fleet again.

I've often wondered, since these exchanges, why my plane was unserviceable. But I didn't think for a moment Percival made that up as an excuse not to send me off again. Make no mistake – he would have sent me out again if he could – that was his job on the day.

As it was, my Channel Dash was over, and I was just thankful I'd got through it. I knew how lucky I'd been, to be able to use the murk to make good my escape. Now I could go to the Officers' Mess, talk to some of the others, and begin the gradual process of recovering from what I'd been through.

But my future gunner Bill Carroll's ordeal hadn't yet reached its climax. Bill and his pilot, Tommy Carson, were still on their way back from somewhere off the Dutch Coast, where they'd been sent to intercept German ships that couldn't be found:

'We got back to Manston and up pulls this damned Shooting Brake and this Fighter Command Wing Commander comes dashing over. "I say, you boys!" He takes Tommy and Mickey McGrath into the Ops Room, while Jack and I stay with the aircraft and get them to put a bit more fuel in.

'Tommy comes back and that's when he informs us: "It's the bloody *Scharnhorst* and *Gneisenau*." I say, "Oh Christ, now you tell us!" Off we go again, all by ourselves, and you can see what the weather's doing, it's murky as hell.

'Jack Featherstone is nervous on the radar; I'm sitting in the damned turret. It was a good job the weather was so bad because we probably wouldn't have got near if those fighters had seen us. We were flying up the Dutch coast and then I hear Mickey McGrath tell Tommy Carson: "We haven't seen a thing; this is as far north as we're supposed to go. We should turn east and go towards the coast for about five or ten miles, then come south again." So that's what we did. We'd just started to turn south; and when you're getting very low, you get a lot of sea-echoes on this radar.

'Jack Featherstone says: "Tommy, you should see the bloody blips I'm getting."

'And Tommy Carson replied: "Oh God! You should see what I can see!"

'There was this bloody great hull and we were right smack next to it! We'd almost landed right on it; I don't know how we got there. I looked through my cubby hole and saw the size of this thing right opposite. And I'm facing backwards, so I see all these destroyers, too. And they didn't like us at all; they were banging away. It's pretty tough to be sitting in a little old Beaufort and go against those big old German ships, you know? I didn't open up. What's the point in using a .303 against a battleship? Which ship was it? Well, we didn't stop to look at a name-plate on those bloody things, so I'm not quite sure. Tommy Carson said it was the *Gneisenau*, I don't know what it was. But I know it was big, and I know they didn't like us. Tommy lets the damn torpedo go and then gets parallel with the *Gneisenau* and we're going alongside her.

'I don't know what the maximum speed of the Beaufort was;

but it didn't feel that great in those moments, let me tell you. And about six hundred yards away is a line of destroyers. We ran nearly one thousand feet. Have you seen the length of the *Gneisenau* on a picture? We were trying to run the full length of it. I don't know how long that damn thing is; but it took us what felt like about half an hour! Anyway we get half-way and all of a sudden there are four god-awful splashes in the ocean; four massive explosions, like eruptions. We all thought, "The silly bastards are firing a broadside at us." We thought it was a bit strange. Then we get hit. This guy puts a couple of shells in the front and one of them came right in the main plane, where the landing light was.

'One hit us smack in the nose. The destroyer, the bugger at the front of the *Gneisenau*, was the one who hit us. We went over on our side and I thought, "What the hell's going on?" You can see the waves; and the starboard wing-tip goes through one wave, which takes off the plastic cover. You're sitting in the turret and this isn't very pleasant, you know? Your head hits the top; it's not a good place to be. You have a leather helmet but you're coming up against metal and glass. Tommy Carson is a big man, strong enough to take this Beaufort through some extraordinary manoeuvres. We go on further, until I think we're out of it. I'm sitting in the turret and I shout: "Skipper, that's the best bloody evasive action you've ever done! Great flying!"

'Carson responds: "What do you mean, great flying? It wasn't evasive action. The bloody thing was out of control!"

'"Now you tell me!" I say.

'We couldn't have had more luck. Imagine running the full length of that bloody thing! Our torpedo had missed, though; otherwise we'd have seen an explosion. By then we were just trying to stay alive, and it wasn't over. Pretty soon our own side was trying to kill us, too. We were flying along and we see two British destroyers circling around another British ship way off to starboard. And we were probably flying at about one hundred or one hundred and fifty feet by now.

'Tommy says to Mickey, "Give me a shell for the colours of the day." It was a thick cartridge you could put in a revolver – you fired the right coloured smoke out of the plane to prove to anyone nearby you were friendly.

'So Mickey gave him the shell and Tommy fires a round up with the colours of the day. As soon as he did that, these bloody British destroyers opened up on us. They didn't like us at all! They didn't seem to like the colours of the day either. About half a dozen shots came too damned close for me.

'"Bloody idiots," Tommy says. I say something worse.

'We were a little bit peed off about it, having our own guys fire at us.

'It was dark when we got back to Manston and the crazy Wing Commander comes up again.

'Tommy says: "We've been hit in the main plane."

'"Oh, it looks OK," says the Wing Commander.

'"Well, I'd better go over and check," says Tommy, who goes over to the control to speak to Thorney Island.

'They say: "Get back over here quick." So we have to take off in the dark. It's late evening when we get back. We report everything to the intelligence officer at Thorney Island, including these four terrific splashes like eruptions from below the sea. And he tells us: "You're mad." "That's what happened," we tell him, and the debriefing is over; that's us finished for the day.

'I just wanted to go to the bar in the Sergeants' Mess after all that. I went to collect my money from the Ops Room. And guess what? My cash had gone!

'I knew what had happened. A lot of the boys had thought we'd gone missing. Dear Moggie Mayne, a friend who'd flown in another Beaufort's turret, must have thought we'd "gone for a Burton" and he'd taken my ten shillings. We're young, and that's the way we behaved. I can't emphasise enough the camaraderie that existed. This was all part of it.

'Anyway, it's nearly 10pm at night, and I walked back into the Mess, and there was Moggie with a pint in his hand, shooting a line with some other guys, with his back to the door.

'I came up behind him and said: "You bugger, Moggie, you've been spending my money."

'"Bill!" he said, turning round. "I'll give it back, you know."

'The other guys look up and one said: "Oh, you're supposed to be missing."

'I put my hand around Moggie's shoulder and grabbed his pint: "Good health, you little bugger," I said. "I bet you bought that with my money."

'Why should I have been annoyed? When Moggie went, I spent his! You saw the guys shot down and we'd get back to the Mess and Asp and I would have a drink to them and say, "Well, all the best, boys." We knew they'd gone. But we didn't cry over it. You've got a group of guys there, most of us twenty or twenty-one years old, we just accepted it as the way things were at the time.'

Moggie, who was to survive being shot down a few weeks' later, remembered Bill's belated return from the Channel Dash more than seventy years on: 'I thought I'd seen a ghost when Bill Carroll turned up in the bar. I didn't quite give him a hug but I was pleased to see him anyway. I think I bought him a drink with his money. I was jolly glad to see him.'

Bill Carroll wasn't the only one to 'return from the dead' that evening, as 217 Squadron's records show:

F/Sgt Banning and crew landed here when we considered
them lost, having done two sorties, about which we knew
nothing until later.

There were plenty of extraordinary stories told in the Officers'
Mess and the Sergeants' Mess that night – all of them true. My
good friend Alan Etheridge wasn't with us to hear or contribute
to them; but mercifully he wasn't dead either. He'd had good
reason to have gone green that morning at the prospect of what
was to come, though. His plane was pretty badly shot up in the
Channel Dash, but he persisted. By the time he had finished
trying to get at the German ships, he had no working undercarriage left. No matter, he flew home, wondering what he
should do next. He kept going round above an airfield he had
spotted, which was called Horsham St Faith. Finally, there was
only one thing left to do – he used his torpedo as an undercarriage.

This wasn't as stupid as it sounds – in fact, it was perfectly
logical. The torpedo's explosives couldn't blow him sky-high
because they could only 'arm' in water after a swim of a few hundred yards. The torp itself was smooth and cylindrical in shape,
and it was still protruding from the bomb-bay, ready to be
dropped. If it was no longer to be aimed at any ship in battle,
what better use for the torpedo than to act as a buffer between the
belly of the plane and the ground? Clever Alan recognised it as
something he could slide on until his Beaufort finally came to a
halt. That's exactly what he did, executing a perfect belly-landing.
A weapon designed to take life had saved Alan's instead.

The maverick Finch didn't come back, though. It was almost
inevitable that he was going to be killed. He was out to get the
VC, after all. Finch, the pilot with whom I'd won the DFC and

watched Mark Lee die, the man who'd almost killed me when he tried to feather the prop, was dead, and he'd taken his crew with him – Sergeant Jackson, Sergeant Buffe and Sergeant McNeil. Of the raiders who'd attacked the SS *Madrid*, my crew and I were the only ones left.

I can't remember exactly when I heard my torpedo had missed; it was probably the following day. That's when I decided that what I'd been taught at Abbotsinch was all wrong. Maybe I'd made a 'bish' of it anyway, I didn't know for sure; but something was telling me their theory was wide of the mark. The main reason I missed was because I did a copybook attack on the beam, I was convinced of it. I shouldn't have been on the beam; I should have gone round to an angle of forty-five degrees and dropped at 800 yards. The training was wrong – I missed and the other pilot, Sergeant Bell, had missed, too.

Everyone had missed. And when poor Bell returned to base, he'd been declared LMF. He was taken off flying and his crew never saw him again.

The whole Channel Dash was a disaster, except for the fact that a couple of mines had been dropped into the path of the *Gneisenau* and the *Scharnhorst* at some point during their escape and damaged them slightly. We didn't score any torpedo hits – and forty RAF aircraft were shot down. Several Beauforts were among that number. Forty aircraft lost, and not a single torpedo hit. The commanders must have been really cheesed off.

I was determined to correct my angle of attack if I had a chance, but I didn't send my own private conclusions up the chain of command. It didn't seem the right time to be complaining about anything. I just realised that I'd need to adopt another tactic in future.

After the Channel Dash, when the news was released that we'd lost forty aircraft, I rang home again, to reassure my parents that I'd survived. In my experience, the BBC was always dead accurate about our losses; they told the truth. That was fair enough, but when the losses were heavy it did mean you had to phone home to reassure people you weren't among them. My mother answered the phone again.

'Arthur!'

'As you can hear, I wasn't one of the forty.'

'Are you all right, dear?'

'Perfectly all right, don't worry.'

From that point in the conversation she was just as matter-of-fact as ever, except I could still hear how relieved she was. It was good to hear her voice, to have some normality.

The inquest into why we failed so badly during the Channel Dash would go on for some time. What wasn't immediately made public was the possibility that some planes had been lost to what would now be termed 'friendly fire'. Tommy Carson's plane, containing my future gunner Bill Carroll, had come perilously close to being lost in that way:

'The day after the Channel Dash, the intelligence officer who'd called us crazy came up to Tommy Carson. "I've figured out the mystery," he said. Later Tommy calls me and says, "Bill, you want to come to the pub tonight? I've got something to tell you." Over a beer he reveals what had actually happened to us. The intelligence officer had checked all the times, and there had been a Wimpy [Vickers Wellington bomber] squadron overhead when we attacked, flying at about twelve or fifteen thousand feet. They were using radar to drop about four 1,000 lb bombs on the *Gneisenau*, but they had missed, and those bombs had landed between us and the *Gneisenau*. So it wasn't a broadside or a clever shot from the Germans, it was the bloody RAF trying to get rid of us! So there it was. In the space of a minute or two, we'd been fired at and hit by the Germans, we'd been bombed by the RAF, and we'd been shelled by the Royal Navy. Somehow we were still alive to tell the tale.'

Bill's account is supported by the words of an Admiralty official called Mr Alexander, who briefed the press at the end of that month of February 1942 about the way events had unfolded that day. Asked if the Beauforts had been sent out too late to support the Swordfish, Alexander replied, 'No. The Swordfish delivered an immediate attack. The Beauforts were deliberately held back for an interval so as to synchronise their attack with that of the high-level bombers and so get a better chance of reaching close quarters.'

It seems almost ridiculously optimistic of our commanders to have expected RAF bombers to release their load only seconds before our Beauforts flew in, and not risk hitting us. In the fog of war, could that ambitious synchronisation plan ever have been realistic? A fancy idea like that might have wiped us all out.

Then again the Germans might have been responsible for those huge vertical splashes themselves, despite the intelligence officer's conclusion. After all, back in May, a day or two before she was sunk, the *Bismarck* was reported to have depressed the guns of her main and secondary batteries to create giant splashes beneath the first wave of Swordfish torpedo bombers.

We'll never know for sure who nearly blew poor Bell out of the water, whether it was friend or foe. But we do at least know why there was so much confusion among the Beauforts about the behaviour of their supposed Spitfire escorts. It emerged later that the order to proceed independently to the targets had been sent by RT radio to the Spitfires – and was duly received by those fighter pilots. That's why they'd taken off into the clouds without us. (The Spitfires specifically detailed to escort Tommy Carson and the rest of us had left the skies above Manston even before we'd arrived.)

So why didn't we know any of this? The reason lay in one basic error. The commanders at Number 16 Group had apparently forgotten that our Beauforts had recently exchanged WT for RT radios. They'd been trying to communicate with us on WT radios, which we no longer had. No wonder we couldn't understand what those Spitfires were playing at.

If stupid mistakes such as these hadn't caused so much suffering, they might almost have been laughable. That's war for you.

Chaos and confusion ruled in the Channel Dash and in my log-book, too. I started out by writing an entry which said I'd attacked the *Prinz Eugen*, because that was what I was originally told. But then I decided it was the *Gneisenau* that we'd attempted to sink, so I crossed out *Prinz Eugen*. Later I crossed out *Gneisenau*, too! I was told that an examination of all the times and positions suggested I'd attacked the *Scharnhorst*.

It was said the *Scharnhorst* was fourteen miles astern of the main fleet; and so the other two blips Alan Still saw on the AVS could have been destroyers in protective formation, though we never saw them as we flew past. I'll never know for sure which ship I tried to torpedo that day. As Bill said, you didn't have time to read the name-plates on those monsters. In the end, I settled for the *Scharnhorst* and that's how the log-book entry for 12 February, 1942, has stayed ever since. I never forgot the date for the rest of my days, that's for sure.

*

The bravery of 217 Squadron didn't go unnoticed. Pilot Officers Carson, Etheridge and Stewart were awarded DFCs within a month. My friend Alan Etheridge, who landed on his torpedo, was decorated for 'persisting' as I recall. That would have been a fairly accurate, if understated, way of describing the attitude of the other two pilots as well.

The news was greeted by 217 squadron's operational record book with a mixture of joy and exasperation:

> At long last the work of the crews of this squadron has been recognised . . . Too long have the efforts of this squadron been taken as a matter of course. I sincerely hope a number of DFMs will follow to the NCOs who have put a terrific amount into their war effort. So far pilots only have received recognition in this squadron.

Bill Carroll would never be decorated, despite the fact that he showed great courage in Carson's plane that day, and in mine later. Being overlooked didn't seem to worry Bill, though. He seemed more annoyed on Tommy's behalf. Of his pilot's bravery on 12 February, he observed: 'Carson should have got the bloody VC for the Channel Dash. He believed he was going to get hell if he failed. He wasn't going to give up, it didn't matter what happened to us.'

11

British 'Kamikaze'

If we thought the Channel Dash was a disaster, events on the other side of the world confirmed that we had reached one of the low points of the war. On 15 February, Singapore fell to the Japanese in one of the great capitulations in British military history. Malaya had already succumbed, meaning that some 138,000 Allied soldiers had now been captured or killed. Burma soon followed as the Japanese swept towards India. It wouldn't be long before Ceylon (now Sri Lanka) was raided, a development which would have a direct impact on my war. For now, we stayed in Britain, looking for ways to recover from our humiliation three days earlier.

There may have been an element of pride involved, with the honour of the RAF having taken a hit, but even before the disaster of the Channel Dash, there was a clear directive from Winston Churchill that a new battleship called the *Tirpitz* had to be targeted off the Norwegian coast. Churchill had written to the Chiefs of Staff Committee on 25 January, leaving them in little doubt about the sacrifices that would have to be made.

'The presence of *Tirpitz* at Trondheim has now been known for three days. The destruction or even crippling of this ship is the greatest event at sea at the present time ... The entire naval situation throughout the world would be altered.'

Since then the *Scharnhorst*, the *Gneisenau* and *Prinz Eugen* had escaped from under our noses, and Churchill must have been desperate to salvage some pride with a successful strike as soon as possible.

We were all suddenly moved from Thorney Island right up to Skitten, near John O'Groats, in the far north of Scotland. For me this meant a change in the line-up of my own crew. Grimmer's wife had given birth to their baby, but it had been no ordinary birth. Normally, having a wife and child to worry about at home would have been no excuse at all when it came to operational duties in wartime. But the birth had apparently been so difficult that it left mother and child fighting for their lives.

Under the circumstances, therefore, Grimmer was given compassionate leave and allowed to stay in the south. I didn't see Grimmer again for the rest of the war. I hope he and his family all survived to be happy together.

Having reached Skitten, we were in a position to attack the *Tirpitz* if a window of opportunity presented itself. On 4 March, the Kriegsmarine's largest remaining ship put to sea, accompanied by destroyers, with the intention of attacking a British convoy as it headed towards Russia. The *Tirpitz* and her friends missed our convoy by 150 miles, and it soon became clear she would have to turn back for Trondheim.

At this point we were sent down to Leuchars, Fife, where 42 Squadron were based. We arrived in a blizzard and the weather didn't improve much for the next few days. On 7 March, Coastal Command's Number 16 Group issued an order for Beauforts to move into position for a possible strike on the *Tirpitz*. Six Beauforts from 217 Squadron were to fly to the desolate Shetland outpost of Sumburgh, along with eight from 42 Squadron and three from 86 Squadron. Most were to be armed with torpedoes.

I led 217 Squadron's six Beauforts north the next day. Unfortunately, a third of the Beauforts didn't make it. Pilot Officer Stevens had to land at Arbroath because he had no oil pressure. Meanwhile, Sergeant Stephens crashed into the side of a hill, the cause of the crash unknown because there were no survivors among his crew. The operations book described Stephens' tragic accident as 'a grim finish to a career barely started'. Even sadder was the case of Sergeant Humphrey Edsell, who lost his life in the same crash. His wife was left with four children, all under the age of nine.

The rest of us landed at Wick and then flew up to Sumburgh the following morning. I have a big colour picture of the Beaufort I flew up in – I've checked the registration and it's definitely the one. The picture is more colourful than Sumburgh. What can I say about that desolate place? It wasn't the most cheerful base I'd ever visited.

Bill Carroll flew up there at the same time with Tommy Carson:

'Sumburgh is rock; and trees don't grow too well on barren rock. It was basically a rocky outpost only just above the waves. I was never there when the wind wasn't blowing like hell. And it is a cold wind. Sumburgh is north of John O'Groats, and the place is bloody cold, especially when that wind is blowing across from Norway. You'd get in a truck from your plane and go to the mess, but I never saw any other houses. There seemed to be nothing to it, apart from the air base.'

That air base was suddenly buzzing when we were brought to one hour's readiness. Then Wing Commander Mervyn F.D. Williams, a tall, skinny fellow with a no-nonsense attitude, briefed us about the mission, which was rather unimaginatively codenamed 'Operation Ship'. Williams was leading 42 Squadron; but it didn't really matter which squadron any of us was from at this point, because it soon became clear that we were all expendable.

Williams had only just assumed his command of 42 Squadron and he hadn't had time to choose his long-term crew or get to know his men. Endearing himself to any of us wasn't high on his list of priorities. There was no reason why it should have been, when we were all very probably going to die in the next twenty-four hours anyway.

The *Tirpitz* had indeed turned back towards Trondheim, and was heading towards the Lofoten Islands, which were on the way. On 9 March she'd been spotted by a reconnaissance plane from the aircraft carrier HMS *Victorious*. Twelve Fairey Albacore aircraft armed with torpedoes had been dispatched to attack the *Tirpitz*. Two had been shot down and the *Tirpitz* had managed to manoeuvre away from the torpedoes dropped by the others. Now it was the turn of our Beauforts to have a go. Williams seemed to think we could do better.

'We're going to attack the *Tirpitz* as it enters Trondheim Fjord. As you know, some of you will be dropping landmines to blow the nets protecting the *Tirpitz*; and some of you have the torpedoes to sink her. I can't emphasise enough the importance of this strike, gentlemen. We have to do everything it takes to achieve success.

'Now, Trondheim is out of our range, insofar as you won't have enough fuel to return to Sumburgh. Therefore after the strike, you are advised to fly across to Sweden and land there. The Swedish border is only about fifty miles from Trondheim. Find an airfield, or any field – crash-land if you have to. As a last resort, bale out and find some friendly Swedes. Each crew will carry money in Swedish krona to assist with this.

'The alternative to Sweden is that you head back over the North Sea, just as far as your limited fuel will take you. We will have dinghies waiting, and air-sea rescue craft will be stationed along the return flight path in the area where your fuel is calculated to run out. Good luck, men!'

How wonderfully vague! We took in Williams' words carefully, to ensure we'd grasped their meaning correctly. Torpedo the *Tirpitz* and then fly across to Sweden ... or just ditch in the North Sea. Neither plan stood up to scrutiny, I quickly concluded. Between Trondheim Fjord and Sweden there were mountains hidden by cloud. And if we got to Sweden, where were we going to land? There were so many forests and so few suitable places that even baling out didn't seem feasible. As for ditching in the North Sea, that was even less realistic. It was midwinter! We wouldn't survive for more than a few minutes. No, this was a suicide mission; a one-way trip. I looked at Williams in some astonishment and said nothing. I didn't hold anything against him personally. But this was Campbell all over again.

Bill Carroll agreed:

'Williams was a regular RAF officer, I would have thought, CO of 42 Squadron. He gave the orders and others cooperated. Would it have pained him to send us to our deaths? I don't think anything pained that bugger, to be honest with you. His manner was clipped, straight. Everything was cut and dried. None of the commanding officers showed any outward sign of being sorry about what they had to do to you, as far as I recall; but some of them had a decent way of telling you. Williams wasn't one of them. But you were a group of guys being briefed, it wasn't up for debate. You have your thoughts ... but you're going to go whatever happens. Nobody wanted to go, but, to be fair to Williams, I think he was going to be flying on the *Tirpitz* raid, too. I don't think he was any chicken. He was going to lead the thing.'

The high probability that we were about to die didn't stop us lining up on the Sumburgh runway in the early hours of 10 March. We were all set, waiting for the green flare which would signal our take-off. And as we all waited, I just felt resigned. I had no feelings at all. I wasn't afraid. I just sat there, totally resigned. I was mentally hardened. No feelings. In peacetime I had felt so much passion for so many things, such as music and art; but this was the war. In Sumburgh, there wasn't much reason to think or feel too much. The fact remained that we were going. It was a suicide mission and the entire squadron was to be sacrificed.

People have compared us to the kamikaze of Japan, who came later; but I don't know. I don't think I could have been a kamikaze pilot, though I know that may sound strange, considering some of the things I was prepared to do. It's true that I pretty much knew I was going to die, along with the entire squadron, when we were preparing to attack the *Tirpitz*. We were probably going to be shot down by the *Tirpitz* or the escorting destroyers. If we weren't shot down, we would fly into the mountains between Norway and Sweden, or freeze to death in the North Sea. So you might wonder what the difference was between me and a kamikaze. Yet I think there was a slight difference – kamikaze brings certainty of death. I faced a strong probability of death, but not certainty. In my case there was a slight hope. A pretty hopeless slight hope, but still a hope.

These were probably going to be the last few hours of my life. I looked up at the sky to see what the weather might bring in the short time that appeared to be left to us. The weather and visibility looked good, which was something. Then the rare peace in that Shetland sky was shattered by an alien object – the flare! Somebody had finally shot the flare into the sky. We all looked in amazement at the enduring glow as it turned the blackness into a recognisable colour. But the bleak night sky wasn't illuminated with green. It had been flooded with a forbidding red. I couldn't believe it. A red flare! We all knew what that meant. The mission had been cancelled.

You might think I breathed a huge sigh of relief and began to hug my crew. Nothing could be further from the truth. I felt no joy or relief. It may be hard to believe, but after we were all tensed up and ready to go, I felt a terrible sense of anti-climax. I even felt disappointment. I certainly wasn't disappointed that I wasn't going to die, I can assure you. I had no death-wish or suicidal tendencies. I didn't even see it as my specific duty to die. But I saw it as my duty to deal with the high probability of my death, and I'd been dealing with precisely that prospect. But now we weren't going, and all that preparation somewhere deep inside for our final mission was suddenly useless – all for nothing.

Bill Carroll couldn't have been happier:

'There was no way we could have made it back. It was ridiculous. We were all very pleased that it didn't happen, because the whole thing was screwy. Jerry would put cables across the fjords, to stop any British aircraft low-flying up there. And if you ran into one of those, you'd know all about it. It was a ridiculous idea, quite desperate, and we would probably all have met our deaths.'

So what had happened to make us see a red flare instead of the anticipated green for go? The simple answer is that we'd been saved by the code-breakers. Our boffins had broken the Enigma Code and so our commanders knew the movements of the

Tirpitz. You could put that red flare down to Ultra. The Government Code and Cypher School at Bletchley Park had supplied the information which effectively cancelled the operation. A decrypted message had revealed that the *Tirpitz* had sought haven in Narvik the previous evening, until the weather improved. A patrolling aircraft was sent out to 'spot' the *Tirpitz* going back into harbour, so that the Germans didn't know we'd broken the code.

We weren't going to get another chance. A few days' later the *Tirpitz* slipped out of Narvik, using bad weather as a screen, just as the other three giants had done during the Channel Dash. She was back at Trondheim and protected afresh by anti-torpedo nets by 18 March. Hitler's Kriegsmarine had outwitted us again ... but at least I could look forward to a little more life.

One of my fellow pilots was not so lucky. For there had been a particularly sad and perhaps unnecessary loss of life three days earlier, recorded in the operational record book:

15th March 1942. Beauforts all carrying torps took off led by W/Cdr Boal DFC. Sgt Watlington, P/O Stewart, F/S Butler, P/O Carson and crew, Sgt Rout and crew. Sgt Rout's machine crashed into the sea ten miles SW of May Island. The machine sank immediately, and P/O Stewart was detailed to go back – found three of the crew, immediately flew to a trawler and indicated that its services were needed. After a maddening delay, the boat got under way, but so slack was the effort made that, even by the time the scene of the accident was reached, the covers were still on the lifeboats. Unfortunately, by the time the men were picked up, they were all dead, presumably from exposure. The fourth member of the crew, Sgt Harvey, who was probably flying as the gunner, is still missing and probably went down with the machine. There is little chance of even proving why the machine went down, but I should like to know why a better result wasn't shown by the Air Sea Rescue, who are supposed to be on their toes all the time, particularly the aircraft of this section.

Bill Carroll suspected mechanical failure:

'The trouble was, the higher your rank the better the aircraft you got, and Rout was only a Sergeant and his aircraft may have reflected that. Let's just say he would get the aircraft that wasn't number one. Something happened, I think mechanical, and Rout went down in the Firth of Forth. I think they were only in the water about ten minutes.'

It was a further reminder of what little chance we'd have had if we'd tried to ditch in the North Sea coming back from the planned raid on the *Tirpitz*. Would rescue boats really have been able to reach us in time? Probably not.

The aftermath of the tragedy was handled by some of the squadron with typically dark humour, as Bill recalled:

'Know what happened at the funeral? Well, Leuchars is a very small place, but right next to the airport is the railway station. They gave the boys' coffins a send-off, everyone was lined up there. Eddie Beesley, the cockney whose money I'd helped to drink at St Eval, was waiting. They were loading the coffins on to the train to go home, and we knew which of the boys was in which coffins. Eddie steps up when Sergeant Rout went by, taps on the coffin and says in a very loud voice: "Don't forget to change at Grantham for King's Lynn." The Wing Commander couldn't believe he'd said it.'

In such a tough, unforgiving environment, people tried to see humour in everything, rather than allow themselves to be dispirited by it. Even the operational record book tried to capture a lighter mood at times:

> 29th March: Today is a day of National Prayer and this morn-
> ing the Church Parade was the longest we've been on for
> years. As usual, 217 had the largest parade and the only
> squadron where officers and senior NCOs were present in any
> number. Everything went along quite nicely until the parade
> tried to march to the unearthly wail produced by the local
> bagpipe team. At a rough guess, I should say that hidden
> somewhere among the mysteries of these bagpipes were var-
> ious decomposed quantities of haggis, which had the effect of
> slowing the time to a beat truly impossible, neither slow march
> or normal pace . . .

Tommy Carson wouldn't have been able to handle even a slow march. The 217 diary for the following day lamented:

> P/O Carson has gone down with a spot of pneumonia as a
> result of being chased from place to place without sufficient
> rest or change of clothing – getting too hot and cold etc. This
> continual standing by is more harmful than actual operations.
> Thus for the want of a few days' rest over a period of a
> fortnight or more, this man will be out of action for some
> weeks.

In fact, it would be months – and an awful lot would happen in that time. In fact an awful lot could happen in your first few days in hospital, if you had a friend like Bill Carroll:

'We were really worried about Tommy. We climbed into the aircraft one day in March and Tommy wasn't in very good shape.

You should have heard the noise he was making; it was the start of pneumonia. He was fevered and Mickey McGrath says to me: "We should say something about him." Mickey had a word with someone, and the next thing we know, they sent him to Perth hospital.

'Mickey McGrath and I decided to go and see Tommy and try to smuggle him in a beer to make him feel better. So in the afternoon we went to see the barman in the Sergeants' Mess at Leuchars and we told him our predicament. "Oh," he says, "just take the respirators out of their cases and you'll find that two bottles of beer fit in there perfectly." We were flabbergasted; but between the two of us we managed to hide four bottles of Tennent's that way.

'We hitched a ride to the hospital with a pharmaceutical salesman, who went out of his way because he said he admired our spirit. So we got to the hospital and this nurse of about sixteen got detailed off to take us to see Carson, who was in a private room. Tommy knows the score and he says to this young girl: "My two friends here wondered if they could have some water, please." So she goes off and returns with two glasses and some water. What we needed were the two glasses, of course, not the water, which goes down the sink.

'Out comes the beer, we'd brought an opener with us, and pretty soon that beer is making us all happy. Then Tommy breaks the news – he has pneumonia and the rules mean he's not allowed to fly for six months. We try to make him feel better; it's just that we must have got a little bit noisier than we should, because suddenly the door opens and in comes this woman, built like a ton of bricks, a matron. Mickey McGrath, Tommy's navigator, was quite a big guy. So she decides to pick on me. She grabs me by the seat of my pants and the scruff of the neck and pushes me into the corridor. Then she gets the nurse to open the door and whoosh – out I go!

'Mickey follows me. We couldn't believe it. Took us about three rides to get back to Leuchars, by which time we'd realised something: Mickey, Jack Featherstone and I probably weren't going to be flying as a crew any more. There I was – a gunner without a pilot.'

12

Bill's New Turret

Even in 2012, Bill Carroll and I were still having a friendly dis-
agreement about which of us asked the other to team up. I say
he asked, he says I did. I'm absolutely sure that Bill came up to
me and asked if he could join my crew. I said yes – but then again
I didn't have any choice, because I was the only one who had a
vacancy for a gunner! Sergeant Grimmer had decided to stay in
England and his replacement in Scotland had only been temporary. I didn't know much about Bill, but I made a very good
decision.

Bill said he was relieved, too, because not having an experienced pilot to fly with could seriously damage your chances
of survival. He and his friends on Tommy Carson's old crew
knew as much – and Bill had the first opportunity to improve
his lot:

'One thing we didn't like, Jack Featherstone, Mickey McGrath
and I, was that we were now a crew with no "driver", because
Tommy Carson was ill. We'd heard the squadron was going to be
posted overseas soon. We'd lost so many crews that new crews
were arriving all the time; and sooner or later they'd be short.
"Oh, Sergeant Carroll," someone was likely to say, "he's not with

anybody – put him with a new crew." The first trip was dyna-
mite for new crews. Unfortunately in those days, quite a few of
the new arrivals who landed on the squadron flew off on their
first trip and didn't return. We had no disrespect for these new
chaps; but we really didn't want to be posted on their crew. We
were a little worried, having done about twenty trips as a good
crew with Tommy Carson.

'Aspinall and I were regular bar-stool neighbours. He knew I
was looking to become part of an experienced crew. Once the
opportunity arose, it was quickly agreed.'

Bill would help make up the crew I'd remember most fondly.
I didn't choose any of them. But if I could have chosen them,
they would have been the ones. Fortunately, having asked me,
Bill went off to make it official, before I could change my
mind:

'Here was a guy who already had a DFC and, by all accounts,
he was a fairly good pilot. Aldridge knew what he was doing.
And he didn't suffer from nerves, mainly because he had this
appearance whereby it seemed like he was asleep some of the
time. He was a very casual chap, he wasn't excitable, and that
seemed like an advantage in a pilot. So on about 12 April, 1942,
I joined the crew of the guy who had needed a haircut so badly
back at Chivenor.

'I asked Arthur, "Had I better inform the Squadron Leader?"

'"You can do that, yes," he said.'

Our commanding officer had changed again less than a
fortnight earlier. Wing Commander Paddy Boal – the genial Irishman who'd been running Chivenor during our time there – had
taken over the squadron not long after the Channel Dash. Sadly
his command didn't last long. On 1 April, 1942, he'd set out for
a strike on German shipping off the coast of Norway and not

come back. Others who survived the strike said that Boal had done a stupid thing. He'd taken too long to select a target among the German convoy, having flown right along the line of ships before finally making a decision. His dithering had cost him his life, though two of his crew had been seen climbing into a dinghy.

Why Boal had not been sharper in his actions was anyone's guess. He'd completed a tour earlier in the war, before he'd had that break at Chivenor; and I suppose it was easy to feel over-confident the second time around. There were also stories circulating that he'd led the dancing at a rather raucous party in the Officers' Mess the night before he was shot down. Whatever the truth, 217 Squadron had lost its top man. Now Squadron Leader Taylor, who'd once been one of the boys in the Sergeants' Mess and had worked his way up through the ranks, was back in charge. So it was Taylor who Bill approached for official per-mission to join my crew:

'Pretty soon I was knocking on the CO's door.

'"Come in," the voice said.

'I walked in and Squadron Leader Taylor was there. Sitting beside him was Flight Lieutenant Carson, and they both had their feet up on the table. Carson was back from hospital but he was still going to be sent home for six months, which was stan-dard procedure for anyone who'd had pneumonia. Squadron Leader Taylor was giving him a few shots of whisky before send-ing him on his way.

'I gave Squadron Leader Taylor a smart salute. Carson looked at me as though I was stupid to have saluted so formally.

'"Excuse me, sir," I said, determined to do this properly. "Mr Aldridge is happy for me to join his crew. Do I have your per-mission, sir?"

'Tommy Carson looked at me and said: "Bill, you stupid

'How dare they?' My mother Melita was furious when I told her the Germans had tried to kill me.

'When can we fly?' As an Oxford student, I spent far too long at Cambridge learning RAF theory with classmates.

Calm before the storm: Tommy Carson (front) and Mark Lee in their 'hay-day', relaxing in Canada before the action started. I was close to Lee; Bill became close to Carson. Sadly neither man pictured here survived the war.

Down the hatch! I entered my Beaufort from above, and landed in the pilot's seat.

Torpedo loaded! The ground crews were the unsung heroes of the war, especially in Malta, where they suffered terribly in non-stop air-raids.

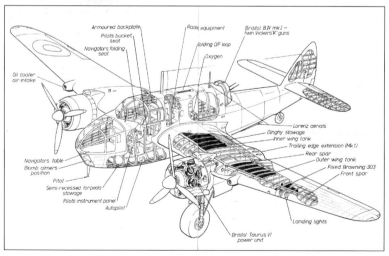

Rooms with a view. Our home in the skies was a Bristol Beaufort – designed to keep us in the air and hurt the enemy but not necessarily built for comfort.

Beaufort 7A Squad – a band of brothers. Sadly most of these brave men died during the war. The author, centre of back row with long hair, somehow survived. So did Bill, third from the right, front row. (There are seven crews here in vertical rows of four.)

What's left of my wing, the tip shorn off by a bracing wire on the SS *Madrid*.

Smile please! New crew member Ken Eades takes a snap of Bill and me during our Beaufort flight to Ceylon. (Vince, centre-front, isn't paying attention, so we just get his back.)

I'm in the shades, still grateful to a smiling Ron Harrison, who always got me to the Luqa air-raid shelter.

Bill Carroll: looking as boyish and mischievous as ever during WW2.

A Beaufort Mk 1 over Land's End from St Eval, 1941. Some found her hard to fly – not me!

The Italian cruiser *Trento* in Venice. But my torpedo doomed her and half her crew.

I sank the *Reichenfels*, a 7,744 ton cargo ship, on 21 June 1942. The German crew was rescued but Rommel was denied vital supplies.

A continuous watch was kept on Brest Harbour and the positions of three major German warships. . This view shows 1) a warehouse damaged in an air-raid has new roof; 2) German cruiser the *Prinz Eugen*; 3) objects thought to be smoke screen canisters.

Royal seal of approval: George VI and Queen Elizabeth (later The Queen Mother) inspect a Beaufort. Bill and I both met the King and considered him an inspiration.

One-way trip. I was briefed for a suicide mission against the 42,900-ton *Tirpitz* in March 1942, pictured here a month before, sheltering in Aasfjord near Trondheim.

Deadly flirtation: It looks like a peaceful scene, but this Beaufort is actually attacking the enemy ship.

Peace during war: Ceylon was an island paradise, and I couldn't have been happier.

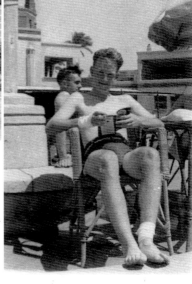

Ungrateful McSharry. I saved the Australian's life and he thanked me by shoving me into a Cairo swimming pool . . . with my watch on!

Des Fenton (left), relaxing with my new crew member Ken Eades in Egypt. Des became a close friend in Ceylon, but was later cruelly murdered by the Japanese.

My lovely mermaid! I met Beryl Jones at Oxford after the war and we had 63 happy years together.

Beryl and I were delighted when a middle-aged Bill Carroll visited us in Malvern.

Bill and Brenda Carroll, still enjoying their 'eternal honeymoon' in later years.

bugger, I thought you had more bloody sense. Aldridge has been at it too long. He's ready. You're not going to make it."

"'Well, sir," I replied. "I looked after your rear-end, didn't I, sir? And Mr Aldridge has got a DFC and he was with us at—"

"'Never mind that. OK," Tommy went on, "that's fine. Sergeant, if you insist, you have my blessing."

'The CO wasn't yet convinced, and said to me, "Are you sure it's wise, joining Aldridge's crew? Are you sure you're doing the right thing? You know he severed his wing-tip, did it a few months ago? You're not going to last long with Aldridge."

'But Carson said, "Well, I can't have you back, Bill, because I'll be off flying for six months."

"'I'm very sorry to hear that, sir," I said, though we'd been through this privately before.

'And at that point the CO said, "Very well, Carroll, you're on Aldridge's crew with immediate effect."

'Before I left, I turned to Carson and said: "By the way, sir, that matron at your hospital was a bit hard on us when we came to visit you."

"'You bastards," smiled Carson. "I've got a bone to pick with you about that. While we're at it, where's that bloody navigator of mine?"

"'I don't know, sir. Why?"

"'Well, after you buggers came to visit, things became a little difficult for me at the hospital."

"'What happened to you, sir?"

"'Don't you know?"

"'No, sir."

"'The matron was so angry, she arranged something for me. At 6pm that very evening, with all these student nurses aged fifteen or sixteen present, I was given an enema."

'"Oh dear, sir." I was trying not to smile.

'"Every two hours until midnight, these young ladies were practising giving me an enema, too. Anyway," concluded Carson, seeming to enjoy the difficulty I was now having in stopping myself from bursting out laughing, "at least the beer tasted fine, while it lasted."

'"Thank you, sir, and good luck," I said, still smiling as I turned to leave.

'Tommy Carson could still laugh about it, because he was such a good man. It was the last time I'd ever see him.'

I made Bill Carroll feel as welcome on my crew as I could, and quickly realised that his outgoing character was only going to enhance the feeling of unity we had on the plane.

The Beaufort was our home in the skies, though we all inhabited our own distinct parts of it. Vince Aspinall entered through the port hatch and had to crouch down to get into the well in the nose, below and in front of me. On the left he had a table, and sliding out of that came his seat. The chart table was over to Asp's left. He had a protective plastic chart cover, holders into which he could roll his maps, and an angle-poise lamp to help him see. Among his small bank of instruments, Vince had the automatic bomb distributor and selector switch on the starboard side. He had to set this correctly before I could drop a bomb or torpedo. As soon as we'd left our own shores, he did just that.

You could say Vince's position in the plane made him more vulnerable and exposed to flak than anyone else. Asp only had a Perspex-panelled window for protection, though two VGOs (Vickers gas-operated machine guns) made him feel slightly more secure. The trouble was, he had to put an ammunition pan into the Vickers to fire it, and that pan only contained 100 rounds. He'd start firing and after what only seemed like an instant, he had to change the pan. The ammunition pans were supposed to be behind him, hung by straps on the wall. When Asp moved his seat, he hit the back of it against the pans, so his solution was to take those pans off their hook and dump them on the floor.

The machine gun was seldom likely to have any bearing on a navigator's fate, though what Asp did with ammunition pans was destined to have a direct bearing on the type of injuries he and I were to sustain a few weeks down the line. An even more redundant piece of Vince's arsenal was a second, backward-firing VGO. The gunner was already at the back, and we didn't hear of anyone who ever fired a backward-pointing gun from the front of their Beaufort.

I was above and behind Vince, though we were both looking ahead as we flew. It didn't feel like we were very far apart and, besides, we had the intercom system, which sounded a little tinny but was usually effective. I could talk to everyone in the plane and they could talk to me, which was particularly useful when Asp was keeping a check on my course.

Right behind me was a sheet of steel, which separated the pilot from the wireless operator. He could still come through to the front by going round that metal panel if he wanted to. In fact, only an armour-plated bulkhead lay between the navigator down in the nose of the aircraft, and the wireless operator up in the middle. To pass through the bulkhead door you just lifted your legs over and bent down at the same time.

The radio seat was a big feature in the walkway on the port side. Stored in the radio seat was all the power required to start the aircraft, in the form of the accumulators, which had to be twenty-four volts. There was a cover on the top, and I'm told that made a nice seat. The wireless operator sat there with the radio smack in front of him. He had a transmitter with a keyboard to send messages if he was using Morse code. Originally we had been using the Type 1083 transmitter and the 1082 receiver, though they'd been replaced by something better. The seat didn't change, though; and if you wanted to move through the plane, you had to climb over it.

The crew tended to put their parachutes a little further along on the left-hand side, if they chose not to wear them. There was never time to clip on a parachute if you were in trouble. You were either wearing one or you weren't. For me as pilot, there was no choice, because the parachute was attached to me – I was sitting on it. If it provided any kind of deluded psychological comfort, it wasn't worth it. This was the 1940s and they hadn't invented a parachute that opened at fifty feet, our altitude for attacking enemy ships. As far as I know, they still hadn't invented one seventy years later!

In the middle section of the aircraft there were two more Vickers machine guns with ammunition pans, one on the starboard and the other on the port side. The port waist hatch was a good place for a VGO gun and its feeds. The gun poked through the hole, ready for use. If the wireless operator wanted to open fire, he just had to lift up the VGOs and blast away. On the starboard side there was a flare chute which you never really used – except perhaps to throw pamphlets denouncing Hitler out over occupied France.

A well towards the back just about allowed the gunner to stand up, though it wasn't easy for him to get into the cramped turret where his Browning machine guns were waiting. The Browning .303 was a far superior machine gun to the VGO. Unfortunately there was nothing superior about the design of the turret. Bill

Carroll's the best one to describe the contortions he had to perform in order to get into position behind his Browning:

'A Beaufort is like a Blenheim, you have to get into the turret from within the plane. With a Liberator and a Lancaster bomber, you have your own door which you can open and close all by yourself; you have space. You even have a place to go to sleep if you're tired and it's safe to nod off. It's much better, being isolated like that.

'But it wasn't like that in a Beaufort. You climb down into this little cramped space. You have to bring the seat right down to get your legs in there, then ease your backside in behind your legs. You're sitting down as soon as you get into the turret, and then you start moving the gun platform around and elevating the guns to make sure everything works. You have to make sure the guns are cocked by pulling up the toggle.

'There's one feature to help you avoid any feeling of claustrophobia – a big porthole with a Perspex cover on it. All you have to do is look back through that and you can see straight through to the front. I prefer the guns to the wireless, because when you're sitting in the middle of the plane, you don't see too much action.

'As for the Brownings, they have armour plating three-eighths of an inch thick. The sight is behind it and the armour has a slot for you to look through. But, the problem is, when you press your forehead up to that, you feel the vibrations. So the first thing many of us do is take it off the armour plating, because it restricts your view and nobody likes it. I'd done it in Tommy's plane and now I did the same in Artie's. It made me feel more at home.'

Later I asked Bill if he had ever regretted joining my crew and he said no. Even so, there was a moment in Scotland, quite early on, when he might have had second thoughts. Our first job together was to fly up to Skitten, near John O'Groats, with Aspinall and Still. Not for the first or last time, a memorable drinking session would precede an unusual turn of events.

It was about ten miles from Skitten to Wick by road; but if you walked along the top of the cliffs, it was only four miles. The prize for making the trek was a good pub, and somehow Bill quickly learned this. It was remarkable how swiftly he was able to pick up local information on arrival at a new base – especially if it meant finding a decent watering-hole sooner rather than later:

'Skitten was a hell of a place. You couldn't get a decent beer and it was almost as bad as Sumburgh, which has been described as the arsehole of the world. Alan Still, Aspinall and I were with Pilot Officer Stewart's navigator, Ted Boreham. We decided to walk along the cliffs and go to the Sergeants' Mess in Wick. On the sea side of the path, there was a big barbed wire fence, and it was all mined. If the enemy was going to invade there, they were going to have to come up those cliffs.

'We found our way along the cliffs safely enough, had a good time at the Sergeants' Mess in Wick, and began to make our way back. It was a pitch-black night, and we don't have any flashlight. Alan Still is walking with me, and I was taking the lead because I could take a drink. Aspinall is with this other guy, Ted Boreham. We come to a fork in the path.

'"We go this way," I say.

'Aspinall says: "Bill, I'm the navigator around here. You don't know where you are."

'He took Ted Boreham and went off somewhere, and I led Still down this path. Our path turns out to be the right one, so Still and I get home to Skitten and go to bed.

'I'm fast asleep at about three in the morning and a bloody corporal comes up and shakes me.

'"Are you Sergeant Carroll?"

'"Piss off."

'"Are you Sergeant Carroll?"

'"What do you want?"

'"The Group Captain wants to talk to you."

'"What does the Group Captain want to talk to me about at three o'clock in the morning?"

'"He'll tell you, Sergeant. Get dressed, please, I have to take you to him."

'"Ah, Christ," I say and get dressed.

'This corporal takes me to the Group Captain's Shooting Brake, which he'd brought with him. I get in there and I'm still half asleep and still half drunk. We drive to where the Group Captain is waiting in his office, and he takes me to the guard room. It is like a jail in there, with bars to the cells and everything. And there are two guys in this one cell.

'The Group Captain says: "Sergeant Carroll, do you recognise those two wrecks?"

'"Yes, sir," I say, with little option but to identify them correctly. "That's Sergeant Aspinall and that's Sergeant Boreham."

'"Very good, Sergeant Carroll, you can go," says the Group Captain, before turning to the corporal to add: "Take these others back to their billet."

'But before they can leave the cells, the Group Captain warns Aspinall and Boreham. "You will appear before me at ten o'clock in the morning, sergeants." By now it's already about four.

'So what had happened? These silly fools, following Aspinall's directions, had got lost. Eventually they ended up in a car park by the Officers' Mess and saw a Shooting Brake and they decided to put their heads down in the vehicle. The pair of them get in and collapse on the back seat. At about two forty-five the Group Captain gets called out, because there's some sort of panic on. He goes to his car, doesn't look in the back, and starts driving to the Ops Room. Aspinall, who is suddenly getting bumped around, wants to be sick. So he opens the door. This is the point at which the Group Captain realises he has somebody in the back, and he shouts: "Don't try and escape. Do not try and escape! Close the bloody door!"

'"But I'm going to be sick, sir!" pleads Aspinall, and it's too late. He pukes all over the back of the vehicle. Fortunately he misses the Group Captain, but they still get put in the clink.

'Later that morning, Arthur Aldridge wants to take his Beaufort up on an air test. You don't need a full crew for an air test, so it's just Alan Still and me who go up with Artie. Meanwhile Aspinall continues to sober up in bed; he's in bad shape. We almost end up in much worse shape in the Beaufort at the end of the air test.

'When we come in to land, the port wheel locks up and the oleo strut – to which the wheel's attached – breaks with the strain instead of acting as a shock absorber as it normally does. You wouldn't believe the mess we got into. Artie still made the perfect landing on the runway. Well, when I say he made the perfect landing, I wouldn't say it was exactly perfect. It wasn't his fault; but you can imagine how much worse things became after the port wheel locked.

'Alan Still is thrown forward and it's just as well. A sharp piece of thick metal shoots up through the radio seat, where Alan had just been sitting. It's the oleo strut which has snapped on land-ing. When he looks up, Alan sees this thing, there's about a foot of four-inch-thick steel sticking up through the seat. He realises it could have been very painful indeed.

'The ambulance comes to check us out, because I had a few bruises, too, from being sent on an unexpected tour of the turret. We're OK, and by the afternoon we're back in the mess. All of a sudden, two guys show up looking like the wrath of God, with really bad hangovers. It's Ted Boreham and Vince Aspinall, and it turns out they've been on a little trip of their own that lunchtime.

'The disciplinary hearing before the Group Captain had been put back to midday and was held at the main aerodrome at Wick. They were on a charge of being drunk and disorderly in the Group Captain's car. But the Group Captain has heard about Artie's crash, thinks Aspinall has been involved, and says: "I'm very sorry to hear about your problem this morning, I'm dismissing the charges."

'So the pair of them were brought back to Skitten; and that's when they walk in and find us there, nursing our bruises. Aspinall didn't have a clue – and neither did Ted Boreham – that we'd pranged. So we're sitting there in the mess and eventually Asp asks innocently: "Hey, Bill, did something happen this morning?"

'"You lazy git," I tell him.

'Inevitably, we went off to have another drink that night to celebrate Alan Still's lucky escape from a backside full of sharp metal. And every so often he would jump up and shout "OOOH!!" as if he really had been pierced in the undercarriage by that metal coming through his radio seat. It was hilarious.'

You could say we were learning about each other! I didn't feel great that I'd knocked my new-look crew about so soon; though I could hardly be blamed for the problem with the wheel. The way we'd spun off the runway had been a bit scary, but in the general context of our war, it was nothing serious. A couple of incidents quickly followed which put our little jolt in perspective.

There was a big naval base up at Scapa Flow. The American fleet came to the Shetlands and Scapa Flow in April 1942, for a joint exercise with the British fleet. Our job was to demonstrate the kind of torpedo attack we did. Onlookers would contrast our approach, coming in low, with theirs, coming in from above.

I was flying our Beaufort and minding my own business when all of a sudden an American single engine aircraft came diving down from about 4,000 feet, maybe a bit higher. That was their tactic; they'd come charging down in a dive, then level out quickly and drop their torpedo that way. But this dive didn't seem right to Bill. In fact, he was so surprised by what was going on that he trained his guns on it. 'What the hell is this guy doing?' he asked me. At that moment, the American just went straight into the drink and died. He didn't pull out in time.

On another occasion we were at Leuchars when there was some formation flying going on. Two aircraft collided and crashed. I didn't see it, fortunately for me, but they all died.

What did our bumps and bruises matter, compared to tragedies like that?

13

The Rock and a Hard Place

Wherever you looked around the world in that British spring of 1942, it was hard to claim with any great confidence that we were winning the war.

After invading Malaya, Singapore and Burma, the Japanese had targeted the British naval base at Colombo on 5 April. A total of 125 Japanese aircraft, including fifty-three Nakajima B5N2 torpedo bombers, had struck. They were under the command of Mitsuo Fuchida, who'd also led the attack on Pearl Harbor. The British weren't much better prepared for the Japanese raid than the Americans had been. Two ships were sunk in Colombo harbour – the armed merchant cruiser HMS *Hector* and the old destroyer HMS *Tenedos*. The RAF lost twenty-seven planes, though they claimed to have downed eighteen enemy aircraft in the fight.

It didn't stop the Japanese from mounting fresh aerial attacks later that day, south-west of Ceylon. HMS *Dorsetshire*, which had sunk the *Bismarck* back in May the previous year, suffered a similar fate herself. Having been spotted by Japanese fighters, she was sunk in eight minutes, at a loss of 234 lives. HMS *Cornwall* went the same way, bringing combined losses up to 424. The next day British steamships called the *Silksworth*, *Autolycus*, *Malda* and *Shinkuang* were all sunk. And on 9 April, the carrier HMS *Hermes* was also sunk off Batticaloa, at a loss of 307 men. Five Bristol Bleinheims were lost trying to bomb Japanese ships, which left the scene relatively unscathed.

Admiral Sir Geoffrey Layton, the British Commander-in-Chief in Ceylon, warned his forces in the immediate aftermath of the raid: 'The Japanese fleet has retired to Singapore to refuel and rearm, and to organise an invasion force, which we think is coming back to attack us ... You men must be prepared to fight to the last man to stop the Japanese.' However, Layton also let slip that he might not be there to lead his men to such a glorious death, because he was going away in search of reinforcements. That didn't impress those he intended to leave behind. He was nicknamed 'Runaway Layton' from that moment on.

The British couldn't just give up on Ceylon, though – and not just because of its vast rubber resources. Ceylon was also supposed to command the Indian Ocean, and protect vital shipping routes to the Middle East and Persian Gulf oilfields. Yet the Japanese looked capable of taking over and seizing the strategic advantage.

The torpedo bombers of 217 Squadron were told that they were to be part of the cavalry coming to the rescue of the island, or at least coming to give it breathing space and hope, while a plan could be hatched to halt the Japanese onslaught. We were going to stop at Malta along the way.

Malta was just about the most bombed and beleaguered little island in the entire world at the time; hardly a safe stepping stone to our final destination. And the Italians – people I'd have considered compatriots as a small child – were making Malta's suffering much worse. Benito Mussolini, the cruel Italian dictator, was still in power and he was helping Hitler to apply a stranglehold around the starving island. It made me feel ashamed.

Despite my roots, I could never have fought for Italy along-side the Nazis. My mother once told me I had dual nationality. I could have been called up for the wrong side if I'd been in Italy when war broke out. If that had happened, I'd have escaped and gone AWOL. No amount of love for Italy would have per-suaded me to help Hitler. If it came to it, I'd fight the Italians who were helping him. I'd fight them without a second thought.

Leaving Britain when she was still under threat wasn't so easy. At least I'd played my part in holding off the Germans when Britain's future was still in the balance. The human cost of our northern European operations had been high among the Beaufort crews, as those of us who'd lost friends knew only too well. But we'd succeeded in keeping the biggest German ships in port for long spells at a very perilous time in the Battle for the Atlantic. And every success we'd had in the seas around Britain helped to tip the balance in our favour.

But the tide of World War Two wasn't yet turning. German U-boats continued to do great damage to our Atlantic convoys. And, although the Nazis had been beaten back from Moscow by fierce resistance and the brutal Russian winter, improved weather in the spring and early summer saw Hitler's army moving men-acingly towards Stalingrad. Meanwhile, America's entry into the war hadn't yet provided the change in fortunes the Free World had hoped for. In fact, they were forced to surrender uncondi-tionally in the Philippines in early May, casting doubt on their ability to win the war in the Pacific.

As for North Africa, there seemed to be no clear winner as the

Allies tried desperately to defend Tobruk. Holding on to Malta was just as relevant to the war in the desert, as we'd discover in time. But we weren't grand military strategists with any great overview of how the war was progressing. We simply had a feeling that, while the war wasn't going all that well, we were continuing to hold our own when it mattered. And, for us, it was time to move on and do that somewhere else.

We were delighted to be told we'd have a brand new aircraft to fly east. A few days before we were due to leave for Malta, we picked up a new Mark II Beaufort, serial number DD598, from the factory in Filton near Bristol. Bill reckons we were probably one of the best crews in the squadron by then; the first crew through all the tests. I wouldn't disagree, though our 'new' Beaufort wasn't exactly a world-beater. It had been fitted with the same type of underpowered Taurus engines we'd had before!

The new plane had originally been built as a Mark II, ready to take Pratt & Whitney engines. But the ship which had been bringing those better engines was sunk in the Atlantic by a German U-boat. So I never did feel the benefit of the superior US engines. I was flying a Mark II with Mark I engines. Still, you make do with what you're given, especially in wartime; and there was no complaint from us. Bill and Asp had finally drunk Britain dry, so it was time to let me fly them to Malta.

We were to take off from Portreath at Redruth in Cornwall and then fly all the way down the border between Portugal and Spain, to refuel in Gibraltar. We very nearly didn't get any further than the rocks at the bottom of the cliff in Portreath. It was one of the craziest, scariest, most harrowing things that happened to me in the entire war.

First of all, we were messed around at Redruth for days, told to come and go away again from that airport so many times that we didn't know what was happening any more. What we hadn't been told was that a huge convoy was being formed for the attempted relief of the besieged island we were going to – Malta. They may have been trying to coordinate our flight with the convoy in mind, perhaps even wanting to keep the convoy a secret from their own airmen.

On 3 June, 1942, we were finally woken up at some unearthly hour in order to leave Cornwall. The Portreath runway was short and we were weighed down with extra-long-range fuel tanks, filled to the top. The plane was also fitted or filled with all manner of things they thought we might need for our new environment. For example, air and sand filters had been added to the front of the Beaufort, and this increased drag. The cruising speed would be considerably reduced in the Mediterranean, for that same reason.

For now, any kind of cruising speed seemed like a distant dream. The runway ended at the edge of the cliff. I tried to get some speed up but didn't achieve enough. We just about took to the air before we fell off the end of the runway, but that wasn't the end of our ordeal – we still dropped like lead. All I could do was drop down and use gravity to gain some airspeed, perhaps just enough to start climbing again. As we continued to fall through the little piece of sky between cliff and rocks below, I realised we were running out of time and space. Quite honestly it was terrifying.

It really looked as though this would be the end of us; if those cliffs hadn't been so high, we would have bought it. Just as in the case of the longer plunge with Finch, there was barely a second or two until impact. We were just twenty-five feet from rocks and sea when we achieved enough air speed to hold our own. Frantically, I pulled her up and avoided crashing in the nick of time. But that take-off from Portreath would remain one of the scariest moments of my life. A little shaken, I flew out over the sea, grateful still to be alive, and climbed into the darkness. It would be years before we saw England again.

The sun was coming up as we reached the Iberian peninsula. I flew across a bit of Spain that I shouldn't have been above, strictly speaking, but there was no other quick way to get into the air space of Portugal, our oldest non-active ally.

It was a perfectly clear day, and we flew along the border between the two countries, staying just inside the Portuguese border all the way down towards Gibraltar. It took about eight hours of continuous flight to go from England to 'The Rock', and that brought with it an interesting challenge: how to fly a plane when your bladder is bursting. There was no George on this particular plane – no automatic pilot. So Bill came up with an ingenious solution:

'Arthur never let anyone take over that pilot's seat; he stayed there. So when he needed to relieve himself, we had a solution. The VGOs had a deflector bag on the side, and all the empty casing went into that. I pulled off the deflector bag and passed it up to Alan, then Arthur sat there and peed in it. Although the bag wasn't designed for peeing in, it was waterproof. Alan passed it back to me, and I tipped the thing out of the port waist hatch. You didn't want to let the thing get too far out or it would blow back on you. All I can say is, I'm glad he didn't need to do anything else!'

It was only when we reached Gibraltar that I became rather annoyed. It was a left-hand circuit to come in there. That meant you were supposed to begin by coming across to the starboard side of the runway, because you were coming towards it from the wrong direction; then by the time you'd come round 180 degrees, you were joining the approach to the runway from the left.

To my irritation, I'd been informed that I wasn't going to be allowed to do that. In order not to violate the Spanish border, I had to do the opposite. I was forced to turn to port to come in tight between the runway and the rock. Pilots are not used to going that way round and I certainly wasn't used to landing in Gibraltar, because I'd never been there before. You would normally come downwind and then turn and land into the wind. Because of Spanish air space I had to turn very sharply if I was going to land into the wind. And it wasn't a very long runway at Gibraltar. In fact it was very, very short. The end of that runway was pretty much level with the sea and seemed to lead straight into it. We almost went for a swim, because I only just stopped on the runway in time. To make matters worse, when I landed they told me there was a leak in my petrol tank and I had almost run out of fuel without knowing it. In short, we were lucky to have got there at all.

The welcome Bill received just about made his day:

'It was the middle of the afternoon, extremely hot, and we weren't used to that sunshine. We were supposed to be in Blues but I didn't have a decent shirt, so I had a khaki shirt on. We were paraded before the commander of the base. He took one look at me and demanded to know: "Why are you wearing a khaki shirt with blue battledress?"

'"I don't have a clean shirt, sir," I admitted.

'"You are not in any outpost of the British Empire yet!" he replied angrily.'

How right he was; and we wouldn't be seeing Ceylon for some time.

*

Although I'd almost flown into the Rock, I decided to climb to the top of it instead. I looked across and saw North Africa, though I had no idea of the part I might play in events taking place further along that coast before very long. In truth, as I relaxed on top of the Rock, I wasn't even thinking of the boys fighting over the water; I just enjoyed the view. Then when I climbed back down again, I made a startling discovery. Oranges! What a luxury. They were non-existent in England during the war. What a sweet, sharp, juicy delight ... I'd almost forgotten.

Unsurprisingly, Bill was more interested in the booze; but first he had a swim, and quickly regretted it:

'The weather was two hundred per cent, there was sea all around, which we loved, so we were immediately straight into it. We went for a swim and suddenly we heard a "whoosh, whoosh" over the top of us. That's when we found out that the army boys we just met had directed us to the beach they used as a rifle range! Having survived that, we went to the Sergeants' Mess where we were told not to buy the expensive bottled beer, because you could get a bottle of rum for 2s 3d. We turned out our pockets and we had about three shillings between us, so we bought a bottle of rum and some lemonade to go with it. Twenty-one-year-olds with a bottle of rum between three of us; we got very merry, drunk – and broke. Fortunately it was near bed time, so off we went.

'The food in the Sergeants' Mess was free and not bad; but we'd come from a hungry England, and we knew there was more on offer in Gibraltar. The next day we were told we had time off, so we went walking, and all we could see were restaurants and bars. Someone told us: "When you go and get a meal there, you ask for a full house." It was a mixed grill for a shilling. For guys who'd come starving from northern Europe this was an incredible opportunity; but we didn't even have that shilling. So Aspinall, Alan Still and I went to Arthur and said, "Pilot, can you lend us some money, please?" Arthur lent us some money, and then some more, but after we had tapped him up three or four times, he said: "No. No more."

'There we were, broke with all this booze around. Anyway, we were walking back to camp when we met a bloke from our squadron called George Lawcock and he was grinning from ear to ear. He had extra money from the RAF and told us how he'd done it. Before we had left England, the RAF had issued NCOs with pay books for the first time. He'd just been to "pay accounts", and when they asked him where his pay book was, complete with his last pay entry, he just said: 'What the hell is a pay book?' So they believed he'd never had one and hadn't been paid. And he got paid again!

'We decided to pull the same stunt, the three of us, and we went to pay accounts.

'"Paybooks," said the number-cruncher.

'"Excuse me, sergeant, what is a pay book?" I said, pretending to be baffled.

'The sergeant says to his boss: "Sir! There are three more of them!"

'They issue us with pay books, and the man asked: "When were you last paid?"

Alan said, "When was it, Asp?"

'"Oh, about three weeks ago," Vince replied.

'They didn't give us three weeks, but they did give us two weeks' pay right there in Gibraltar. So we thought about Arthur refusing to give us any more money and we said: "To hell with you, mate. Now we have two pay books!" We didn't have to bother him after that.

'We were drunk a lot on Gibraltar, even when we were invited onto a warship, which had been in a battle on their way to the Rock. They'd lost some crew and quite a bit of damage had been done to the ship. When we saluted the quarterdeck, one of our crew disgraced us because he was promptly sick all over the deck, which was disgusting. I won't say who it was.'

Fortunately I was nowhere near my crew when any of this happened, and perhaps it was a good thing it was time for us to be on our way.

Gibraltar to Malta was another eight hours. The flight took place on 10 June, 1942, and came with dangers of its own. Not everyone arrived alive.

Bill Carroll recalled: 'Sergeant Denis Norman, a twenty-eight-year-old married man, was minding his own business on the radio in Sergeant Jimmy Hutcheson's Beaufort when he was killed with one shell to the heart, fired by a Messerschmidt 109 just south of Pantelleria. One bloody shot, straight through him, and only one other struck the plane. Jimmy thought they'd all got away with it, so did Freddie Moore, his navigator, and the gunner, Sergeant Henry Parry.

'Nobody knew that Norman had been shot dead until they landed. You'd be shocked to find a colleague like that, wouldn't you? That's what poor Henry Parry was faced with when he came out of the turret. Remember, just as pilots and navigators were partners on a Beaufort crew, so were the radio man and gunner. There's Parry's partner sitting there, looking normal as anything, except that he's got a bullet right through his heart.

'After that tragedy you had to watch what you said to Parry on Malta. You'd sit there and you'd be bullshitting away, and Parry would suddenly take your head off about something you had said. That's not normal, especially among a bunch of characters like we were. Then someone told us what Parry had been through the previous year back in Scotland, and we began to understand why he was so edgy.

'While doing his torpedo training at Abbotsinch, Parry's aircraft had been turning for a dummy run on the range when it clipped a mountain in low cloud, flipped over and caught fire. His pilot and navigator burned to death, while Parry managed to kick his way out of the wreckage and save his injured wireless operator. That happened only a month after we'd left the place.

'If you look at a Beaufort and imagine the turret upside down you get a sense of the challenge Parry faced. How the hell do you get your legs up and kick that bloody Perspex out of there and crawl out of that hole? That's what Parry managed to do and it was some feat.

'So we understood why Parry was jumpy – once you realise what's happened to a bloke you become more sympathetic. But, after a while, when you get a bunch of young men like we were and one odd-ball, you find it's best to leave him alone. When the rest of us were together in the Sergeants' Mess we couldn't give a damn about anything! A merrier group of buggers were hard to find and then there was this one. I don't doubt that he was brave to carry on, though.'

Indeed he was. The operational records suggest Parry had acted heroically in his turret – and not for the first time, bearing in mind his exploits defending Pilot Officer Stewart during the Channel Dash – because the Me 109 which had killed Norman on the way to Malta had been 'driven off on his third attack'. All that gutsy resistance – and yet this time a good friend had still been killed.

I didn't know Parry like Bill did, because I was in the other mess, but his story gives you a further idea of some of the things we'd already seen and been through as individuals, even as we landed on Malta. Some of the men had been pushed close to the limits of their endurance – and it was only going to get much worse for all of us. There would be many more cruel twists of fate before the few of us lucky enough to survive our ordeal finally left Malta.

14

Bombs, Songs and Weevils

As we reached Luqa airfield, I might have guessed we were going to be needed around the place when we saw all the bombs exploding by the runway. The air base was being attacked. I thought to myself, 'We're coming to the wrong place here. Better go back to Gibraltar.' But it was too late to turn back and, fortunately for us, by the time we actually got to Malta, the bombing raid had finished and the runway hadn't been badly damaged; otherwise we might have had to ditch in the sea.

The raid reinforced what we'd already been told: Malta was under siege. We were regarded as the senior 217 crew by now; and that meant we were the first duty crew when we arrived there. The whole squadron was put on immediate stand-by and it wasn't long before the qualities of the AOC, Air Vice-Marshal Sir Hugh Pughe Lloyd, shone through. Bill was one of the ben-eficiaries of his kindness:

'We got to know what he was like the first time we got to Malta. The rule in the air force was that you had a meal before you went on a trip and you also had a meal when you came back. The Sergeants' Mess had civilian cooks and at about 6pm they buggered off. They didn't want to hang around and get bombed. But the Officers' Mess had RAF personnel to cook for them and they had to stay.

'As the duty sergeant, it was my job to tell the NCOs when to eat. But because of this situation with the cooks, there was no meal in the Sergeants' Mess to go and get. I mentioned the situation to one of the Canadian pilots, who went straight up to Sir Hugh Lloyd and gave him hell.

'Sir Hugh Lloyd didn't get angry, he just told this Canadian: "Send the sergeants to the Officers' Mess." The boys didn't believe they were allowed to go at first. When they realised it was true, I nearly got knocked over in the rush. After that, every time we came back at some unearthly hour and there was a meal out of time, the NCOs went to the Officers' Mess. That tells you Sir Hugh Lloyd was a good man.'

The first chance I had, I went down to Valletta, Malta's main port, to take a look. I was shocked to see that all the buildings were in ruins. The main street in Valletta was nicknamed 'The Gut' and it had been bombed to pieces – even the opera house. I felt the horror of it – the place had been reduced to rubble. Houses were devastated all over the town. It was horrendous, a terrible sight, and all the Maltese people were going through this; they were suffering greatly.

I bought a little silver Maltese cross from somewhere, and decided to wear it on my uniform to show my solidarity with the local population. I thought it looked rather nice. Officially, I wasn't meant to have the cross; but the authorities turned a blind eye. It's strange to think how deeply I felt about the plight of the Maltese people, not even knowing at the time that my mother, Melita, might have been born there. And it soon became clear that we wouldn't be going on to Ceylon; at least not just yet. The situation was too desperate where we were.

With or without British help, Bill couldn't quite understand how the island was surviving:

'It was a tiny island, bombed night and day. The war was going badly in North Africa, most of Europe was under Nazi occupation, and still little old Malta stood up to Jerry. The stupidest thing that Adolf Hitler ever did was never to take Malta. If they'd done it like Crete and sent paratroops in, they could have walked all over us. They killed anyone on Crete who wasn't any good to them. Why didn't they do that with Malta? Rommel would have won easily in North Africa if they'd taken Malta and no one had been attacking his supply ships.'

Rather than take Malta, they seemed content simply to destroy it from above. And we were going to spend much of our time over the next few weeks dodging bombs or shells while they went about their evil work. Either we'd be in the air above and around the island, or in the air raid shelter beneath its limestone. Occasionally there'd be enough respite to go to the mess for a meal, though sometimes we wished we hadn't.

We quickly fell into a routine early each morning in the Officers' Mess. We'd go into breakfast, and one of the airmen would say, 'Will you have your slice of bread now, or later?' I always said, 'Now, please,' just to make sure of it before anything happened.

We used to hold these thin slices of bread up to the light. And in the bread you could clearly see weevils. They're little beetles that love flour. We'd pick them out meticulously, at least at the start of our time in Malta. Bill Carroll insists that habit didn't last:

'By the time we left Malta we all used to leave those little animals in the bread, because it was the only fresh meat we were likely to get!'

I'm not sure we ate them in the Officers' Mess, because I

remember joking, 'If we ever get back to England, I bet we'll still be holding our bread up to the light and trying to pick things out of it, just out of habit.'

The food was just about adequate, though we were on minimal rations. I would have my one slice of bread, and then later on we were dished up bully beef for lunch. It was horrible, and Bill Carroll thought he knew why:

'There were tins of corned beef at the side of the mess in Malta and the date on them was 1914. This stuff had been there since the First World War!'

I don't know about that, but I do remember how the piece of bread and the bully beef tasted, and neither was very pleasant. We did have one luxury, though. Luckily they cultivated tomatoes on Malta, so we had a good supply of those. They were lovely, and the NCOs were given some of those tomatoes, too. Perhaps the pilots were generally better fed than their crews over in the other mess. I sincerely hope not, but Bill suspects that was the case.

Despite the general food shortage, the arrival of more crews to feed could only be a good thing for Malta's future. Another six Beauforts and their crews joined us from Gibraltar the day after we arrived, having encountered no hostility in the skies. And on 12 June, the total of fifteen Beaufort aircraft which had arrived from Gibraltar had their auxiliary tanks taken off, and torpedoes fitted. Hungry or not, we were building up a fighting force. By the next day, all the planes were fully prepared for operational work. We were getting ready for battle. But before we went to work, there was time for some play.

Any relief from the heat was going to be welcome. Though Luqa airfield was built at the island's highest point, it was still only about a hundred feet above sea level. The sun was relentless, and it was very hot. You had to be very careful about touching metal because it would burn. If you'd wanted to, you could have fried an egg on the wing of your plane. So imagine our joy when we heard we could go down to Valletta, trudge through the rubble-filled streets, and cross over to bathe in beautiful Sliema, just along the shore. I'd always loved swimming, ever since I'd first entered the pool at school in Ramsgate. Learning to swim there had been one of the most enjoyable experiences in my life; over-arm, side-stroke, breaststroke ... and just being able to float on your back – sheer bliss! Now such pleasures were available in warm sea and sunshine.

Bill remembers the strange contrast between war and relax-ation:

'On the second or third day, the "Queen Mary" went through the camp. That was the name we gave to the big RAF trailer which was used to carry aircraft. The Queen Mary used to go very slowly, and we were given permission to run alongside it and then jump on. We used to hitch a ride down to Sliema and swim off the rocks there. It was great! Aspinall and Alan Still didn't swim much; I went with people like George Lawcock. We couldn't believe we'd found a place which made you feel like you were on holiday, even for a few hours.

'We had to walk back, though. And on the way back that day, we saw a very welcome sight. Spitfires, maybe thirty or forty of them, were coming in to land at the airstrips in Malta. They'd been flown in off an aircraft carrier, which may have been lost, and come several hundred miles to Malta. The next morning Jerry got a shock when he came over with his usual good morn-ing greeting. Two 88s were welcomed by the Spitfires, which gave us hope that the tide could be turned, and the RAF could take back the skies above Malta.

'In the meantime, after the luxurious food of Gibraltar, we searched for a solution to the nagging hunger we were beginning to feel. There was an experimental farm on Malta run by the military. It was breeding pigs so that the forces could get meat to eat – not that we seemed to be seeing any of it. This farm had barbed wire all around it. Every time we went past it, we saw these little piglets the other side of the barbed wire, and we wanted to eat them.

'George Lawcock was a Yorkshireman and he said: "I'm a butcher – you let me into that piggery and I know where to stick a pig." One night, one of the boys got a pair of pliers, they cut the barbed wire, and George, who had sharpened his knife especially, went in to stick one of the piglets and get the thing out of there.

'I was outside keeping an eye out, but the problem was inside – because they encountered nothing but pig shit. They started crawling around trying to grab a piglet and they had crap all over them. George said: "Grab one by the ears, boys, and I'll dispatch it." But they couldn't grab a piglet by the ears when they had all this crap all over them. It was a disaster so we got out of there in a hurry before anyone found us. No piglet. No food. So much for George the butcher. I think that was our first week in Malta.'

Despite Bill's little set-back, morale was still relatively high at this early stage of our summer on the island. We needed to keep it that way, too, because there was the unspoken feeling among us that we were going to be in a very tough fight, indeed, before long. If unity was to be the key, the Sergeants' Mess had the solution.

The non-commissioned officers of 217 Squadron formed a choral group under Sergeant Harold 'Taffy' Hole. I heard about it but I wasn't involved with the group, despite my love for music. They were in the other mess and, besides, they weren't short of singers. There were twenty-eight of them in that hut and they all joined in.

Bill Carroll liked a sing-song as much as the next man:

'Taffy was a music teacher and he was a very, very happy fellow. If he'd survived, Taffy would have been a Headmaster in no time. He was closer to thirty than most of the rest of us. Still, we were grateful to Taffy Hole for giving us some amusement while it lasted. Welshmen are famous for the quality of their singing, and Taffy would give us hell if the bass or the tenors went wrong. We sang our favourite old songs, such as: "Pack Up Your Troubles in Your Old Kit Bag." One of the lines in that song says: "What's the use in worrying? It never was worth-while." But some of those poor guys would be cracking up within a few weeks; and a lot more, including poor Taffy, would be dead. He was a very nice guy, though different from most of the NCOs because he didn't drink.

'Taffy was excellent for morale, and there were others on hand to offer us spiritual comfort if we felt the need. The padre of the station – I think they called him Monsignor – used to come in and talk through the next church service with Aspinall. That padre liked his little brown jug almost as much as Asp, which could only have strengthened their bond. He was a very nice guy and he was always in our billet with Aspinall. He must have been about fifty-five, from another generation entirely, and he would say: "Bill, we haven't seen you in church." My father was a Catholic but that didn't make me as religious as Aspinall, so these moments could be a bit awkward. "Very sorry," I'd reply a little lamely. "I'll go with the other boys."

'In fact, Aspinall did enough worshipping for all of us. If there wasn't a service at the airfield on Malta for any reason, he'd find a church in a local village – Malta was Catholic – and he'd attend the service there instead. The Catholics in the squadron were keener than the Protestants to lay on a service. Given the amount of bombs that were coming down from the sky, we probably all should have been praying as much as Vince was.

'Every building seemed vulnerable; even the little Intelligence Office, which was used as an Ops Room. Like our hut, it was covered by nothing more than a corrugated iron roof. At least the air raid shelter below it was pretty solid, carved out of the local limestone. That was just as well, because for the first month we were there, Jerry still had command of the air.

'There'd be so many air raids that we didn't know whether we were listening to an all-clear or a fresh warning. We were heavy sleepers and the Ops Room wasn't very far. So when we heard the siren go, one of the twenty-eight would run to the Ops Room and ask: "What's the plot?" If there were fifty-plus enemy aircraft coming, we'd make our way to the air raid shelter. Otherwise we tried to stay where we were.

'Often there wasn't any warning at all. These Junkers 88s would come from Sicily or somewhere, flying in at fifty feet like we did, so the radar wouldn't pick them up. Completely unannounced! You'd hear the guns before you heard the siren. An 88 is roughly the size of a Beaufort but it's about 100 miles an hour faster. Wow! We really didn't know what was going on half the time. Inevitably there were some near misses and some tragic hits when the bombs came down.

'An airman called Ken Eades led a charmed life. One time he was playing the piano and we were teasing him about slouching. "Sit up straight when you're playing," we joked. Suddenly a bomb landed and a piece of shrapnel the size of a plate was embedded four inches into the wall just where his head should have been. If he'd been sitting upright instead of crouching over the piano, it would have taken his head off. That same bomb killed a cook outside, a local Maltese man.'

The officers' hut wasn't far from the air raid shelter. If your bed was near the entrance, you could usually make it before the bombs came down. My bed was at the back of the hut, right at the far end. That made me rather naughty about the air raid shelter, because all I did was stay in my bunk when the air raids were on. I didn't care. I was too lazy to get out of bed to go to the air raid shelter. I just felt resigned to my fate. What was the point of disturbing my rest to join the scramble for the shelter? Either a bomb was destined to hit me, or it wasn't. We all had our different ways of coping with Malta, and this feeling of resignation was my own defence system, I suppose. It was probably how I maintained my own morale. Not that I really thought about it at all. We were men of action; we didn't think or feel any more than we had to. Except that in this particular instance, I was perfectly happy to be a man of inaction. I just lay there as the sirens wailed and the bombs fell . . . and I tried to go back to sleep.

15

The Sinking of the Trento

We weren't just going to sit there and take the bombing indefinitely. The time was fast approaching to hit back. On 14 June, 1942, the operational record book stated:

> Standing by; the Squadron was fully briefed on the situation which will develop tomorrow.

Malta was only about twelve days from having to surrender due to a lack of food and fuel. Realising how desperate the situation was, the War Cabinet had sent two convoys towards the island simultaneously from different directions. Eleven battleships, accompanied by ten cruisers, twenty-seven destroyers, and half a dozen other ships, were trying to reach Malta from Alexandria, Egypt, in what was codenamed Operation Vigorous. A smaller convoy of eight ships had left Gibraltar at roughly the same time to try to reach Malta from the opposite direction. The idea was to split the enemy attack and halve its severity, though the onslaught would be brutal enough when it came.

The Italian fleet, including their battleships, was steaming out of Taranto to intercept the British convoy coming from

Alexandria. But thanks to intelligence coming from Bletchley Park, we were on to them straight away. We were going to attack the Italian fleet with whatever we'd got. On 15 June at 04.00hrs, we were sent out to find them. Wing Commander Davis was to lead us on what was going to be one of the most important strikes of our lives. Engaged to be married back home, Willie Davis was in charge of 217 Squadron by now. He was a pleasant and steady enough chap, without ever being quite the force of nature that Malta's desperate situation demanded if we were to prevail in the long run. Davis didn't lack courage, though, and we were prepared to follow him into whatever storm might be waiting for us.

The idea was to form up at 500 feet over a lighthouse on the nearby island of Gozo, adjacent to Malta. When we were all ready, Wing Commander Davis was going to waggle his wings and everyone would set off for the target, which was calculated to be somewhere to the south-west of Crete.

As we made our way to our Beaufort, the night was still dark, with no moon and barely a few stars. The aircraft were housed in dispersal pens, which were bricked around to protect them from bomb blasts. June in the Med was warm even at night, so I was in shirt-sleeves, an open-neck shirt and tailored shorts. Flying would give us some relief from the heat, if nothing else.

Unfortunately, my plane was blocked by another Beaufort on our way along the taxi path that led from the dispersal pens to the runway. The other aircraft had engine trouble and they couldn't restart it. You couldn't just go around it, because there were crater-holes all over the place and the Beaufort wheels were made of relatively soft rubber. Alan Still and Bill Carroll got out and helped the ground crew push this thing off the taxi track. In the meantime, I stayed in our aircraft with Aspinall, keeping our engines running as we considered our options.

Bill remembered his exasperation:

'We'd got up at two or three in the morning, hardly had any sleep, and we were buggering around pushing an aircraft out the way.'

As we watched the rest of the squadron take off and disappear into the black sky above us, we realised the chances of making up enough time to join the others in formation over Gozo were diminishing by the minute. Aspinall said what the rest of us were thinking: 'Pilot, we're twenty minutes late, the others have taken off without us, and we can't possibly catch up now. We'd best head straight for the point of interception.'

I knew he was right. 'OK, Asp, set the course,' I told him. From that moment on, we knew we might have to go up against the Italian fleet all alone. We were certainly going to have to try to find it by ourselves. Asp handed me a piece of paper with the required bearings, which I put in front of my P4 compass before setting the course on my gyro. We took off and climbed to about a thousand feet. It felt good to be on our way; yet within a few minutes, Aspinall was expressing his dissatisfaction.

'Pilot, we're flying two degrees off course.'

Had the gyro strayed, due to the rotation of the earth on its axis? Had I taken my eye off it? You couldn't watch it all the time.

'OK, Asp,' I replied, making the necessary adjustment.

On the way, Bill fired his Browning guns, normal practice just to make sure they were working. Otherwise we were all quiet – focusing on our jobs, waiting for whatever might come our way in the next few minutes. We were still flying quite high, at about a thousand feet. Even though it was nearly six o'clock in the morning and we could see dawn just breaking ahead of us, it was still dark in our part of the sky. Then I spotted them to port; four gleaming cruisers, in perfect line astern. The convoy! What a beautiful sight! '*L'ho trovato io!*' as I might have said as a child in Italy – 'I've found it!'

'Look ahead!' I told the others on the intercom. They took in this magnificent sight in silence. Like me, they'd never seen anything quite like it in their lives. The sea was calm and the ships so serene that the whole scene barely looked real. The cruisers were protected in the bow by two destroyers, and astern there were two more destroyers. But this wasn't the time to think favourably about the country of my birth, the home of the art I most loved, or the Italian people on those cruisers. No time, no feeling. This was war, my life was on the line; they were trying to destroy our convoy and starve Malta. There was a job to be done, these Italians were my enemy. They didn't seem to know it, though, because they weren't going very fast. Perfect timing. We'd be able to use the dark – for those ships down on the sea it wasn't even starting to get light yet.

I passed with the fleet on my left and turned gently away to starboard, losing a little height as I did so. This wasn't the time to arouse suspicion. I wanted to come right round again so that I could attack out of the dark half of the sky. I didn't want to be silhouetted against the light of the dawn.

As far as I could tell, they still thought I was friendly, part of their patrol, precisely because I was circling like this. A Beaufort looks rather like a Junkers 88 if you haven't seen one before and they probably hadn't. They were going to remember this one, though. We were in luck – there was no ack-ack whatsoever. Now it was all a question of timing.

As we circled, Asp gave voice to what was going through all

our minds, though the decision would be mine. 'Pilot, should we attack alone? Shouldn't we wait for the others?'

'The others may not find them,' I replied.

From the middle of the plane, Alan peered at our prey through the gun hatches and said: 'I think we should go in now.'

Not one to be left out of any conversation, Carroll yelled from the back: 'So do I!'

It was good to hear that the crew were broadly in agreement with what I'd already decided.

'The others may not find the fleet,' I repeated. 'We're going in.'

I focused on the leading Italian cruiser rather than a destroyer. That's what I had been trained to do – go for the most dangerous, the biggest ship. This cruiser was the biggest, so it was the one to aim for. It had more fire-power, as well, which was going to make it a dangerous beast once it sensed a threat. And there was another minor problem: I was going to have to fly low across the bows of the leading destroyer to get at the cruiser.

Asp had two Vickers K machine guns down at the front. He prepared to take off the safety catches, but didn't want to fire until the moment was right. He knew how vulnerable he was, right in the nose of the plane. He wasn't about to get trigger-happy, and he didn't want anyone else to, either.

'Don't open up on them, Bill,' he said.

'I'm not bloody stupid, you know,' Bill replied.

Carroll recalled the tension of these moments, as we waited to strike:

'The Italians must have been fast asleep. But if they woke up there'd be blokes down there with eight-inch cannons. These were real guns, not like what I had, and there were eight of them. They had sixteen more to call on if they had time, less than half the size but still lethal enough. So it was in our interests to get this strike right. We circled around, and Arthur made a perfect job of it, flying in an S-shape as we turned inside the destroyer. It was just off to our port side, I was only fifty yards away from the thing. I could have thrown a bottle on to the deck and I could practically see the colour of the men's eyes down there.

'The freeboard [the height of the ship's deck above the water level] on the destroyer was unusually high, and I could see these four Italians running for the cannon they had on the port side. The alarm must have gone up because they were running like hell towards this 3.7 gun. No one said anything on our Beaufort as we waited for them to open fire. And then – you wouldn't believe it – they just stood there! They never moved an inch to fire their gun. Their captain must have decided we were friendly after all. Arthur spun the plane around and went in while the going was good. The cruiser, our target, was to port.'

I was going to do this my way; I'd made up my mind. I'd failed with my torpedo during the Channel Dash. Now I'd adapt my tactics. The training was wrong at Abbotsinch, I was sure of it. This time I'd attack at forty-five degrees and slightly ahead of the ship's bow. Take advantage of the converging speeds, that'd increase my chances.

The Italian cruiser seemed to have slowed down slightly. Even better! I opened the throttles to get my speed up to 140 knots, the right speed for dropping the torpedo from a height of 60 to 80 feet. Now it was all about timing my release. My finger was on the button. The cruiser was lined up. A thousand yards, nine hundred yards ... I was going to aim off but not by much, because my target wasn't moving very fast. Eight hundred yards. I pressed! It felt right.

'Torpedo gone,' I said. Now science and design took over. The two wires and the drum control gear began the destructive process. The wires spun for a second and came away, sending the torpedo into flight with its nose slightly down. The torpedo weighed 1,650 lb but still managed to fly 250 yards in two or three seconds, helped by its tail. It entered the sea at a downward angle of seventeen degrees to the horizontal. The tail detached on impact, its job done. At this point the torpedo seemed to take on a life of its own. It reared up and dipped back down, before finding its cruising depth at fifteen feet below the surface. Powered by its own little engine, it was ready to swim at a sea speed of 40 knots. The fan blades in its nose whirred in the water for 350 yards, and automatically armed the torpedo. The warhead was now ready to detonate on impact.

We still didn't know whether we were going to score a hit, but already we were trying to find a way to leave the scene quietly. At last the Italians realised what was coming their way, and they tried to shoot us down. The flak arrowed towards us.

'Take avoiding action!' said Aspinall.

'I am,' I told him. 'Can't you see I'm skidding?'

'Are you turning enough?' he persisted.

I didn't want to raise my wings to present a bigger target. I was performing the usual evasive manoeuvres, swinging from right to left and back again, though perhaps a little more extremely after Aspinall's pleas. We passed the bows of the enemy cruiser. We were so close now that Still could see people running about in a panic on the deck. They knew all too well what was about to happen.

In his turret, Carroll was struggling to watch the drama unfold:

'I was craning my neck but when you've got that damn tail there, you can't see the torpedo running. I could hear the guns, though. The Italians had woken up and realised we weren't friendly after all, but they were firing over the top of us, which was a good thing. We went between the bow of the cruiser and the stern of the destroyer, and we were skidding. Since the Italians had woken up, I opened up with a few bursts back at them. That's when I spotted a wake in the water, as our torpedo closed in on the ship. I couldn't see it until we were skidding away. Over to my right, I could see the bow of the leading cruiser out of the corner of my eye, and I saw this flash. I realised the torpedo had hit home. Then there was a whoosh – a blast of air coming from the explosion on the cruiser, the draught from the torpedo. The bang came last, we all had headphones on but we could still hear it.'

I knew the torpedo had scored a hit, because I felt the buffeting from the explosion just after I passed the cruiser. Smoke and debris shot upwards with a huge jet of water. There was fire, too, and we knew we'd inflicted some serious damage. I felt satisfaction. We'd achieved the right position to drop the torpedo, it had hit the target, and I'd done it by going against what we'd been taught. I wasn't a rebel and I wasn't going to go around telling other people what I'd done, I just wanted to try it my way, without making a fuss about it. It had worked! It had been a close-run thing, though, because I'd hit the bows, and that meant I'd only just found my target. If I'd aimed off any more I wouldn't have hit it. We weren't out of danger, though. From the turret Bill had spotted fresh fireworks:

'All of a sudden I could see ammunition going off all over the place, behind us. I said: "What's the matter with them? Now they're shooting at each other!" What I didn't know was that the rest of the boys were coming in from the other side, led by the Wing Commander. The Italians were firing at them. We'd dropped our "torp" so we left them to it.'

The Italian fleet were shooting in all directions because the rest of the squadron were now attacking from all directions! The Italians were in disarray as I turned to starboard to get further away. But suddenly they opened up on us again, and the tracer was getting closer.

Asp was guiding me, 'Turn to starboard ... now back to port ... back again ... We're getting clear but keep low!'

The Italian gunners weren't great shots – not like the Germans. Besides, we were out of their range by now. It was too little too late from their point of view. We'd done it! We'd left the chaos behind us! But which cruiser had we hit and neutralised?

'I think it was the *Gorizia*,' said Aspinall, who'd learned the names of the biggest ships in the Italian fleet. But he was wrong. It turned out to be the 10,000 ton cruiser *Trento*. I'd gone for the right target, because a destroyer might only be 1,500 or 1,800 tons. You are trained to go for the biggest and the *Trento* had certainly been the biggest ship in the section of the fleet I'd encountered.

What we didn't know was that by flying a little further to the north we might have run into the battleship squadron, and been at the mercy of even greater monsters. The *Littorio* and the *Vittorio Veneto* were 35,000 and 45,000 tons respectively, real giants of the sea. Other British aircraft would have to face that formidable pair, if they could avoid the eight destroyers screening them. As for us, it was time to head for home.

When we landed at Luqa, two of the ground crew followed us down one of the taxi tracks and jumped up on the port wing. Carroll put his head out of the port waist hatch to deliver the good news over the sound of the engines. Bill has fond memories of these moments:

'We were the first ones to land and this little ground staff bloke came running up, and he could see that the torpedo was gone. The other ground staff looked equally elated by the fact that they couldn't see the torpedo. The ground crew in Malta were very resilient. We air crew had it tough; but for them it was terrible. Anyway, this first bloke pulled himself up by one of the handholds, got on and sat in the crutch of the wing at the back.

'"Did you get one?" he asked.

'I said, "Yeah, this big Eyetie cruiser, and we've blown the bows off her!"

'He was so happy when I said that. He started telling all his mates and there was joy all around. You don't score a big hit like that every day, you know. It was a joyous thing. The maintenance men pumped their fists in the air and cheered. Luqa had been taking such a pounding, and they'd been so busy round the clock fixing planes and filling in bomb craters, that any news of success against the enemy provided a terrific lift. The ground crew were real heroes, especially out in Malta. They were working and being bombed all the time and they just got on with it. This was their reward.

'Everyone on our crew was ecstatic, too. I think we were the only ones in the squadron out of about nine aircraft who actually got a significant hit. It was an excellent result for F/O Aldridge – his finest hour.'

The operational record book claimed more hits for 217 Squadron:

Nine Beauforts took off from Luqa at 04.15 hours this morning to attack the Italian battle fleet about 200 miles east of the Island. The enemy fleet was in two sections, the leading section consisting of two battleships, two cruisers and seven destroyers.

W/C Davis led his formation of F/O Goodale and Sgt Hutcheson in to attack the first section, encountering intense flak but, it is believed, scoring two hits on a battleship. A piece of shrapnel hit F/O Goodale's aircraft, setting off a Very cartridge, which was quickly extinguished by the navigator and W/OP. S/L Lynn attacked with Sgt Dale from the opposite direction. He scored a hit on the same battleship, while Sgt Dale hit a destroyer, which was last seen listing to port. F/O Aldridge attacked the leading battleship in the southern force, or first section, scoring a hit. Sgt Nolan also attacked alone, aiming his torpedo at the same battleship, but observed no results. Lt Strever attacked the northern force, dropping amid intense flak which wounded his gunner, Sgt Grey. He had to belly land on his return.

The only torpedo that hit the cruiser squadron was mine – I'm absolutely convinced of that. And I'm not so sure the rest of the boys had as much success against the battleship squadron as 217's official account suggests. It's funny, because the way I remember it, no other pilot had any success at all in hitting the Italian fleet that day. Perhaps in all the chaos they were mistaken. The official account certainly seems to be unreliable, not least because it claims I hit a battleship, rather than a cruiser.

I had the best opportunity of all, catching the enemy unawares, and I took it. By the time my colleagues had arrived just after me, the Italians had been ready. I suppose I did mess it up a bit for the rest of the squadron, looking back. But I had to go in alone, because there was no guarantee that the others were going to find the fleet. I never heard anyone express annoyance at what I had done; quite the reverse.

We walked into the Operations Room, pleased with the job we'd done. I didn't tell my superiors how I'd deviated from the training we'd been given. I suppose I should have said something, but we didn't generally go into that kind of detail in a debriefing. In fact, I don't remember any debriefing where pilots and their intelligence officer went into specific details of technique. I'd had some success on this occasion, but I didn't consider myself important enough to be going around telling other people what to do and how to do it.

What I did believe was that Bill deserved a beer – though he wasn't going to get one. Life was never quite so straightforward on Malta that summer:

'There were two problems. The first was that we couldn't celebrate with a beer because even if there was any beer around, it was too expensive at 1s 6d a bottle. The second problem was that we hadn't finished our day's work. We were told to prepare to be sent out again with more torpedoes. The mission was to locate and hit the Italian fleet a second time that very evening. This was news we didn't really want to hear.'

As we rested before trying to hurt the Italians again, another important development took place at Luqa. Squadron Leader Pat Gibbs and a detachment of 39 Squadron from the Middle East arrived. Taking off from Egypt, Gibbs had led twelve Beauforts on a strike against a 35,000 ton battleship. One of the aircraft in his formation had been picked off by enemy fighters on the way to the target. And, as Gibbs dropped his torpedo, his aircraft had been so badly damaged by fire that he'd had to crash-land on his belly at Malta. I remember him doing that belly-landing. It was quite an entrance and Gibbs was a man none of us would forget – he had a fanatical look in his eyes.

Observing the newcomer's demeanour, Bill Carroll was immediately wary of the new arrival:

'Gibbs didn't take over right away. He was basically 39 Squadron and he was like a bull in a china shop. You don't cross someone who has got angry eyes like that.'

Gibbs had reason to feel angry almost immediately. Unbeknown to us, the convoy from Alexandria had already turned back after taking substantial casualties. Gibbs learned this news in the Officers' Mess, just as we in 217 Squadron were preparing to take off and attack the Italians again. Had we also been given the bad news, we would probably have shared his sense of disappointment and indignation. Surely the Alexandria convoy had already come through the worst of the ordeal it was to face? There seemed little point in its about-turn at this late stage. After all they'd suffered to reach Malta, it might have been no more dangerous to sail on towards the island and see the job through. Still, the decision had been made; and apparently it didn't change our basic objective, which was to see off the Italians.

As we climbed wearily back into our Beauforts on what had already been a very long day, our commanding officer probably spared a thought for home. Once he had led us through our convoy operations, Wing Commander Davis planned to hand over to his second-in-command and return to England. Davis was due to be married and had already missed his original wedding day. When the time came for him to fulfil that pledge, it was Gibbs who was destined to fill the power vacuum in Malta. In the meantime, Davis and the rest of us had a job to do – and a dangerous one at that – if, indeed, we found our Italian targets again.

16

Into the Wall of Fear

We took off at 19.30hrs to search for the enemy again. The Italian fleet was heading back to port, but we wanted to make sure they never came back for more.

This time we were part of the formation following Wing Commander Davis. Unfortunately, his navigator had got his sums wrong and my navigator soon realised. 'He's miscalculated,' Asp kept saying. 'We're on the wrong course. The Italian fleet is further north.'

'Are you sure, Asp?'

'Of course I'm sure. We need to break off and go it alone again. Or get them to follow.'

Looking back I should have trusted Aspinall enough to have set our own course. We would probably have found the Italians again. I did trust him, but I didn't want to get into trouble with my commanding officer. There wasn't any radio contact between the aircraft, so we couldn't tell the leader of our concerns. But Bill puts my obedience down to a lack of natural rebelliousness:

'Even if we'd been able to tell the lead man he was off course, I don't think Artie would have said anything. Arthur watched his Ps and Qs. I have an idea that Sergeant Fred Dennis was the cocky navigator chosen by the Wing Commander for that evening effort to find the Italians. Wing Commander Davis was a good guy; but that little navigator, Fred Dennis, he didn't have a clue – he was lousy.'

I should have listened to Asp and gone on my own. I could and should have waggled my wings to try to get the others to come with me. But what if I'd gone off on my own and the others had stayed with the commanding officer, and then they'd found the fleet without me? That might have caused a serious problem for me.

In the end, we didn't find the Italians again. And if I'd followed Aspinall's advice I think we would have done. Bill wasn't sorry we didn't get a second bite at the cherry, though, for all his griping:

'We knew they'd be ready and waiting for us this time. I don't think Asp was too angry that Arthur ignored his advice to break away and follow a different course. To be very honest with you, we thought we'd got away with it in the morning, and we were very tired. Don't forget the rations on Malta were pretty poor and we'd been up in the very early hours. By the time we returned to Luqa, it was one o'clock in the morning, so we'd been on the go for about twenty hours.'

On 16 June, the squadron rested after the previous day's efforts, but remained on stand-by. It was then I heard that a submarine had finished off the Italian cruiser I'd hit. The *Trento* had been doomed from the moment we left her like a sitting duck. Our attack and the subsequent chaos had all been watched by a British submarine the HMS *Umbra*. Later that morning, they finished the job I'd started by firing two more torpedoes into the *Trento*. She sank and 544 Italians lost their lives because of what I'd set in motion. Almost half the *Trento*'s crew of 1,151 men were killed.

When I sank the *Trento*, I had no feelings at all about fighting the Italians, the people I'd lived among for the first five years of my life in Florence. You just had to find the Italian fleet and sink it. You were in danger and you didn't think about the people on board. Even when I realised there must have been a high casualty rate, I still didn't feel anything. I was part Italian, I'd spoken the language like a native as a toddler, I'd fallen in love with the gentle hills and endless rows of Tuscan olive trees; yet none of that mattered in wartime, it had all been pushed to the back of my mind. Only much later, after the war, did I consider the consequences of my actions; I wished more Italian sailors had survived. And if there was to be such a big loss of life resulting from any of my actions, I wished they could have been German lives not Italian.

The price in Italian lives was high, but there were favourable consequences for Britain's war. The Italians never put to sea again as a major force after the *Trento* was sunk, and my success might have contributed to that reluctance. Lack of fuel was also an issue, though I don't think the Italians were all that keen on fighting us – at least not as keen as the Germans were. Maybe that's why they weren't given so much fuel. It was only because of Mussolini and his cronies that the Italians had joined the wrong side. The rest didn't want to be allied to the Germans. No way! Once Mussolini was overthrown, the Italians joined the Allies.

But how could I possibly be expected to worry about Italians and their unfortunate situation at the height of the battle for Malta? Our situation looked desperate once our convoy from the east had turned back. And that, in itself, was a reminder that, despite the huge Italian loss of life, British losses had been far greater. Meanwhile, the convoy from the west had limped on, though only the SS *Orari* and SS *Troilus* had reached Malta with their supplies of fuel and food. It wasn't much, but it was better than nothing; and what got through kept the island alive for a little longer.

With the convoy operation over, Gibbs learned that 217 squadron was going to be moved on to Ceylon. He wasn't having it and he went straight to see the AOC on Malta, Air Vice-Marshal Sir Hugh Pughe Lloyd. 'Hughie Pughie' was a larger-than-life character, ready to entertain any sensible plan for the aggressive defence of Malta. But the feisty Gibbs offered more than defence. He insisted that the Germans, for all their recent advances in North Africa, could still be stabbed in the back by the retention of as many torpedo-laden Beauforts on Malta as possible. We could hit Rommel's supply lines when he most needed them – and help save the island at the same time. It was a persuasive argument and one Hughie Pughie promised to pass up the chain of command. Gibbs had made the correct call, though the consequences for 217 Squadron would be devastating.

On 19 June, four more Beaufort crews arrived from Gibraltar after an encounter with enemy aircraft south of Pantelleria. Among them was a pilot friend of mine, Ron Harrison, who also doubled as a navigator. We'd been together at Chivenor, had been posted up to Abbotsinch in the same group, and we got on well.

The trouble was, almost as soon as he arrived, I began to put him in danger – just by doing nothing. Ron's bed was nearest to the bomb shelter and he knew I was at the other end of the hut, furthest away. I still couldn't be bothered to go to the shelter during night raids but if anyone expressed concern I used to say I'd be there in a second . . . and then I didn't move. Ron didn't trust me to go to the shelter on my own and he was right not to!

But the way he responded to what he saw as a problem was self-less in the extreme. He started coming all the way to the back of the hut to fetch me and bring me to the front and then out to the shelter. By doing that, he didn't get to the shelter as quickly as he could have done.

One time, as we were rushing to the shelter, we heard the bombs whistling down. We threw ourselves on to the stony path. We could hear the explosions all around us, even on the airfield next to where we were. Somehow we were able to pick ourselves up unscathed, dust ourselves down, and go belatedly to the shelter. If Ron had gone straight to the shelter, he would have been safely in there before the bombs struck. Of course, I couldn't let him carry on coming to get me like that. It wasn't fair for him to go on risking his life for me. So I behaved myself after that and rushed off to the shelter at night with everyone else. What a marvellous gesture Harrison had made. No wonder Ron became one of my closest friends in the entire war.

On 20 June, there was a heavy air raid during the day, and we lost one of our squadron right there on the ground at Luqa. Bill Carroll knew the victim:

'Jack Walworth could have been a professor, he was older than us, a very sage, studious type. He was Des Fenton's navigator, and Des would become good friends with Arthur and me before long. Poor Jack, he was walking to Valletta, because he was interested in culture and archaeology. A bunch of butterfly bombs dropped all around him. The Germans would come in low and drop these things like the modern-day cluster bomb, fifty or a hundred at a time. Hinged wings would open at the top and leave what looked like a tin below, which was packed with explosive. They didn't drop them from a height, because then the tins would have gone off immediately, so they dropped them from about fifty feet. The tins had a spring at the bottom with a band around it. When the band got knocked off, the whole thing went whoosh! Poor Jack was crushed against a wall and that was the end of him – he was killed outright. They were horrible devices, these 2 kg cluster bombs, which the Germans called *Sprengbombe Dickwandig* or SD2s. And they claimed many victims on Malta. It was terrible because Maltese children would come along and kick these tins like a football and they would be killed, too.'

Life was no easier in the skies between Malta and Italy that week. During a strike by twelve Beauforts on the toe of Italy, Sergeant Bob Dale's rudder blew off, so he returned. Two other aircraft, piloted by Flying Officer Minster and Sergeant Hutcheson, were late on take-off and were attacked by four Ju88s. Sergeant Hutcheson managed to beat off the two that attacked him and returned to Luqa, but Flying Officer Minster failed to return.

Bob Dale, a quiet, well-educated Londoner who was housed in Bill's hut, must have known what a lucky escape he'd had that day. But if the experience had shaken Dale, he chose not to share his feelings with Bill, Asp or Alan Still. Dale had his own small circle of friends, and didn't even play cards with my crew when they invited him to do so. No one could force Dale to be friendlier with the wider group, and my crew had already learned to tread carefully around certain individuals. Henry Parry, Hutcheson's gunner, was another who seemed withdrawn at times. Yet when it had mattered, Parry had pulled out all the stops yet again to prevent their aircraft from becoming a second victim of the Ju88s. Even so, these narrow escapes were quietly taking their toll on the men, and there was no end in sight.

On 21 June, 1942, the Wing Commander gave us details of an operation regarded as vital if we were to stop Colonel-General Erwin Rommel's Afrika Korps from being resupplied by sea. An enemy convoy had left Naples the previous day bound for Tripoli in Libya. The ships were off the Tunisian coast and the convoy was trying to reach the German regiments who were dishing out so much punishment to our own army in North Africa.

There were two merchant ships, the Italian *Rosolino Pilo* and the German *Reichenfels*, escorted by two Italian destroyers and a torpedo boat. We were told what was going to happen. We were to strike with nine Beauforts, each carrying a torpedo. Squadron Leader Robert Lynn, who Bill remembers well, was to lead the first vic:

'Squadron Leader Lynn was a fantastic guy. He was from Inverness, but he spoke perfect English! He was tall, six foot plus; a handsome-looking bloke, and a gentleman, too. No bullshit ordering you around. Everybody liked him.'

I was to lead the second vic, while Flying Officer Stevens, a Canadian whose company I very much enjoyed, was going to lead the third. For the first time we were going to be escorted by Beaufighters. Though the six Beaufighters were welcome, no combined tactics had been worked out, other than the obvious role they would have in trying to protect us from enemy fighters.

Bill had his concerns; the escort might make us more detectable by radar, and there'd be no cloud cover:

'The operation was going to be done in broad bloody daylight. You might not think that makes any difference when you're flying in at fifty feet above the waves. But the Beaufighters were to be stacked up above us, at elevations five hundred feet and one thousand feet, and so on; and the clear skies would make it easier for enemy fighters to spot us.'

We just had to accept the conditions as they were and get on with it. Hugh Pughe Lloyd gave us a pep talk at the end of the briefing. We liked Hughie Pughie and sometimes he could be quite an inspiration. 'Pop 'em in the bag,' Pughe Lloyd always used to say. But this time he overdid it.

'Pop 'em in the bag for me, men! I know how brave you are, each and every one of you, and you're going to need all your courage to make a success of this today. I can't emphasise enough just how important this is. Good luck to you.'

I couldn't help thinking this pep talk was potentially counter-productive. A talk like that could make people feel more afraid. It didn't have too much of an effect on me, because I was quite resigned to my fate anyway. But I thought his words might have sounded a little unnerving to some of the newcomers. It was one of those occasions when we'd already been fully briefed, and all we needed to hear from Hughie Pughie was a heartfelt 'good luck'.

He hadn't talked about the amount of firepower we'd face, or anything specifically frightening. And Hughie Pughie certainly hadn't told us that we might not all come back. They may say things like that in the movies, but no flyer in their right mind would ever say it in a real briefing. No way. However, by talking about the strike's extreme importance and the courage we'd need, he simply made us more aware of the danger we were going to face. We didn't need anyone to tell us it would be dangerous.

We knew what could happen when something was of supreme importance. The aborted strike on the *Tirpitz* had taught us that we were regarded as expendable under extreme circumstances. If we were being told this was so important, you couldn't help but think there was a greater chance our lives could be sacrificed. After a certain amount of information had been delivered, we didn't need to hear any more – at least I didn't. We knew what we had to do. We knew Hitler and his generals had to be stopped.

It was all very well telling us we had to pop this convoy in the bag at all costs; but he wasn't the one who was going to have to pop 'em in the bag – we were. We took off at 11.15hrs; three vics, a total of nine aircraft. I was leading a vic on the port side of Squadron Leader Lynn, who was spearheading our formation. To starboard was the vic led by Stevens. Our chances had been slightly improved by the fact that one of the escorting destroyers, the *Strale*, had run aground near Cape Bon.

But the *Reichenfels* and the *Rosolino Pilo* were still escorted by the destroyer *Da Recco*, and they were all hugging the Tunisian coast on their way to Libya. They were watched over by three twin-engine Junkers Ju88 A–1s, which could be fighters or bombers, depending on any given situation. On this day they'd be fighters. The ships were also protected by a Sparrowhawk or *Sparviero*, a three-engine bomber, and a Cant Z.501 – an old-fashioned flying boat. These aircraft were less likely to hurt us.

We flew west for the Kerkennah Islands and the Gulf of Gabès, and Vince noted the island of Lampedusa on our right. We stayed low at fifty feet, while the fighters above us looked for opponents coming in from the south.

I spotted the killer specks on the horizon, hoping to sail unnoticed against the hazy Tunisian coast. When we were close enough to attack, Lynn waggled his wings and tried to lead in the first vic ... and that's when all hell broke loose.

Poor Robert Lynn took a shell right through him, and from that moment on the entire first vic was doomed. His plane lurched violently as his navigator Dick Dickinson tried in vain to shift his big body and wrestle with the controls. Their aircraft struck the sea, but not before their torpedo had separated from the plane and rebounded off the water. Lynn's death had already forced another Beaufort in his vic, piloted by Sergeant Smyth, to veer sharply and fly only feet beneath us. I climbed for my life to avoid that collision after hearing Bill's warning. But poor Smyth, having narrowly avoided my Beaufort, flew straight into the path of the rogue torpedo from Lynn's plane. Though there was no explosion, the torpedo did enough damage to send Smyth crashing into the waves. Flying Officer Phillips was taken down by flak at about the same time.

So the entire first vic had been wiped out in seconds. And we could so easily have joined them in the drink. In all the chaos, it was a wonder we were still in the air.

Bill Carroll still puts our survival down to our quick reactions:

'My shouts; I think they're what saved us. It was broad daylight, the most perfect day and you're in the Mediterranean, and you see this aircraft coming straight for you. Wow! We were only thirty or forty feet off the water. And I could see those shells coming in from the enemy ships – they weren't very friendly, those Germans. I watched this joker come straight in at us on the same elevation, and I'm shouting to Arthur to get up and he pulls the thing up and this guy goes straight underneath our tail.'

We'd avoided a friendly collision, but there was still the enemy to deal with. And when I saw the greeting they'd arranged for us in the form of that dreadful, seemingly impenetrable wall of flak, that's when I felt it. The empty, queasy feeling in the bottom of my stomach, the unwelcome stranger – fear. All I could do was fly on, knowing the next few seconds were going to be deeply unpleasant.

I flew into the flak at a speed of 140 knots. There were puffs of smoke everywhere and I realised I was now inside it. Locked inside a wall of flak, which surrounded us, darkening everything. I knew a more final oblivion could come at any moment. I couldn't hear anything, not even the shell bursts, because I had my headphones on. The explosions didn't rock the plane or invade it with the smell of cordite. The puffs of smoke, black and grey and all around us, rendered us almost senseless. Yet I could see enough to know why I was afraid. They couldn't come any closer, those bursts, or we would die.

Bill Carroll was still feeling typically positive back in the turret:

'The flak was grey, bursting here, there, all around, but at least we could see it. The flak you don't see is the flak that hits you. These German guys were very good. There was a hell of a difference between a German gunner and an Italian gunner. These were German gunners and they knew what they were doing. One Kraut was even bouncing the ammo off the sea, something we'd never seen anyone do before. I tell you, they were shooting their shells deliberately to create ricochets off the sea. I was in my turret and when I looked forward I could see the flak all over the place.'

And then we came straight through. None of us in that plane will ever know how we managed it. Somehow we were clear, momentarily, and nearing perfect torpedo range. The supply ship was taking evasive action; it was turning away to starboard, thus presenting no deflection shot. That meant I wouldn't have to aim ahead of the ship to anticipate its path at all, not even slightly. Aim straight for the ship and you'll normally miss because you haven't allowed for its movement. But not this time. This one was slow, and after what we'd been through, I was determined to get it.

I rose to between sixty and eighty feet and aimed at the bow. With no deflection necessary, I could go for the jugular, the point of maximum damage. This was going to be perfect. 'Time it right, Arthur. How's your distance?' Eight hundred yards ... gone! I'd pressed the button on my control column and dropped the torpedo at a distance of about 750 yards from the ship. For the second time in a week, this felt just right; but there was no time to wait and see what would happen. The flak was still horrendous. It was all about trying to stay alive now. But I was rattled, and I wasn't thinking straight.

I just wanted to get out of there. I wanted to get the hell out as fast as I could. I was so rattled that I did a stupid thing. When you take evasive action you normally snake from side to side. That's what I should have done; take the usual evasive action, skim low over the water, skid as you go. But, like an idiot, I panicked and banked to starboard; I banked so steeply that I presented some very angry Germans with a better target. They couldn't miss now ... and they didn't.

17

The Price of the Reichenfels

What a silly thing to do; bank like an idiot! Now we were paying the price. An explosion! Another, a third, and a fourth! We'd been hit by four cannon shells; I saw sparks fly and felt my plane go out of control. One shell had struck the starboard tail plane, another the port wing-tip; and a third had hit the leading edge of the starboard wing, putting one of the ailerons out of action. The starboard aileron control wires had been severed, that's probably what had caused my loss of control. The shell that had done the most damage to the crew had struck one of the ammunition pans that Aspinall had taken off its peg and put on the floor.

The shell's argument with the ammunition pan had created shrapnel from the exploded casing, and now a piece had hit me. It might have been even worse if the pan hadn't been there to absorb some of the shell's impact. A splinter had entered my right forearm. It wasn't very painful but the blood worried me for a fraction of a second, until I realised there was no time to worry, because it looked like we were about to slap into the sea. We were less than eighty feet from the waves by now. We were going in.

A thought flashed through my mind: 'We're not too far from

the coast.' I was thinking of the coast of Tunisia. 'If I have to ditch, we're not too far away. And the sea is calm. Maybe we can still make it.' It was a stupid thought because I wasn't even in control of the plane any more, so how could I ditch safely? I was out of control, yet the thought persisted in my mind: 'If I survive the impact, we are not too far from the coast. I have my Mae West on, which is good, because there's a strong possibility that within a few seconds, I'll be in the sea, trying to inflate that life jacket.' I didn't have much on to help me survive at night, though. I was in shirt-sleeves, and it'd be cold out there in the dark.

We had a dinghy, as long as we could release it from its storage point in the port wing. You pulled a piece of handgrip and out the boat was supposed to come. It'd be more use than the parachute, that was for sure, because we weren't much higher than fifty feet.

There was a Perspex top to my cockpit above the pilot's seat, which I could slide off if I was still conscious. That way I could get out and I wouldn't drown by going down with the plane. I could probably have jumped out right then, before impact, but the rest of the crew wouldn't then have had much of a chance. I decided to stay where I was and try to regain control. I might have been slightly wounded, but both my arms were still working and I was going to fight until the last possible moment.

The starboard wing was edging ever-closer to the sea, almost touching it. When it hit, that'd be it. Instinctively, I opened both throttles wide. For a moment I felt as though I was managing to get the Beaufort under control again. How could this be? My port aileron was out of action. But, by sheer luck, that act of opening the throttles had given me the slipstream over the undamaged aileron to allow me to regain control. I'd only been out of control for a few seconds, but it had felt like so much longer.

A bit of extra slipstream. That was the difference between getting shot down or not. Having been given a second chance, I didn't hang around. I did all I could to gain enough height to fly us out of there. I still only had one aileron functioning; but that didn't seem to be causing a major problem. Good old Beaufort. Our sturdy planes could certainly take some punishment.

Now I wanted to stop that blood from seeping out of my right forearm. It was coming from a gash a few inches above my wrist.

'I'm hit,' I told the others.

'Me, too,' shouted Aspinall.

I was grateful we didn't have to wear battledress out there in the Mediterranean in June. Since I was in shirt-sleeves, the wound would be easier to dress. Alan Still came forward from the middle of the plane to bandage my arm. I realised it was very minor, and I'd been more disconcerted by the blood than anything. Good old Alan, what a wonderful chap – there when you needed him. This wound probably wouldn't even leave a scar – unlike the ice-skating head wound.

Asp had been nicked below an eye. More than being injured, though, he seemed stunned. But there was no time to worry about that, because I'd noticed a more alarming sight over to my right. A Junkers 88 was chasing a Beaufort, which wasn't taking evasive action. The Ju88 was just pouring bullets into the Beaufort and there was no defensive fire at all coming from the wretched victim.

'We're going over,' I announced immediately. 'Bill! Open fire on the 88 as soon as you can; I'll try to give you a good shot.' I didn't come up alongside the other Beaufort, but stayed just below it, so that Bill could shoot upwards into the Junkers without taking our own tail off. Just after I got there, I heard Carroll open up. He didn't need a second invitation:

'And as we went over, I realised that the Beaufort had two of my good friends inside, a New Zealander called John Wilkinson and another Sergeant named Ray Brown. I knew 'em as "Wilkie" and "Brownie" – and they were in big trouble. Their Beaufort, piloted by an Australian called McSharry, had been trying to fly parallel with us back to Malta. This Junkers had sneaked in behind them and an 88 is much faster than a Beaufort, so it had closed in rapidly. This enemy pilot was pretty smart because Wilkie in the turret couldn't fire at him at all. His own bloody tail was in the way, and you couldn't go shooting that off. I suppose the Junkers pilot knew that, too. But he couldn't stop me from having a go at him.

'The Junkers was going through my gun-sights from right to left, and I had to press a pedal with my left foot to get the guns an extra fifteen degrees further round. In the turret you're on a big plate. The whole thing rotates through eighty degrees either way, but if you want the extra fifteen degrees you use one of the pedals. There's an ammunition case on your right and there's one on your left, too, so there isn't much room to manoeuvre. But in a second or two I managed to swing round to where I needed to be – and then I opened up. We were just above the waves and as you bring the guns up, you see the bullets hit the water first and then you've got him. All of a sudden, smoke started pouring from the Junkers' port engine. Yes! I'd hit him and he was there for the taking now ... then I felt my guns jam.

'I was still on the pedal, because this bloke was moving faster than we were, and that's when the Brownings do tend to jam. I cursed the bloody Brownings and their ammunition belts. It was a continuous belt, but if you had your finger on the trigger for more than eight or nine seconds it used to jam up. The ammunition was fed in at an awkward angle. The design forced hundreds of rounds per minute to go all round the houses. They had to come up, starting from the inside, then out and round, and in over the top again. If it sounds complicated, it was.

'I had two Brownings; but usually if one jammed they'd both go, and that's what happened. If you get a gun that jams, you've got to put the long cocking pin in the front of the Browning and pull the damn thing back. But in a Beaufort you've got the turret wall behind you and you can't bend your elbow. So you've got to drop the bloody seat, the guns are sticking up in the air, and you're up and down all the time.

'Just as I began to contort myself to cock my guns, a new plane came over the top, about 100 feet above us, and it scared the pants off me. I wasn't too sure if it was ours or theirs; he was moving at about 250 miles per hour. Then I saw the 88 go in the water. A Beaufighter had come in to finish the Junkers off, which was very nice of him. He pulled up and was gone again just as quickly.'

We'd done our bit to keep the other Beaufort in the air; but McSharry had been hit in the throat, severing an artery. Blood was going everywhere and his crew would have to help him fly that plane home, because it was all he could do to stay conscious. Though things weren't nearly so bad in my Beaufort, they weren't ideal either. Aspinall was still in a daze. Although we could give him a few moments, we were going to need him to come to his senses if he was going to help us plot a course home to Malta.

'Pull yourself together,' Still said. Alan being Alan, he even said that in the nicest possible way. As if to urge Asp to snap out of it, he pointed out, 'We're off course. Look, that island is too far away!'

Still had realised we'd flown much nearer to Lampedusa on the way out from Malta, so something was now awry. Asp needed to focus if we were going to get back on course. I still wasn't all that worried, though. I knew he wasn't badly hurt and I was too busy doing the flying to think about what might happen if Aspinall didn't pull himself together. Was it for situations like these that they'd sent me to Canada to teach me how to navigate? Fortunately for us, Asp came to his senses, so what I could or couldn't remember from my lessons on Prince Edward Island didn't come into play.

When I felt I was back on course, I wanted to check what had happened back there.

'Asp, did we score a hit? I was a bit busy struggling with the controls to be sure.'

'Yes! I saw the torpedo explode on the ship's port side; but the funny thing was, there were two explosions,' insisted Aspinall.

Good. A secondary explosion caused by ammunition on the ship. Even better; though how that came about I wasn't sure, because I'd been aiming for the bow.

Now that Aspinall was communicating normally again, I could give him some bad news. 'Asp, my ASI's been put out of action.'

If his ASI (air speed indicator) had suffered similar damage and he couldn't give me my air speed, I'd risk stalling and crashing when we tried to land. There was a nervous silence while he checked.

'Mine's OK,' he replied. 'I'll keep reading out the air speeds then.'

True to his word, he gave me the data I needed as we approached Luqa; and he didn't stop until we came in to land.

The last reading was 80 knots, the same speed at which I'd taken off. Plenty had happened since then.

Despite the gash on my arm, I managed a perfect landing. We climbed out of the plane, which could have become our tomb an hour earlier, and I looked at the faces of my crew. I noticed how very white they all looked. Poor crew. I'd been flying, I'd had something to do, but they'd just been sitting there most of the time, watching the flak explode all around them. No wonder they were white.

'I don't know how you got through that flak on the way in,' said Aspinall, shaking his head. 'I just don't know how on earth we got through it.'

Bill remembers sharing that dazed feeling:

'They always took us in a bus to and from the aircraft, and it was throwing us around a bit on the way back. There was no place for me to sit down because it was so full with returning crews. One of the surviving pilots, Des Fenton, could tell I was feeling weak so he just said: "Come and sit on my knee, Bill." A kind little gesture from a good man; one I remember. I would fly with Des within a few weeks; he was made of strong stuff. In contrast, another pilot who survived that day, Bob Dale, seemed very quiet. I think he was nearing his limit.'

Everyone had been pushed to the limit on that strike and Bill remembers my face looking just as pale as anyone's from our plane. We went in to the debriefing. You had to climb up some stairs to get to the Ops Room and I remember feeling a bit shaken. My legs hadn't completely turned to jelly but I wasn't exactly one hundred per cent either. It wasn't the loss of blood, because that looked worse than it was. The shock of it all, I suppose.

Bill was getting over it, because he quickly claimed half of the

Junkers 88. The Beaufighter pilot who took it off us when Bill's guns jammed was there with us in the same room and had no complaints. He even came over to meet Bill:

'The Beaufighter pilot was a good-looking young man with a silk scarf and his top button undone. He was also the gunner, because in a Beaufighter everything's in the front. They've got four cannons and six machine guns.

'I told him: "You couldn't bloody well miss with that lot." He laughed.'

Bill and the pilot were congratulating each other when Sir Hughie Pughie came up and put his arm around the pair of them. Hughie Pughie officially gave them half a kill each.

Bill Carroll was perfectly satisfied with that carve-up:

'Sir Hugh Pughe Lloyd was pleased, too. He was always grinning and smiling, especially if we had faithfully carried out his instructions: "Pop 'em in the bag for me." We'd done just that. So he popped his big old arms round us and congratulated us.

'I said, "Excuse me, sir. If I bring my log-book would you please sign it for me?"

'"Certainly," said Lloyd.'

Nobody saw fit to mention any eye-witness account of the possible premature release of a torpedo as we lined up to attack. An official report later mentioned all the downed aircraft, including Smyth's, with confirmation that a form of 'friendly fire' had played a part in his demise. I didn't mention anything at the time. I hadn't seen what had happened with my own eyes – I had just heard the rumours from other eye-witnesses when we got back to Malta. There was so much more to take in and I still felt a bit shaken up.

The Australian navigator in Smyth's Beaufort had survived the impact with the sea and was rescued by the enemy. Later that year in Stalag IVB in Germany, he still felt bitter that he had effectively been made a prisoner of war by the involuntary actions of someone on his own side.

Meanwhile no one blamed Asp for the shrapnel that hit us from the ammunition pan. Had the shell continued upwards into the cockpit, it could have been carnage – and I might even have ended up like Lynn. As for the bloody scene in the other Beaufort, we still didn't know whether that was going to end in another pilot's death.

Bill Carroll remembers:

'McSharry was barely alive when they came in; the navigator landed the aircraft. I don't think they could lift McSharry out of the pilot's seat. I remember old Ray Brown told me they sent an SOS to Malta to have an ambulance ready. You imagine getting hit by a piece of shrapnel in your main vein. I saw his parachute afterwards when they took it out of there, and it was just dripping blood. He was pretty much dead . . . and yet a few weeks later he was back to normal.'

Others we'd assumed to be dead were still alive, too. The flak had been so bad that it was hard to imagine how anyone could have survived a hit but there were some who hadn't gone under with their aircraft. Apart from Smyth's navigator, who must have drifted to a place where he was spotted early by the enemy, those survivors were still in the water.

Bill Carroll heard what happened to them:

'There were three of them still in the drink from Lynn's plane: Pilot Officer Dickinson and Sergeants Frith and Horn. I knew 'em all and they were in the Med all night. One of them, Horn, wasn't in good shape; he'd been hit. They all tied themselves together overnight but, in the end, they had to let Horn go because they knew he was dead.

'The other Sergeant, Frith, was one of our characters, you know. He'd recently refereed a soccer match and he still had the whistle in his pocket. Dickinson and Frith were still bobbing around in the Med the next day, the two of them tied together. Lo and behold they saw an Italian launch coming around, looking for survivors from the aircraft we'd shot down. It turned out the crew in the German Junkers had been Italian.

'The rescuers didn't find any Italians, but they did find two Brits. Or at least, they heard a referee's whistle. Frith had pulled the whistle out of his pocket and was blowing his damn teeth out.

'The Italian crew finally found them and came over. And the Italians were very nice people. They put the ladder out of their launch and the exhausted pair climbed on board. According to Dickinson, he thanked the skipper, who could speak English, and the captain said: "You're lucky, we weren't looking for you. We were looking for our own crew members." Otherwise these two guys would probably have had it. Anyway, they got taken prisoner of war.

'If Arthur hadn't gone over and we hadn't hit the Junkers 88, enabling the Beaufighter to finish it off, Dick Dickinson and Frith wouldn't have been saved, because the Italians wouldn't have been out looking for their Junkers crew.

'I believe Horn's body was washed ashore in Libya. The Italians contacted the Brits, because he still had his name-tag on. They said that when they found him, he was breathing. It was the Italian army and there was a medical man there, who was supposed to have confirmed it. The *British Medical Journal* covered the case and said it was impossible for him to be alive after being in the water nearly forty days.

'The Italians contacted the British again and said: "No, this body that got washed up, the guy was definitely alive, because when they rolled him over, he was breathing." But it was just the air coming out of his body. Although he was dead, he had floated because he had a Mae West on.

'Dickinson and Frith survived the war. Squadron Leader Lynn's wife got hold of Dickinson somehow down in Cornwall, where he was a printer. She lived in Inverness and she was very worried that Robert had been badly injured or had suffered terribly for a long time before he died. He said, "No, he got a cannon shell right through him and didn't even stand a chance; he probably never knew what happened to him." So that put her mind at rest, as far as these things can.'

Poor Lynn had been beyond help long before we left the scene. As for the others, their story might make you wonder why we didn't go out looking for them ourselves, but the sad fact is, we'd assumed they'd all gone for a Burton once they were down in the drink. The sheer ferocity of the enemy fire, sustained with an intensity we'd never experienced before, may have clouded our thinking. You can replay these things in your mind but you can't change them. Our consolation was that our strike had not been entirely in vain.

I knew I'd sunk a merchant ship, which could be used to carry cargo, troops or both. After a while I found out it was called the *Reichenfels*. Only much later did I hear it had been carrying 4,000 tons of munitions and 600 tons of fuel for Rommel's war effort, and had been bound for Tripoli. The *Reichenfels* weighed 7,744 tons and was 485 feet long, with a beam of 62 feet and a draught of 31 feet. Only six years old, she was a valued cargo vessel, and many decades later there were even claims she'd been carrying a new type of Panzer tank when she went down. She was the first of many Axis ships sunk by Malta-based Beauforts. Luckily, even though I sank the *Reichenfels* near land, just off Kerkennah, they had no chance of raising her. All the 246 men on board made it away from the ship safely, though – probably a Panzer platoon or two among them.

Looking back, it seems a shame that so many Italians had died when I torpedoed the *Trento*, while all the Germans from the *Reichenfels* survived. I wish it had been the other way round; all those lovely Italians. At least Rommel wasn't supplied from the *Reichenfels*, though – and he was very short of supplies by then. At the time, we didn't know Rommel by his nickname, 'The Desert Fox', nor did we know much about him at all. Although, we'd soon hear of his latest breakthrough.

Luckily, we'd also hear about 'Monty' – our own General Montgomery – before very long. And I like to think I must have helped Monty quite a bit.

18

Morale Slips

You wouldn't have thought we'd done any good at all, if you'd been fighting in North Africa at the time of my successes. On 15 June, the day I helped sink the *Trento*, Rommel's advance had reached the North African coast, cutting off any Commonwealth forces still in Gazala. On 21 June, the very day I sank the *Reichenfels*, Rommel took Tobruk – all that stood between the Axis powers and Egypt. He was made a Field Marshal for that.

He was advancing deep into Egypt, and seemed on the point of taking the entire country. Had he been able to do so, Rommel would have been free to turn north-eastwards to secure the oil-fields of the Middle East. The frightening prospect of him linking up with other German forces already besieging the Caucasian oilfields seemed all too real. Hitler would have had all the fuel he needed to do his worst. What's more, he might have been able to link up with the Japanese coming from the other direction, if both invading powers had continued on their path of destruction.

But with a delayed effect, the successes of raids like the one we carried out on the *Reichenfels* began to pay off. Rommel had stretched his supply lines, while the Allies were destroying up to two-thirds of all the Axis supplies which embarked for North Africa. The Germans were destined to lose momentum and stalled a few months later at the First Battle of El Alamein, when Rommel wrote: 'Fuel shortages! It is enough to make one cry.' He'd also admitted: 'The bravest soldiers can do nothing without weapons, and weapons are nothing without ammunition. But in terms of mobile war, neither weapons nor ammunition are worth much without the necessary volume of fuel for engines.'

The Germans would get what was coming to them at the Second Battle of El Alamein in October, by which time both Rommel and his dwindling supplies had been pushed beyond their limit. Churchill called our victory there the turning point of the war.

Back in June, as the Mediterranean sun seemed to burn even hotter than before, our efforts seemed to have little effect, and Rommel still looked capable of claiming more territory for his master, Adolf Hitler. Malta didn't show any obvious signs of improvement after the two successes I'd had in the space of a week either. If anything, the island seemed to be edging towards the brink of even greater desperation. And the airmen were beginning to suffer almost as much as the local population.

Bill Carroll never forgot just how tough things became:

'From the moment those convoys failed – apart from the two ships that got through – we were on siege rations. Those weevils were almost becoming a delicacy. Aspinall got dysentery badly and I got sandfly fever. Talk to the Spitfire pilots and they'd tell you they saw clouds of them coming over from the desert, at up to 30,000 feet; clouds thick with these damned sandflies.

'We all got sick one way or another. When you get sandfly fever, all your joints ache and even your eyeballs feel like they've got sand in them. The MO [Medical Officer] would tell the NCOs that he'd got nothing to give them. "You're stuck with it," he'd say. It was different for the officers, though. They'd be sent away to convalesce. We were one of the best Beaufort crews and if we were idle for any period of time there was a reason. It was because we weren't all healthy enough to function as a crew any more.

'You got the shits every other day in Malta, too. The sergeants would eat anything we could because we were so damned hungry, and that's why we fell ill. George Lawcock and I were ill at the same time, and we headed for the outhouses up on the hill. Christ, it was terrible – we'd go to the outhouse up there, turn round to come down again, and say to each other: "What's the point in going back down? We're only going to have to come straight back up and do it all again." So we stayed there and started bullshitting between the pair of us; bullshitting while we carried on shitting.'

At the end of the runway there were quarries. If an aircraft had a bad landing and pranged, that was probably the end of it. The shortage of parts made it difficult to repair anything on Malta, so they'd get the bulldozer and push the badly damaged planes right off the end of the runway and into the quarry. Some of the boys were starting to feel like wrecks ready to be pushed off the edge and down into that quarry, too.

Pat Gibbs was back from a short trip to Egypt; and it became clear he was going to be taking over from Wing Commander Davis as our commander before long. He certainly didn't lack courage. The bombs kept raining down on Luqa, but Gibbs was completely fearless during these air raids. Others were rushing around heading for the air raid shelter and he'd just stand there nonchalantly and say, 'Oh, what's the time? Five o'clock in the

morning? Oh good, plenty of time to have a bit more sleep.'
With him it was fearlessness, with me it had been laziness.

Gibbs was charismatic. He was a flyer, whereas Hughie Pughie
wasn't flying. Gibbs was absolutely incredible. The raids he did
were fantastic. Gibbs was inspirational, a wonderful man. Davis
was still there in charge; though you already had the feeling it was
Gibbs whose almost superhuman standards had to be met, as 217
Squadron was combined with 39 Squadron for fresh strikes.

Just two days after the horrors of the strike which sank the
Reichenfels, Sergeant Bob Dale, who'd been very quiet when we
returned, was sent out again with those still fit enough to carry
out another attack on enemy shipping. The squadron record talks
of another Sergeant Carroll, who was a pilot – not to be confused with Bill:

W/C Davis, F/O Sangster, Sgt Mercer, Sgt Nolan, Sgt Grey,
Sgt Carroll and Sgt Dale, with five aircraft of 39 Squadron,
took off at 11.15 hrs to attack a convoy of two merchant vessels and four destroyers off the toe of Italy. Hits were scored on
both merchant vessels. No 39 Squadron lost two aircraft. Sgt
Nolan was hit in the leg by shrapnel, which also wrecked the
hydraulics. He crash-landed on his return to base.

Bill's close friend Mickey McGrath had been navigator in Nolan's
plane, and that crew had all been lucky to survive. It was hard for
anyone to escape the thought that their time was probably
coming, sooner or later. To lose two aircraft and their crews, and
have another return in tatters with a wounded man, was actually
a better-than-average result in the context of recent events. Since
the costly *Reichenfels* raid, we pilots had discussed in the Officers'
Mess the price being paid for our successes. I don't think it was

over a drink, because I don't think there was much to drink in
Malta. In fact, there wasn't much of anything in Malta – except
tomatoes, weevils and danger.

One in three Beauforts were being shot down on each strike.
By the law of averages, you're not going to last very long, are
you? Your life expectancy is going to be short. The first three
planes had been shot down on that *Reichenfels* strike. I was
lucky to survive because I'd almost been shot down, too. I tried
not to think about the odds, I just felt general resignation.
'Steve' Stevens was one of the pilots I talked to about this.
There was a slight feeling of morale not being at its best. In fact,
it was sagging. There was no grim humour about it – just resignation.

What could you do? You couldn't go to your commanding
officer, complain about the odds and urge a change of plan. Of
course you couldn't. We were there for a good reason. Malta was
an important strategic island; from there we were able to attack
the German convoys and Italian convoys. It had to be held at all
costs. The fighter squadrons were doing a terrific job in wrest-
ing control of the Malta skies from the enemy. We all had to
make sacrifices; but how could the fighters and Beaufort crews
work better together? We'd had a few Beaufighters with us when
we hit the *Reichenfels*; we just hadn't really thought out the best
possible strategy for combining fighters and torpedoes. After all,
we'd still lost a lot of men in the downed Beauforts, despite the
proximity of the Beaufighters and their best efforts.

Unbeknown to us, that *Reichenfels* raid was one of the last in
which the Beaufighters had a purely defensive role. A change in
tactics designed by Pat Gibbs ensured that they diverted some of
the attention away from the torpedo-carrying Beauforts. Instead
of being there simply to provide an escort and take on enemy

fighters, our Beaufighters were going to start attacking the ships, too. They would go in first to draw enemy fire and give the ships something new to think about. The Beauforts carrying the torpedoes could then steal in behind them, with a better chance of success and survival.

But these strategic changes were still a work in progress; and we hadn't yet felt the benefit of this more intelligent planning. It was too late for most of the original crews of 217 Squadron, as the dwindling numbers in our huts only confirmed.

It was understandable if morale had slightly dipped and things felt a bit dodgy at times. That was when the Canadians, who'd joined us in the Officers' Mess, seemed to give us a boost. We had a gramophone player in the mess but not much to play on it. But two Canadians I'd struck up a really good rapport with – Steve Stevens and his friend Hutch – got hold of some old 78 gramophone records. How they got them, I don't know. Stevens put a record on in the mess; it was an Artie Shaw tune, and I was told that Artie Shaw was one of the kings of swing. When they introduced me to swing, it opened up a whole new world to me musically. I lapped it up. I liked it almost as much as classical music, which seemed such a distant pleasure at the time. It lightened the mood, just when we needed it.

Hutch was a wonderful chap and he became a great friend, even closer than Mark Lee had been. The Canadians were good guys. There was something about them that really lifted morale. You needed a sense of humour in that situation – and they had it. Moreover, they reminded us that we had a sense of humour, too. Life was much happier and more cheery when the Canadians were playing their music. Artie Shaw's music helped us, and Steve and Hutch even started calling me 'Artie'. I liked that, because I wasn't particularly fond of the name Arthur.

The Canadians knew how to keep a cool head under fire, too. I remember sitting on some steps with Hutch, just inside the bomb shelter, when we were told that there were two unexploded bombs – one right above us on the shelter roof, the other on the roof of our billet – the hut where we slept. Hutch and I just looked at each other as we sat on those steps; half-smiling, knowing the bombs could go off at any moment. Then we ran to the only place left – the Officers' Mess. I think some brave souls must have defused those unexploded bombs, and there was no lasting damage. But Hutch was a good person to be alongside in that sort of scrape, because he had a positive attitude, like the rest of his compatriots.

I'm not saying more people would have gone LMF if the Canadians hadn't been there, because I don't think that would have happened. But they definitely made life a little more enjoyable. How were they different from the Brits? They were more out-going, a bit like the Americans. They raised morale at just the right time and I really admired them for it. Bill Carroll reckoned there was something they liked about me, too, and I'm just pleased to know I could give something back:

'I've got to say; those Canadians were as impressed by Artie as he was by them. Some of them would come up to me and ask, "Whose crew are you on?"

'"Flying Officer Aldridge," I'd say.

'"Hey, we know that guy! The one who can speak four or five different languages, right? He's quite a guy!"

'To them, Artie was a breath of fresh air, just as they were to him. People were kind of feeding off each other to keep their spirits up.

'But then we found out that a certain bloke was taking and not giving anything back to our group at all. We didn't find out until about the third time it happened. As I've said, the padre was a very nice and very honest man; but he had a sidekick who was a Leading Aircraftsman. If we lost a man, we used to take the kitbag to the padre's office, and then the padre was supposed to handle it all from there. His assistant packed up everything, and since the padre was without doubt a good man, we trusted the process entirely.

'That was our mistake. When this Leading Aircraftsman saw these kitbags come in, he knew there'd always be a few personal items placed at the top, because it was pretty obvious that the whole big kit bag wasn't going to be sent back to Britain. This assistant had started going through the personal effects of the dead man and anything of interest or value, like money or a nice fountain pen and all those kind of things you didn't get just anywhere, he pocketed.

'We found out because somebody went to take in some more stuff and they saw him doing it. We didn't report it and we didn't think it would have done any good if we had. But he'd been found out, along with his nice little earner. To say we were angry is an understatement. Pretty soon we realised there was no point in letting money and valuables get as far as the padre's office, because his sidekick would steal it. So we used to take the money out and split it between us. You might think that was just as bad, but it was what we wanted as a group of friends all taking risks together. The padre's assistant wasn't part of that; he had no right to any pickings from our kitbags. If we went for a Burton, we wanted our friends to benefit, not him.'

We couldn't be on perpetual 'stand-by', ready to fly at any moment. There had to be some kind of respite. Mercifully, the squadron was stood down on 25 June, presumably because there were no targets to go for, and there wasn't another strike until 3 July. But, as soon as the squadron went back to war, the grim reality of our predicament hit home again.

On that fateful day, Beauforts piloted by Sergeant Russell Mercer and Sergeant Jimmy Hutcheson went missing after attacking a convoy off the Greek coast. This wasn't Hutch, who survived the war, but the other Hutcheson, a friend of Bob Dale. Unfortunately Dale had been even closer friends with Mercer; so what happened was always going to be tough on him.

Twelve Beauforts with the usual Beaufighter protection had taken off early in the morning to intercept a convoy off the Greek coast. The search had proved fruitless and the aircraft returned at midday. But that kind of failure was never going to be acceptable to Gibbs, who organised another attempted strike for that very evening.

The official account didn't tell the full story:

At 18.30 hours S/L Gibbs of 39 Squadron led eight Beauforts to attack three merchant vessels and eight destroyers off the Greek SW coast. A last-light attack was made. Hits were observed on at least one merchant vessel but visibility made observation difficult. Sgt Mercer and Sgt Hutcheson left the convoy but failed to return. S/L Gibbs crash-landed on the aerodrome, owing to damage by AA [anti-aircraft] fire from the convoy.

But Bill Carroll remembers what happened behind the scenes, and he always considered it shameful:

'I'll tell you what happened – it was disgusting actually. Mercer and Hutcheson hadn't been downed by the convoy and they might have been able to find their way home, especially with a little help from Luqa. And they needed all the help they could get, because one of the planes had that terrible navigator, Fred Dennis, on board, the one who'd set the wrong course to intercept the Italian fleet after we'd hit the *Trento*. The other was Harold 'Taffy' Hole, the twenty-nine-year-old sergeant from Blaina, Monmouthshire, who'd been our choirmaster.

'To find Malta at night is tough. The Med has tiny puffs of cloud up in the sky and on a moonlit night they cast shadows like islands. You'd see thousands of little islands dotted around there anyway. These lost crews may have tried to go for anything if they became really desperate. They didn't receive the help they needed and they didn't come home that night. For all we knew, they'd survived ditching and they were in the sea; but we couldn't do anything until morning.

'When Alan Still and I looked around our dorm that first night, there were only ten left of the twenty-eight who had slept there a few weeks before. Back then the padre of Malta had been walking along the road and he heard us singing in the hut. He'd come in, sat down with us, and told us he was so impressed that he wanted us to give a concert. We'd all been ready to oblige, and you could see how proud Taffy Hole was. That concert date was just coming up; and now it looked like we'd have to cancel because poor Taffy and the others were gone.

'These were the kind of thoughts that went through our heads during a very long and sombre night. If Taffy wasn't there to organise the singing any more, it was certainly going to be quieter than we would have liked. Before he did that for us, it had been a little dull on the base. We'd just be playing bridge or sitting there with nothing to do. Now it looked as though we'd be going back to that kind of boredom.

'As we lay in our beds, we pictured Sergeant Hole, this lovely little Welshman, the music teacher from Wales who loved to sing; we imagined the group of twenty-eight men we'd been so recently, with nothing else to do at night but join in with him. It used to get dark by about 7pm or 8pm, and we'd sit there and he'd say, "Come on now, boys." You missed that kind of thing when it disappeared. We missed it already and we wanted it back.

'Taffy and the others were down, but when dawn broke we hadn't given up on them completely. For all we knew, they might have survived the night out there somewhere. First light brought some kind of lingering hope that we could go out and rescue them. But first light also allowed a disturbing story to start coming through from the radio people to the crews at Luqa. The stricken crews, the ones now lost, had made contact the previous evening and asked for a QDM – a magnetic course, a heading to get them back to base in Malta. And despite hearing the request, the powers that be at Luqa wouldn't allow anyone to give these crews the QDM that would have saved their lives.

'There was a policy of radio silence, and they insisted it had to be maintained. So basically our friends went down when they shouldn't have gone down. All the rest of the crews were spitting mad about this. We were really pissed off that nobody had put out a helping hand for men on our squadron when they needed one. We were only allowed to go out searching for them after we raised hell about it. It was worth searching that day and the next, because they might have ended up in a dinghy.

'We took off, we searched and searched, but all in vain. After a couple of days, we finally had to accept that Taffy Hole and the others were dead – their Beauforts probably on a sea bed somewhere under the Med, with our friends still in them, for all we knew. The choirmaster was gone and so, therefore, was our choir. We all felt it; but Dale was probably the most devastated.

He'd lost eight friends from his barracks, including his two closest pals.

'Russell George Mercer was only twenty-one and his youngest crew member was a nineteen-year-old Canadian called George Leonard Hodson. Another crew member, Leonard Alwyn York, was only twenty-two. The oldest was Hole at twenty-eight. Jimmy Hutcheson had been a volunteer who hailed from Newcastle. Sergeant Fred Dennis, aged twenty-five, was his navigator, and the WOP/AGs were a New Zealander called Frank Stuart Weaver and Dennis Melville Davis. Though I have no proof, I've always suspected it was Dennis who set the wrong course for home, just as he'd set the wrong course in search of the Italians a few weeks earlier.'

The operational record book suggested that everything possible was done to bring the missing pilots home. The entry for the day after the mission against the enemy read:

'Two Beauforts and two fighters went off to search for Mercer and Hutcheson. They searched in vain.'

The next day it merely confirmed the search continued:

'Four Beauforts searched today, but with no results.'

Only the airmen who survived remember the anguish and conflict behind those bleak times.

Depleted and jaded, 217 Squadron was released from day-to-day duties for ten days to rest and recuperate. Bill remembers how Bob Dale used that period, which started on 6 July, to come up with an unconventional plan for survival. Dale was desperate to avoid joining his friends on the growing list of those lost in action:

'Bob Dale was just like anybody else to look at, he was my height and well built, but I don't think he thought like the rest of us. He wasn't happy-go-lucky, and I don't remember him even having a pint of beer with the boys. In fact, I don't know why he was in the bed next to me, because you sort of slept as a crew, or next to people who were your friends. But Dale was next to me, and that's how I found out about his plan to avoid more misery.

'He went down to "The Gut", the nickname given to the main entertainment street in Valletta – and he went with as many working girls as he could find to do business with down there. His plan was to catch a dose, so he could get off flying. He's in the bed next to me and he keeps looking at his tool, and you think, "What the hell is going on?" Then I realised. We didn't go with Dale to see those ladies when he was having that problem of his, but I realised what he was up to. However hard he tried, though, the plan didn't work. He certainly didn't manage to catch anything serious enough to provide his escape route.

'When we weren't out and about, most of us were back to playing cards in the hut. Of course, some of the songs we'd rehearsed with Taffy still stuck in our minds. But we just didn't feel like singing them any more. It was just as well we'd pulled out of the concert, because by the time the weekend set aside for it actually came along, there weren't even ten of us left any more. It was more like five or six.'

I was fairly tired by this time, but was I desperate or close to cracking? No. I'd felt that awful feeling in my stomach before flying into the wall of flak to hit the *Reichenfels*; but it hadn't stayed with me, or even stopped me from going on at the time. Was I close to losing my nerve now that I had more time to think about it all? No way. I was resigned to whatever was going to happen. It helps you to cope when you think like that. But that didn't mean I wasn't in need of a good rest.

Now that we had some leave, I was allowed to go to the rest-house the RAF had for exhausted pilots in St Paul's Bay on the north-west side of the island. I wasn't burnt out by any means, but it must have seemed like a good idea to send me there while we had this period of unexpected leave. The garden ran all the way down to the shore's edge. I went bathing there and enjoyed myself, the water was warm and relaxing. It was a wonderful place. I enjoyed being able to sleep late some mornings after all the air raids and early starts at Luqa. St Paul's Bay was a nice little break for me, though I was only there a few days – a week at the most. You could see why Malta might make a good place for a holiday one day. What a pity we were there for a war.

19

Farewell to Alan

I heard in the second week of July that I'd been awarded a Bar to my DFC for what I'd done in Malta. They announced it back home, too.

The citation for the Bar to the DFC reads:

> Flying Officer Aldridge has attacked shipping on several occasions and in spite of heavy fire, he has achieved great success. During three attacks in June, in the Mediterranean, he hit an Italian warship, which later sank, and disabled another. On the last occasion Flying Officer Aldridge defied an extremely heavy barrage of shells.

It was strange, that wording, because as far as I can remember I was only involved in two significant attacks in June – the ones which sank the *Trento* and the *Reichenfels*. At any rate, I'd won the DFC and Bar by the age of twenty-one. I'm sure I wasn't the youngest to do that, but it was still quite an early age when you look back at it. Would I have been able to do the things I did had I been older? I can't answer that question. Some people say you get more afraid as you get older. The war came when I was young, and since I wasn't destined to be involved in another, it's not something I can confirm or deny. As far as my crew and I were concerned, we'd just been getting on with the job.

There was a little ceremony and Lord Gort, Governor of Malta, gave me my DFC during a parade. It was quite awe-inspiring to see the man in the flesh. Lord Gort had won the Victoria Cross in France in 1918 and he'd been with the British Expeditionary Force before Dunkirk, so he cut quite a distinguished figure. We were all lined up in a square somewhere in Valletta. The parade wasn't just for me; there were a few others, too. We had to go up one by one to receive our award; I was next to Steve Stevens, my Canadian friend, so that was nice. When it was my turn, Lord Gort pinned a ribbon on my chest – we weren't given our medals at that stage. He didn't say anything to me, but then no words were necessary when you were in the presence of Lord Gort. That was enough in itself!

I didn't tell Bill Carroll or the crew about it; I didn't want a fuss or a booze-up. It might have sounded conceited if I'd gone around telling people about it; and I didn't want to highlight the fact that I was being singled out when they had been through exactly the same experience. My parents probably heard because the *London Gazette* carried a little announcement on 14 July. And my crew found out soon enough, much to Bill Carroll's surprise:

'Arthur didn't tell us about the Bar to his DFC. Then all of a sudden, we see it in the *Malta Times* the next day, a little something at the bottom of the page in the local paper: "Flying Officer Aldridge has been awarded the Bar to his DFC … " I said to him, "Well, why the bloody hell didn't you tell us?" He went there to collect it and never said a word to anybody.'

*

The squadron was put back on stand-by on 17 July. Perhaps ten days off had given some people too much time to think, because Bill bore witness to the extraordinary events in the sergeants' hut:

'Bob Dale had lost his big mate Mercer, a big old farm boy. Sergeant York was gone and Sergeant Hall; and Sergeant Hutcheson had gone for a Burton, too. They'd all been on the same course. Sergeant Dale had been through a lot considering all these blokes were new to the squadron – I don't think they'd done many ops before. But I still didn't see what was coming.

'As I've mentioned, Dale didn't do much with the boys; he was an introvert and perhaps that was his problem. He never really spoke very much to anyone outside his little circle. We didn't ostracise Dale, though I don't know whether the boys were happy with him exactly. It's not a lot of fun for anyone when you lose friends. You just wanted to get some beer down you, and get it out of your system. But he wasn't taking it well.

'We didn't give a damn about what would happen to us, whereas he was worried about it. He wasn't married, he was our age, I would say; maybe even a bit younger than me. But he wasn't happy-go-lucky like us, things stayed with him; and the effect of losing one friend after another must have built up inside him.

'Sergeant Dale was in the bed next to me and one evening he sat up mumbling and groaning to himself. It was hard to understand his muttering, but it gradually became clear that Dale was not very impressed with the way we were losing people. Alan Still, Aspinall and I were looking at each other and wondering what we should do about his behaviour. Amazing, it was.

'Then Dale stood up and surprised everyone with an announcement. He looked at us and he said: "I'm very sorry. I'm no longer able to fly. There's nothing anyone can do about it. I'll tell the CO first thing in the morning." No one tried to talk him out of it, we just respected his decision. I don't remember him having nightmares or anything in the build-up to that day. He just suddenly started mumbling and then made his announcement.

'Henry Parry came off flying at about the same time. He'd been jumpy ever since he'd reached Malta and found his friend Denis Norman dead by the radio. In fact, he'd been jumpy even before that, having survived Abbotsinch and watched his friends die in the crash up there. This poor chap Parry started getting the shakes after all he'd been through and all he'd seen. He had proven himself as a gunner in aerial combat, but now he was a physical and mental wreck. Probably not before time, he said he couldn't do this flying business any more. It was no great surprise when Parry said it; but with Dale, none of us saw it coming.

'Both had our sympathy, but especially Henry Parry. People may think these men were ostracised by us the moment they said they couldn't carry on, but that wasn't the case. We felt sorry for them. For anyone to come off flying took a lot, you know. Personally I couldn't imagine doing it; but they were in such a nervous state by then.'

Had they been able to stick it out a little longer, they might just have had the feeling that the worst for 217 Squadron was nearly over. There wasn't any more action for anyone in the squadron until 21 July, when a combined operation with 86 Squadron and 39 Squadron, all led by Squadron Leader Gibbs, attacked a south-bound convoy off Cephalonia. The attack was successful, the merchant vessel and one destroyer being left in difficulties, and all the aircraft returned safely. My crew and I could only watch them take off and land, because ill-health within our little number meant we were still grounded.

Illness was so widespread that it was difficult to get a crew together. They used to look at crews in such a way that a pilot and navigator were deemed virtually inseparable. If my navigator wasn't fit, that was me effectively grounded. After recovering from dysentery, Vince was now sick with sandfly fever, which was devastating while you had it, because it left you so weak. So I was grounded because I didn't have enough crew.

On 22 July came the anticipated change of leadership. Wing Commander Davis left the squadron to return to England, and Wing Commander Gibbs assumed temporary command of the squadron. All the Beauforts on the island were now functioning as one unit, with Gibbs our inspirational leader.

Between 25 and 27 July there was another lull, which gave Wing Commander Gibbs the opportunity to stamp his authority on the Beaufort airmen of Malta. I didn't witness what happened next, but Bill did – and he didn't like it:

'It was about ten days after Dale and Parry had reached their limit. But he wasn't prepared to let the two men leave quietly, or treat them with any respect at all. Instead he was determined to humiliate them publicly, to make an example of them. So Gibbs got all the NCOs together outside, brought out Parry and Dale, and tore them off a strip in front of all of us. What a shit. Gibbs was a bloody nut as far as I'm concerned. There he was, nervous and all worked up, and he just launched into them.

'He stripped them of their stripes, quite literally in Parry's case. Gibbs made sure they were both classified as LMF. "You bloody pair of cowards! I'll have you buggers," he yelled. "You've turned your back on the face of the enemy! You'll be cleaning shit out in my shit-house for the foreseeable future. And when you've finished doing that, you'll be cleaning other people's shit, because I'm going to send you to the bloody desert as AC2s."

'To be demoted to Aircraftsmen Second Class was one thing, but this public humiliation out in the open didn't go down well with us. We knew he was trying to make it so unpleasant that no one else would want to go LMF but I don't think there was a single man among the rest of the group who was close to cracking anyway. None of us would have refused to do anything we were supposed to do.

'Personally I could have kicked Pat Gibbs up the arse, for standing there and saying that to those guys. He wasn't normal like us. He was a heck of a good pilot and all that, but he was a crazy bugger. He got the DFC and Bar in about three weeks, I think. He used to come back and crash-land on Malta, he was gung-ho, hell-bent for leather. He wasn't human like some of the Wing Commanders. As a person he wasn't great; he was too brutal. And after another month or so he had to come off flying himself, which was very annoying. I think the guy was a nervous wreck and he got posted to England and they got rid of him.'

Pat Gibbs did live on his nerves and that did take its toll eventually. But he never refused to fly any ops, and he was inspirational to me as a charismatic leader. I don't think it's fair to Gibbs to compare him with Dale, just because he got taken off flying. I don't want to judge or condemn anyone in any shape or form but Gibbs didn't go LMF. He didn't experience fear at all, as far as I could see, let alone react to it – not while he was at war. That was the difference.

Perhaps Bill and I had different perspectives because I was an officer and he was a sergeant. The officers weren't asked to witness the public humiliation of Dale and Parry by Gibbs but I imagine Gibbs was trying to act in the best interests of the squadron. A man under an enormous amount of stress cannot always get it right. The despair felt by men who simply couldn't take any more must have been sad to see. But Gibbs had other priorities, brutal as that sounds. He was trying to maintain an effective fighting force at all costs, with numbers dwindling.

That said, Bill and I share a feeling of compassion for the men who developed psychological problems due to the stresses of the war. There were so many of them; how can we just write off these human beings? Overall, the RAF was suffering 3,000 cases of nervous breakdown each year during World War Two. A third of these occurred at Flying Training Schools, before the airmen had even gained experience of operations. Dale and Parry had lasted a lot longer than that. So you could see why there was anger in the Sergeants' Mess about how their cases were handled.

Yet the perspectives of officers and NCOs are bound to be different at some points in a war, even if you're on the same crew. Officers carried more responsibility and were therefore sometimes insensitive to others, which in turn could fuel resentment. They also received better treatment at times – even though that shouldn't have happened.

Bill Carroll never forgot the inequality because he, too, regarded it as unfair:

'If the sergeants had a bad case of fever then you went to the MO and he would give you an aspirin, as long as the submarines had come in with a supply of them. But then ten days later he would have none left, so he wouldn't give you anything. When the officers went sick, the MO would say: "Oh, you'd better go to St Paul's Bay to recuperate."

'Contrast that to when George Lawcock and I had dysentery on Malta, and we were so ill we thought there was no point in getting off the toilet and going back down the hill because we would only have to climb all the way back up again within a few minutes.

'Aspinall also had a very bad stomach, though if the truth be told it was sometimes self-inflicted. He didn't take very kindly to the local moonshine, which was called Ambid. That drink proved to be a bit rough. "Come on, Asp, cheer up for Christ's sake!" we'd tell him. But the sandfly fever, the trots from the local booze, and the general lack of food hadn't left him in good shape.

'We were all on starvation rations for so long on Malta because virtually no supplies were getting through; so eventually one's natural resistance to illness was compromised. I lost forty pounds while I was there, nearly three stone in a couple of months – and I wasn't overweight when I arrived! But I was still able to fly most of the time. So was Alan Still, though he had a different kind of problem.

'There was a Canadian, Frank Perry from Calgary, who'd just come out of hospital. He told us that a number of men were in there with scabies. Alan Still started scratching away, so I said, "Alan, do you think you should go up and see the MO?" Alan was a real gentleman and didn't put up any resistance. So he went up there and, sure enough, he had scabies.

'The MO asks, "Who is in the next bed to you?"

'Alan said, "Bill Carroll."

'So the MO says, "Well go and get the bugger."

'The MO tells me, "Carroll, take your clothes off."

'So he examines me and he couldn't find any of the incriminating spots you get with scabies. He gives me a little brush, like a scrubbing brush, and a tube with some green lotion in it. And he says, "Come with me, you two."

'We went into the next room and they had a bath there. It seemed like the MO was the only person on Malta who had fresh water.

'"Still, get undressed and get into the bath," he orders.

'Then he turns to me and says, "Carroll, take your brush. See all these spots on your friend's back? If you look hard enough you'll find there is a little bug in each one. I want you to take the green lotion and put it on these spots, and then scrub them with the scrubbing brush until they bleed. That's the way to kill these things."

'So I had to scrub Alan's back really hard. Now, Alan was a mild-mannered man and he knew it was for his own good; but he was spitting mad about what was happening because it hurt! So he was swearing away at me, I was doing my best to make him bleed, and we were supposed to be the best of friends. It would have looked hilarious to anyone else. Maybe the MO had a little smile to himself in the next room.

'When he'd had his scrub, Alan Still carried on flying, because he was very much in demand. When another crew needed a wireless operator on 28 July, they pinched Alan for the strike. I was meant to be on the same crew because the gunner and wireless operator were always a good team together, but it didn't work out like that this time. Ordinarily, no one allowed Alan in the turret because he couldn't hit a bloody barn door; I certainly wouldn't allow him to do so. But on this occasion he fancied the turret. The pilot on this op was called Butch Dawson, who had a bit of a reputation for low flying. Anyway, the PA system goes off: "Would Still and Carroll report to the Operations Room."

'Alan saw his chance and said, "Bill, will you let me fly in the turret, just this one time?"

'I replied, "I don't mind, Alan, but if we get in any trouble just get out of that turret quick and swap places with me."

'So I went to get all the radio equipment, and joined Alan and Butch Dawson at the aircraft. Before take-off the wireless operator always gets in and checks out the radio, so that's what I did. Then I heard this kerfuffle going on outside.

'Alan came in and said, "Hey, Bill, the Wing Commander wants to talk to you." What on earth had I done this time?

'Wing Commander Gibbs was standing there. He said, "Sergeant Carroll, Pilot Officer Head here says he is normally on this crew. He has brought his complaint to me because he thinks he should fly in place of one of you two."

'Then he looked at Head, who was very smart and wore a silk scarf, a public school type. Gibbs was effectively asking Head to state his preference. Head said to the Wing Commander, "I'm usually on the radio, sir."

'That was a lie. He never flew on the radio.

'But Gibbs just said, "Which of you two men has got the radio?"

'"I have, sir," I said.

'"Brief Mr Head," said Gibbs.

'That meant tell Head how far I'd got with the radio check and then stand down to make way for him. So Alan went out on the strike with them and they were coming back late at night. I saw the planes coming in; I counted them in and there were two missing. And I knew right away that one of them was Dawson and that Alan was with him.

'When some of the lads came back into the hut, they confirmed Alan was missing, not that they needed to. You see, when the boys went out and someone had changed in a crew – that was always the plane that was going to be in trouble. Everyone knew that Alan's aircraft would be one of the missing pair. Everyone knew that if you change your crew, you change your luck.

'Our beds were only a few feet apart; Alan, Aspinall and I had been in a row – three crew members together. We had done everything together, before Asp fell ill, and now Alan wasn't there either. I was a little upset because he went instead of me. It should have been me in the turret. Also, he was wearing my shoes when he went! But was I moved to tears? No chance. "Where's his money, let's go and have a drink." That was my attitude. But nobody wanted to come with me that night.'

We didn't know if Alan had survived, but as far as we were concerned we'd lost him. It was pretty awful. We were both very upset, because we'd been through so much with him. We'd always been together, but then this had happened when he'd been pinched by another crew. That made it even worse. You lose many people in wartime, but when it's a member of your own crew and there was nothing you could do to protect or save him, that's not easy. Alan Still, the nicest person I'd ever met, was gone. I wanted to be left to my own thoughts, while Bill wanted to drown his sorrows and say goodbye in his usual way:

'There was a little village called Qormi facing Luqa. It had a little restaurant and the lady who ran it – a little mamma with a very big chest – would feed you black market pork for a price, which some of us crew were very pleased to pay because we were starving. We would go in the back room to eat it, maybe two at a time. She would send her kids to all the corners around the restaurant to check if the police were coming.

'We drank that terrible Ambid firewater, too, with lemonade. If we had stayed there for another month we would probably all have been blind. Anyway, since no one else wanted to come, I went down there on my own and received the usual warm welcome from the mamma.

'"Where are your friends?" she asked.

'I didn't want to say who had gone for a Burton, so I just said: "Sick."

'She looked sad. Although she didn't speak English, she had one of her children translate for her. I had a drink and a meal and when I got up to pay, there was a nice brown paper bag sitting there waiting for me. I looked inside and saw five hard-boiled eggs and two cans of condensed milk.

'"For your friends," she said.

'That choked me up a bit and I thanked her. But I picked the cans of milk out of there and said, "I can't take these. Keep them for your little children."

'At this point she grabbed her huge breasts and started wiggling them around. Her eight-year-old son started to translate, not that he needed to: "Mamma doesn't need cans of milk. She is big woman. She has lots of milk to feed her babies."'

Alan had gone for a Burton, but that didn't mean he was dead. We knew he was missing but, until you know for sure, there's a difference between dead and missing. The operational records described the events which led to Alan's disappearance like this:

Target for today was one merchant vessel and two destroyers near Sapiéntza. There were six torpedo Beauforts and three with bombs from the three squadrons. W/C Gibbs led the attack, which was fairly successful, at least two hits being observed. Lt Strever and P/O Dawson did not return, but some people were seen climbing into P/O Dawson's dinghy.

Bill Carroll only knew part of the story from the sketchy details still coming through:

'People were seen getting into dinghies, we heard that much.

But of course we didn't see the report, so we assumed it was Wilkie and Brownie from Strever's plane.

'In fact, only one man, the Canadian navigator called Doc Sutherland, got trapped on Dawson's plane and went down with it. Apparently, Alan was lucky. Head got him out of the turret just before impact, having spotted oil leaking from the port engine. When they slapped into the sea, Alan had gone flying forward into Head's leg, but both had stayed conscious and survived to release the dinghy.'

I can't remember exactly when or where we heard the news that our grief had been misplaced. We were so relieved when we learned Alan was alive. It was obvious he was going to have to be a prisoner of war, though, with all the suffering that entailed. He spent a week in hospital in Greece, recovering from his injuries, and was then transferred to Italy.

Fortunately for him, he was shot down by Italians, and they were also the ones who had rescued him. The Italians treated Alan and the others like long lost brothers. Even though he was a sergeant, he was taken to the Officers' Mess, stood drinks, and they had a wonderful time. But, of course, the Italians had to hand them over to the Germans in the end. And they got different treatment from the Germans. That's when they really did suffer.

The Germans had started shooting at downed crews, while the Italians continued to rescue them. I think we had an arrangement with the Italians, whereby we would let them know if we saw a dinghy from one of their planes, and they would let us know.

At least Alan had been picked up by the Italians. And he still had his secret weapon – that skin condition. Bill Carroll told me:

'When Alan went for a Burton he still had all those scabies spots on him. With a bit of luck, he gave a few to the Italians and Germans!'

20

Malta Saved

Alan Still was destined to survive his POW ordeal in Germany; but life in the camps pushed everyone to the limits of their endurance, and in some cases beyond. Captivity could be boring, dangerous and degrading. It wasn't unknown for a prisoner to rush at the wire in despair, so that he could end his torment with the help of a German bullet.

Back on 28 July, 1942, it was the anticipation of such horrors that probably made the crew of the other downed Beaufort, piloted by the feisty South African, Lieutenant Ted Strever, so reluctant to be taken prisoner. As far as their friends back at 217 Squadron were concerned, there was no way back for Ted and the others – there never was. As was the custom, therefore, his fellow airmen were soon rifling through Strever's locker to acquire spare socks and shorts. After all, if you don't come back from a strike, you're never coming back – at least that had to be the assumption.

Once this ritual had been carried out, Bill and his big Yorkshire friend George Lawcock returned to their increasingly empty hut and found it utterly depressing. The next day, they decided to cheer themselves up by going to Sliema, the beautiful beach across the bay from Valletta, for a swim. Bill and George were sitting there on the rocks, sunning themselves after a splash in the Med, when all of a sudden, at about noon, they heard the sirens go off.

Bill had seen his share of war in the air by then, but didn't expect to see any more while he was sunbathing:

'We see this float plane coming in. We knew there were no three-engine float planes that were British, so it had to be the enemy. Above this intruder were three Spitfires closing in for the kill. I couldn't help but think of the airmen in the float plane, poor sods, in their last moments. Sure enough, the leader of the Spitfires peeled off, swooped down and we heard the cannons going. It turned out they put forty cannon shells in the wing before the float plane landed on the water in submission a good distance away from us. For a few moments I wondered whether the float plane's crew had been lucky enough to survive, and then I forgot about it. We ambled back to the camp and when we reached it, somebody told us to get over to the Officers' Mess, because there was nothing but booze over there. They were right – and Strever and his crew were back!'

Bill would do anything for a free drink so he came in and joined us, and found Strever standing on the table in the Officers' Mess. This great big South African was telling us what had happened, and quite a story it was, too. Strever and his crew had been picked up by Italians in a dinghy somewhere in the eastern Mediterranean, and were put on a sea plane. They were being flown back to Italy in a Cant Z.506B, their eventual destination probably one of those German POW camps. Before they had flown very far, they decided to hijack the plane. They made signs to each other and then made their move for the Italian wireless operator's revolver. Wilkinson, a big New Zealander, thumped the man as hard as he could, while Strever grabbed the revolver from its holster. It was quite a dramatic moment, because Strever began pointing his revolver at the pilot, only to see that the pilot was pointing a revolver at him. Now it was all down to a test of nerve – and neither man cracked; until the Italian flight engineer blocked his pilot's line of fire. That's when Strever and Wilkinson charged their captors and took over the plane. Once the Italians were subdued, Strever flew them all towards Malta. Brown, the other New Zealander, took over the turret. Bill Dunsmore, a Liverpudlian who'd been slightly wounded in the initial crash, kept an eye on the Italians with Brown.

Listening to all this I couldn't have been more delighted. Not only was I quite friendly with Strever, but I'd played a part in keeping Wilkinson and Brown alive a few weeks earlier. They'd been in the plane with McSharry when the Australian had been hit in the neck and chased by the Junkers 88. It was fair to say that Wilkinson and Brown had been through some fairly unusual experiences of late. And they clearly still had nerves of steel, even though a few hours before this spontaneous celebration, they'd almost been killed by friendly fire. That, of course, was the spectacle which had temporarily captivated Bill as he relaxed over at Sliema:

'I'd seen the plane come in, pursued by Spitfires. Now Strever told us how the restrained Italian crew had been terrified they were about to be shot down. Strever's crew saw their point. Dunsmore had taken off his white vest and tried to wave it out of the plane, to show they were friendly. Meanwhile, Strever had jumped out of the pilot's seat and forced his Italian counterpart to land in the sea not far from our base at Luqa. The Italian pilot had the presence of mind to throttle back on the engines before they could be completely shot to pieces by the Spitfires. This manoeuvre caused many of the Spitfire's bullets to miss the main fuselage. The added bonus of getting down in one piece was that the Italians had been about to go on leave, and they had suitcases full of wine and various other types of booze, which were now being drunk by 217 Squadron.'

I wasn't particularly interested in the wine, but I was interested in what Strever had to say. He gave us a tremendous talk about how they had won back their freedom, only interrupted by the familiar wail of an air raid siren. Reluctantly we headed for the shelter, our spirits high after such an unexpected reunion. And when the air raid was over, people had to give Strever back the things they had pinched from his locker. They were cheerfully apologetic, of course. How were they supposed to know Strever was going to hijack the plane that was taking him to captivity?

Strever didn't mind too much, and personally I didn't mind the thought that my fellow squadron members would rifle through my stuff a few hours after I was shot down, if ever that was to be my fate.

Strever's hijack was quite a morale-booster – especially after what had happened to our dear friend Alan Still. I wasn't doing any flying, because Vince remained unwell, but Ken Eades, the wireless operator and piano player who'd defied flying shrapnel on more than one occasion, knew I'd be back in the air sooner or later. Eades had been on Bob Dale's crew, all of whom had to find new homes after Dale went LMF.

'Can I join your crew?' Ken asked me.

Well, there was no other crew to join, so I said, 'Yes, I don't see why not.'

Ken became a very good friend, but he wasn't Alan Still. And when I think of my wartime crew, I always think of Asp, Alan and Bill.

*

Having endured the public humiliation Pat Gibbs had dished out, it was time for Bob Dale and Henry Parry to leave Malta. They'd been isolated from the rest of the NCOs since being stripped of their stripes, except when ordered to clean toilets at unearthly hours. Finally, on 13 August, 1942, Dale and Parry – no longer sergeants – left for the Middle East.

Bill Carroll knew what happened to at least one of them:

'They were sent to Egypt as AC2s – Aircraftsman Second Class – just as Gibbs had promised. They had been reduced to the lowest of the low in the RAF pecking order, the lowest form of animal life. You were sweeper up, toilet cleaner – anything. Dale saw out the war like this in Egypt, as far as I know. He certainly survived the war, because I met him in central London through a mutual friend from the squadron, Harry Mallaby. Dale never apologised for what had happened. He'd done his best to forget about it. He said he'd had enough of losing his friends in Malta, sometimes being shot down right in front of him, he was fed up with it, and couldn't go on like that. He didn't go into more detail.

'We respected the fact that he obviously wanted to put it all behind him, and not another word was said about it.'

On 14 August, Gibbs blew up a ship called the *St Andrea* but he had reached his own limit, mentally and physically, and he was rested from actively taking part in strikes after that.

Thanks in no small measure to his tireless work and his intelligent, highly aggressive way of taking on enemy shipping, the besieged island of Malta had been thrown a lifeline. Beaufort crews were starting to feel the benefit of synchronised attacks, as Beaufighters took on more responsibility. The Beaufighters weren't just strafing ships with their guns now, they were bombing them, too. This all gave torpedo-carrying Beauforts more chance of scoring a hit and coming home unscathed but losses would continue to be high and the responsibilities of leadership acutely felt.

As he finally ran out of that extraordinary energy and strength which had made him such a character, Pat Gibbs must have known that Malta was also running very low on supplies. The Allies had just a few days' fuel left. Once that ran out, Malta would have to surrender, because we'd have nothing with which to fly the aircraft to defend her. A convoy simply had to get through, or all would be lost on this vital strategic island – and perhaps in North Africa, too.

Our brave sailors never stopped trying to reach the island in its hour of need. They formed a convoy in the second week of August and headed for the Straits of Gibraltar, knowing it was now or never. The convoy, originally made up of the American tanker *Ohio* and twelve fast merchant ships – was then joined by an escort of seventy-two British naval ships, including three battleships and four aircraft carriers. But after setting sail for Malta, the massive convoy was soon getting pounded from above and below. Dive-bombers, torpedo-bombers, U-boats and E-boats joined forces in multiple attacks – and the enemy enjoyed considerable success.

We on Malta knew what was happening, but 217 Squadron wasn't called out for some reason. The strange thing is this: records show that between 11 and 14 August, 217 Squadron was either at full readiness or on stand-by to defend the convoy. Yet 217 Squadron wasn't called upon. Perhaps it was because there was no obvious enemy shipping target, due to the Italian fleet's continued absence. The fighter squadrons bore the brunt of the battle instead.

Three transport ships got through on 13 August and another

the following day; but the most dramatic events took place on 15 August. The *Ohio* appeared on the horizon near Valletta, damaged and in danger of sinking. That was the tanker which had to get through if Malta was to avoid surrender within days.

I saw the *Ohio* approach as I looked down from a high point above the Grand Harbour in Malta. It was quite a saga; the *Ohio*'s crew were ordered to abandon ship, even though they were so close to bringing Malta the vital fuel she needed for the continued defence of the island. The *Ohio* was on fire and carrying petrol, so everyone knew there could be an almighty explosion at any second. These were the moments when Malta's fate hung in the balance; when her freedom would either be secured against the odds, or she would finally be forced to submit to occupation. The *Ohio*'s crew abandoned the ship, got back on again, abandoned ship and got back on again. It was absolutely amazing; unbelievable to see such a vital tanker in that terrible state.

And when the crew finally nursed their stricken ship into harbour, the locals took off their hats and bowed. They did so out of gratitude and respect. It was very moving and very important; a wonderful moment in history. The fuel was saved and so, effectively, was Malta. We in 217 Squadron knew we'd played an important part in the island's salvation, even if we hadn't been called upon during those crucial days. Had the Italian fleet come out to join the fight against the convoy, it's very doubtful whether any of the ships would have made it through. Luckily we had dented their confidence earlier in the summer.

Bill Carroll didn't regard the Italians as committed fighters, especially after we'd done them some damage:

'They would get attacked and run back to port; they didn't

care to fight it out. Hitler said: "I'm not allowing you to have any more fuel," and so they were stuck in Taranto Harbour. It was definitely partly down to Artie and the raid on the *Trento*.'

Many people helped to keep Malta supplied; and many were still flying dangerous missions from the island weeks and even months after I was effectively grounded, due to the lack of a full crew. At one stage Bill went off to crew for another pilot, Des Fenton, a really nice chap I'd get to know much better within a few months. Mercifully Bill and Des didn't encounter any serious problems when they teamed up on Malta.

In the long run, Beauforts were still going to be needed for the further defence of Malta; but what did the future hold for our squadron? Some key reorganisation was being considered behind the scenes, with Pat Gibbs still at the centre of everything, even though he was no longer flying.

Bill Carroll is reluctant to accept that, before he left, Gibbs saved the remnants of the original 217 crews from probable death on Malta. 'I don't believe Gibbs was personally responsible for moving us out,' Bill argues.

Yet Gibbs insisted after the war that he'd deliberately defied the spirit and intention of an order he'd received to retain 217 Squadron's most experienced crews on Malta. Instead he apparently made play of some ambiguous wording in the instructions from his superiors, and decided to send what was left of 217 east. For that to happen, he had to fill a new squadron with less experienced but fresher crews. It was an audacious gamble – and I, for one, believed his claims that he took the decision on our behalf.

The deteriorating condition of the remaining 217 crews made Gibbs' decision the correct one, in my view. Bill Carroll offers a graphic summary of our time on Malta and its effect on many of the men:

'When we left Malta we were complete wrecks. Those forty pounds I'd lost were about average for the rest of the boys, too. Our losses at Malta were unbelievable. When we got there, our big, long billet, made up of blocks of limestone with a corrugated iron roof, was full. By the time we left, only a handful remained. The Beauforts took an awful beating, too. We only had three of our original aircraft left; but history tells us we won.'

Later, when I met Gibbs at a reunion in the RAF Club in Piccadilly, I told him: 'Thanks for saving my life. I wouldn't have lasted much longer.' Before he could react, I added: 'You probably saved my life by moving me out of Malta and sending me on to Egypt. Thank you.'

Gibbs was well enough by then to smile in acknowledgement, daring to remember what we'd all been through. But back in mid-August, 1942, he'd already begun to suffer from nervous exhaustion. He stayed on Malta until September, inspiring his pilots as best he could until he knew he could do no more. Then he headed for home; although, you could argue that a large part of him never left the island. He once wrote: 'You must have known that I would die in Malta; you must have known that it was a ghost which made the journey home, a ghost which was haunted not by the past but by the dark shadow of an unknown future.'

It was only when Gibbs returned to London, a hero justly decorated with a DSO, that he had a nervous breakdown. Even the administrative job they gave him in the Air Ministry in late 1942 wasn't enough to calm those nerves. He was destined to be medically discharged from the RAF in 1944, but he'd already done far more than I did for the war effort. Despite his explanation, Malta must have come back to haunt him when the pressure was off. For a long time, he couldn't cope with the contrast between the life of constant danger he'd known in the Mediterranean, and the sedate existence behind a desk that typified what he viewed as his increasingly frustrating contribution to the war effort back in England.

Just before his powers deserted him, towards the end of that dreadful summer of 1942, I'm convinced it was Pat Gibbs who decided my fate. The man who'd originally urged his superiors to keep us on Malta ensured our departure. We took our cut, bruised bodies, in some cases diseased and half-starved, and dragged them wearily on to planes for a new life elsewhere. Like Gibbs a few weeks later, we, too, were flying towards an uncertain future; but we were still very much alive.

21

Egypt to Ceylon

We left Malta on 19 August, 1942. One of the surviving aircraft caught fire after take-off and crash-landed. The pilot was the irrepressible Strever, who emerged unscathed yet again.

Many of us were ferried to Egypt in a Dakota, leaving the Beauforts that were still serviceable behind, because they'd be needed on the island. I felt relieved to be on my way. How had I survived Malta? For that matter, how had I survived since the previous December? I'd been lucky on Malta, especially during the *Reichenfels* raid. No one knew how much longer their luck would last; and for a year or so I'd been resigned to whatever fate had in store for me.

All we knew was that Egypt was to be our stop-off point on the way to Ceylon; Cairo would be a place where we could rest. Of course, we could always make ourselves useful to the war effort there if called upon. Bill Carroll remembered the glorious abundance of food and drink – and what it did to him:

'We landed on a strip somewhere in the desert on the road between Alexandria and Cairo. They had this great big tent and great big letters on it: Officers' Mess. They left us standing there, and there was food piled all over tables just inside the tent. The Wing Commander comes by and says: "What are you sergeants doing standing there? Go on in, this is all for you." I went in and half an hour later I was outside being sick as a dog – we'd eaten so much so quickly. From there we were trucked to a transit camp called Al Marsa, which is south of Cairo.

'I had a sinus infection when I got to Egypt and that, combined with the weight loss, made me think it was a good idea to go and see the MO. He just said one word: "Hospital." Next thing I know, I'm in the RAF hospital in Cairo. After a while I got "hospital blues" along with a fellow patient, and so we began to sneak out to all the drinking joints in Cairo. My drinking partner was a big bloke; he could handle himself, so we didn't get into any trouble. You had to have a pass out of hospital, but we forged them and earned some freedom in the bars.'

We all had some leave in Cairo, whether you were sick or not. Unlike Bill, I didn't frequent the bars, and if I ever went near them I would only have a tomato juice. For fun I preferred bathing at a place called the Gezira Club, where I became the victim of a coincidental encounter. The Australian pilot McSharry, whom I'd helped save from the unwelcome attentions of the Junkers 88 on 21 June, was lying by the pool. His neck had healed and the blood that had left his parachute dripping just two months earlier had clearly been replaced. Remarkably, McSharry was in high spirits and I wondered whether he was going to thank me for stopping that Junkers from finishing him off. Sure enough, he did thank me – by pushing me into the pool. Fortunately, I had my swimming trunks on; unfortunately, I was also wearing my watch, an expensive present from my parents. That was McSharry's thank you to me for saving his life. No wonder we'd had to push the boundaries of sportsmanship to beat those Australians in cricket's Bodyline Series a decade earlier!

McSharry went on to live a long and peaceful life. He became a bank manager – heaven knows how – and I heard he was still doing jobs for that bank well into his eighties. Back in Egypt in that August of 1942, we still weren't expecting to live long lives. In fact, we had no idea what might happen from day to day.

There was a strange atmosphere in Cairo because the recent German push so deep into Egypt had given some of the British in the capital the idea that the country was going to be overrun completely. They were burning all sorts of documents; they destroyed everything they didn't want the Germans to lay their hands on, as though the Afrika Korps might come in and start knocking down doors at any minute. It really did look as though the Germans might get through.

I may not have got drunk with Bill, but I did a couple of things with the other two members of my crew while we were in Cairo – probably while Bill was supposed to be in hospital. Aspinall and I went to a concert of classical music, though no one was playing live. An airman put some old 78s on a gramophone. We listened to the music together and it was simply wonderful to hear, after all that we'd been through in the previous weeks and months. Music! It reminded us there was still a normal life to be had, somewhere beyond the war. Then I went to a wonderful French restaurant with Ken Eades, my new wireless operator.

Some squadron members went to the Holy Land during this period of leave. On my own, I went to something a little closer instead – the Great Pyramid. It was quite an impressive business, though I never fell in love with Egypt itself. The trouble with Egypt was that there was too much sand and too many flies. As for the Egyptians, all I can truthfully say is that I was more struck by the wonderful, darker-skinned immigrants who had come up from Sudan, and seemed such fine upstanding fellows with such obvious natural dignity.

After about ten days in and around Cairo, I was getting fed up. Having kicked my heels there for so much time, I wanted to get on to Ceylon – and so did the other pilots. Quite why we were in such a hurry to get closer to the Japanese is anyone's guess. We thought we were needed in Ceylon to defend an island wanted by the Japanese as a stepping stone for the full-scale invasion of India. In the face of an overwhelming enemy force, our chances of survival in our Beauforts would be slim if we bothered to think about it. But we didn't bother to think about it. Personally, I didn't feel anything about the prospect of facing the Japanese; I just wanted to get out of Cairo because I was fed up with twiddling my thumbs. That's the way we all felt about it. We didn't think about the Japs.

Looking back, I must have been mad to want to fly into the storm of a potential Japanese invasion of Ceylon. But we were just frittering away time in Egypt; it was becoming tedious. If Ceylon was where we were needed, why didn't we just go? Part of the squadron delegated me to go to the RAF headquarters in Cairo to hurry things up if I could, as their unofficial spokesman, you might say.

On arrival, I was about to go into the appropriate office when I saw a name on the next office door: Squadron Leader W.R. Hammond. Wally Hammond. Wow! The greatest cricketer of all time! Wally Hammond, the poet who made Australia's finest, Donald Bradman, look a mere clinician. I almost gasped. I wanted to go into his office just to see him, meet him, and then excuse myself by telling him that I'd made a mistake, entered the wrong office. (He probably wouldn't have believed me. People probably did that to him all the time.) I'd like to have said, 'Thank you very much for a wonderful day at Folkestone, Squadron Leader Hammond, where I saw you score an immaculate 184!' I'd have looked at him in awe. The great Hammond, my boyhood hero! Unfortunately for me, W.R. Hammond never got to hear those thanks for a happy childhood memory. After all the mighty ships I'd confronted around Malta and Britain, I hesitated; frozen at the idea of meeting one human being, sitting unarmed behind an office desk. But Hammond was more than human to me, he was a hero, and I hadn't got the nerve to go in. Seventy years later, I was still wishing that I'd gone in – just for the chance to talk to him. I could never have talked to my other boyhood hero, Beethoven – he was long gone. But Wally Hammond? I had the chance . . . and didn't take it.

So what happened in the office I did have enough courage to go into? I went in and said what I was supposed to say, that the chaps had sent me to ask if we could be pushed on rather more quickly than seemed to be happening. The officer listened and said he would do what he could to speed things up. It's not pos-sible to tell whether my visit made any difference because the time might have come to move us on anyway. But within a few days, we were on our way – though not to Ceylon just yet. We were to join 47 Squadron, which was stationed on the Bitter Lakes, part of the Suez Canal. I wasn't entirely unhappy to have something new to do, though my memories of the long weeks spent in Egypt are more closely linked with frustration and bore-dom than anything else. That's probably why Bill remembers some of the specifics of our temporary attachment to 47 Squadron better than me:

'We were based at Shandur on the Suez Canal. We endured the awful flies around the Bitter Lakes, but at least we were soon airborne ourselves. The crew was now Arthur "driving", Vince Aspinall sufficiently recovered to resume his duties as navigator, Ken Eades having replaced Alan Still as wireless operator, and me in the turret, as usual. Eades liked the radio, which was a good thing because, as with Still before him, he couldn't hit a bloody barn door with the guns.

'Rommel had pushed the Eighth Army back to El Alamein; German ships were coming in mainly to Tobruk. We used to fly to a strip that was just ten miles east of the El Alamein line, right on the coast. In the heat of the afternoon we would refuel there with four-gallon tins, topping up the tanks through shammy leather with a funnel. In the hot sun, the fumes from the gas tank were awful, but we had time to recover before taking off again at night. We tried to arrive at Tobruk at first light, to hit any enemy shipping that might present itself as a possible target. We tried on several occasions and luckily we never took any fire. If the Me 109s had spotted us we'd never have stood a chance. They were fierce buggers. Unfortunately we never found any suitable targets either, so we never dropped any torpedoes.

'There was a certain Squadron Leader out there trying to give everyone a hard time. He'd just come from England, had white knees, a brand new uniform, brand new officer's hat, he was pucker and he'd come to smarten us up as a squadron. He didn't come out with a bed roll for desert nights, though, and he had to sleep with the rest of us on a concrete floor. (We weren't allowed to sleep in the sand outside because we were only ten miles outside El Alamein. The Krauts used to send people out to find people who'd taken a chance and slept outside to give them a good sticking on the quiet.)

'This Squadron Leader, he only had one blanket, didn't wear any underpants, and when he woke up after a rough night everything was dangling out. A navigator woke up just as the officer got up, and was therefore confronted by the unappealing sight of his superior's testicles. "My God," said the navigator without thinking, "I always thought the bloody things were golden!" The rest of us couldn't suppress our laughter. The officer, a chap called Carr, was a bit more human in the way he behaved towards us after that.

'It was about 20 October, we were still based around the Bitter Lakes at Shandur, and the Eighth Army was getting ready to run the Krauts back across North Africa. That's when Arthur called up to give us the news.

'"Pack your bags!"

'I said, "What the hell is happening?"

'"Someone has realised at last that we're supposed to be in Ceylon!"

'We were taken by truck to another landing strip on the Alex–Cairo road, a distance of about 230 miles. Ken Eades had been commissioned, so he and Arthur went straight to the Officers' Mess there, while Vince and I made do with the Sergeants' Mess. It must have been 21 October when something happened that I won't forget. I'd just had my evening meal and a quick drink with Vince. Just after 7.30pm, the sergeant running the bar said he was closing for the night. Very reluctantly, Asp and I made our way towards our tent and decided to relieve ourselves in the sand before we got there. At this point, Aspinall suddenly said something you would never, ever expect him to say:

'"Bill, we have to stop drinking."

'"What?" I couldn't believe what I was hearing.

'"Well, I've got to stop, then." He looked worried.

'"What's the matter, Aspinall? What on earth's brought this on?"

'"I could have sworn I saw those tents down there moving."

'"What do you mean, moving?"

'"Moving. They're moving."

'I said, "Asp, we've only had a couple of pints!"

'Out of curiosity, I looked over as well. "Bugger me! I think they are!"

'Sure enough, there were several tents moving very slowly. Except they weren't tents, they were camouflaged tanks. The Eighth Army were edging them up on the quiet, in preparation for the Second Battle of El Alamein. Hours before we left Egypt, we had witnessed the first move in the battle that was going to win us the war in North Africa once and for all.'

Since I'd left the old one in Malta, I was given a new Beaufort to fly out to Ceylon. As we began our long journey to Ceylon, we also heard that Montgomery had not only halted the advance of the Germans, but gone on to defeat them at El Alamein. Churchill later claimed that before El Alamein, the Allies had never experienced victory; after El Alamein, the Allies never experienced defeat. The tide had well and truly turned. Something was going right for the Allies at last! What a boost to our morale that was, as we flew to halt the advance of that other enemy of the Free World, the Japanese, who were at the Burmese border.

It was a wonderful flight, with its various stop-offs and contrasting surroundings. It took us a few days, and they were filled with a sense of freedom and anticipation. First we flew to Habbaniya in Iraq. I remember walking around some very beautiful gardens there.

As usual, Bill Carroll judged each place we stopped at by the availability or otherwise of beer:

'Habbaniya was the first stop, a very modern air force station. It was also the crossroads of the world, where even the Germans used to come to get parts. If you wanted a beer you could see it written in just about any language you could imagine. Aspinall got ill again and ended up in the sick bay, so we were there for two or three days. It was Ramadan, and the Iraqis would fire their arms and we would wake up and wonder what on earth was going on.

'The day we took off from there, we landed on Bahrain Island at about noon. That's the hottest place I've ever been. We went to get out of the aircraft to refuel, but the outside of the aircraft was so hot we had to look for a pair of gloves. From there we went to Oman and then on to Karachi, which was mainly an American base. The Americans don't have beer or any other type of alcohol in their messes, but Aspinall said: "Bill, we'll have to have a drink before we go to bed." We hitched a ride into the town of Karachi and found the necessary stuff.

'On the way back there was this Indian lady, one of the untouchables, I think. She had a baby in each arm and a toddler on her hip. Aspinall, who loved children, went up and started stroking the head of a baby ... whereupon she gave him the baby and took off! Aspinall was landed with this baby and there's the mother, hightailing it down the road. I had a job to catch her up. When I finally caught her and pulled her back, she wasn't very happy at all. Aspinall handed back the baby – and that was our first welcome to what was then India. From there we flew to Bombay.'

We stayed two nights there because I didn't want to fly on, due to cloud around the high hills we would have to go over.

Eventually, however, we went on to Bangalore, a place as green as England. There was a bottle of whisky up for auction at some do in Bangalore, and I had the right number on my ticket. Anyway, I went up and got it, because I knew a crew member or two who might appreciate it. We carried on down to Ceylon and approached Ratmalana, the airfield about ten miles south of Colombo in a coconut plantation. My crew were unusually nervous; they told me to make a good landing because of this bottle of whisky. They were worried it might break. 'Be careful, be careful!' they kept saying. I did the best landing of my life, so smooth you could hardly feel it. Perfect, it was; and for a while I was their hero – until they opened the whisky and discovered it tasted so bad that it was undrinkable. After all that we poured it down the sink. What a waste of a good landing!

At least we'd arrived in Ceylon. We were a little late, you might say, and there had been one or two hiccups on the way over. We'd taken off from Portreath in early June ... and it was now late October. Still, Ceylon would prove to be an unforgettable place, with some of the best and worst – mostly the best – of what the world had to offer.

Bill Carroll's memories are still vivid, and he paints the scene with typical humour:

'We landed in a grass field on a very short runway, surrounded by coconut trees. Nobody came to see us so we left the plane with the mechanics and one of them pointed us to the headquarters. We started walking and a python about fifteen feet long slithered across our path. Welcome to Ceylon! We walked around in a big loop to avoid it, and reported in at the HQ. We're soon told that the place we're due to go to – Minneriya – is so terrible that it's nicknamed 'gonorrhoea'. When we reached it we found it really was the back end of the world, an unbelievable place. Malaria, dysentery, you name it – everything could be caught in Minneriya.

'At this point we have to remind ourselves why we're here. Winston Churchill is convinced the Japs are going to take Ceylon. In fact they could have walked in there. The Ceylonese were very nice people; so nice that they didn't even bother killing snakes that would slither through the dining room from time to time. Their fishermen didn't even kill the fish they caught, they preferred to let the sun do it for them – they would lay the fish in the road to die rather than be violent against the fish. These were very gentle people. The Japanese could have walked in; they were at the height of their powers.'

The Japanese wouldn't have received much resistance from the local population had they wanted to take Ceylon. The natives – the Singhalese – were incredibly friendly, as pleasant as any people you could wish to meet – even though theoretically we were the occupying power. Unfortunately, there wasn't much the locals could do to improve our first station. It was terrible in the jungle in Minneriya, full of disease. I fell ill there with stomach problems, sweats and chills. Everyone was going down like flies. I went to Kandy Hospital and found I hadn't got malaria, as originally suspected, but very probably dengue fever instead. You feel similar symptoms and I was to have repetitions over a couple of years, until the bouts finally died off altogether. In the meantime, we learned to live alongside the local wildlife, though rather surprisingly Bill Carroll didn't feel at home:

'Minneriya is in the middle of the island, not far from Kandy. Ceylon is famous for the number of animals per square inch and, for a boy from London who had never even seen a snake in his life before, it was a real eye-opener. As sergeants, Asp and I were put together in this one hut along with quite a few other sergeants – same as ever, wherever we were. Initially we were all posted to the Beaufort Squadron which was already there, 22 Squadron.

'A member of the ground crew had been out there for years when he got some good news – he was told to report to Colombo to pick up the plane that was taking him back to dear old Blighty. He was in a flap, the train left at 5pm – so we volunteered to pack his kit for him. We saw a snake, killed it and put it in the bottom of his kitbag – just to remind him of the place that had been his home for so long. Nice of us, I thought. Hope he appreciated it!

'We found these two unused condoms and threw them out of a window, though, because his wife wouldn't have appreciated finding those when he got home. Then we watched as four monkeys, two senior and two junior, took these things up into the trees. The noise was unbelievable at night in the jungle and these monkeys, having chewed the rubber, had the hiccups. Nothing is more annoying than monkeys with the hiccups at night, and we all got up with small side-arms and started blasting away at them. But they saw us coming and dodged the bullets. Their hiccups lasted for two nights, and we didn't sleep a wink.

'Arthur's flying is OK, but his idea of driving a car is to put it in top gear and go as fast as he can. This can be very alarming, especially when you come belting round a corner and suddenly see a panther with a cub in its mouth, caught in the headlights and crossing the road as calm as you like. Arthur applied the brakes in time to spare mother and cub, and we worked out why this panther had come so close to camp. Her other cub had been nicked by one of the ground crew the week before; he had been trying unsuccessfully to sell it to the zoo in Colombo. As soon as he heard the mother was back looking for her missing cub, that little cat suddenly became free for anyone who wanted to take it off his hands.

'No one got attacked by the mummy panther, as it turned out, but plenty of the boys were getting bitten by mosquitoes. Not my crowd, though, I noticed. I told the Medical Officer about this pressure lamp in the tent, something that Wilkie had rigged up after scrounging it from somewhere.

'"The boys near the lamp haven't gone down with malaria but the boys further away from it have, sir," I explained. I thought I had stumbled across a startling scientific discovery.

'"You boys near the lamp are also the drinkers," he replied. "Take a look at your arms right now. You're perspiring. Do you think a mosquito is going to want to drink stale beer? It is not amphibious, it doesn't have floats, and it doesn't like booze."

'So I said, "What you're telling us is to keep drinking the booze, sir?"

'"Doesn't seem to have done you any harm so far, does it?" replied the MO.

'It wasn't a scientific breakthrough . . . but it was just the news we wanted to hear.'

22

Paradise – and No Japanese

To contribute to the war effort we knew we first had to play a waiting game in Ceylon.

We did searches for Japanese U-boats off the east coast of the island. I remember on one occasion, when Aspinall was sick again, we had another navigator. But generally we stuck together as a crew and enjoyed our flying while we could, wondering when a formidable enemy force might turn up to try and shoot us out of the sky.

We were certainly ready to do our best against the Japanese; and at first it wasn't a question of 'if' they turn up, but 'when'. They had bombed Colombo a few months before we arrived; so the moment we reached Ceylon, we knew there was a very real threat of a Japanese invasion. If the Japanese invasion of Singapore was anything to go by, just about everything and everyone in Ceylon would be destroyed or subjugated with unimaginable cruelty.

If the Japanese were coming, it was going to be much worse than Malta, which was saying something. We would have to attack their fleet with our torpedo bombers, just as we'd attacked the Germans and Italians. The odds of survival against the

Japanese would probably be even worse, though we didn't think about it at the time. It's hard to make people believe how relatively unconcerned we were by the Japanese. If they weren't there – and they weren't – we generally didn't think about them.

We assumed we'd have some kind of warning when the time came for the Japanese to attack. Surely it wasn't going to be like Pearl Harbor – or even Colombo in April – all over again? The weeks passed . . . and no warning came. And unlike Pearl Harbor or Colombo in April, the Japanese didn't come either. For some reason they seemed to have made themselves scarce, apparently concentrating their resources on more important and immediate targets elsewhere.

The longer they stayed away, the more often we heard a little joke doing the rounds among the men. 'The 217 Squadron was posted to Ceylon because of the Japs. But once the Japs knew that 217 Squadron was coming, they left Ceylon alone.' That was the joke. 'What? The 217 are there? We're not going to take them on!'

For some, though, either the prospect of the Japanese invasion, or more likely the haunting memories of what they'd been through already, was too much. Bill Carroll certainly remembers an LMF case in Ceylon:

'There was one LMF bloke I used to visit in hospital in Colombo. When I went to see him there, he was sitting on the edge of his bed. He'd drawn some chickens on the wall. And he was breaking pieces of bread and throwing it down there towards this wall. I said something to him but he didn't respond; the fellow was gone. It was a shame. He'd come off flying but, even then, he still wasn't really in our world.'

And some might have argued that we were no longer in the real world either – at least not in the world of the war. Then we had a terrible reminder of what was going on elsewhere – and Bill was hit hardest:

'We had an officer join us and his name was Ed, a Flight Lieutenant with the DFC. He came walking over in my direction, looking serious.

"Bill?"

"Yeah."

"Have you heard?"

"Have I heard what?"

"Oh, I've got some sad news. Carson didn't come back." My heart sank. "He was flying a Beaufighter and he went down in the North Sea somewhere. Sorry."

'Tommy Carson loved his low flying and he was a good pilot. No one knows what happened. We'd been through so many ops together, so much danger, and so much fun, too. He was a really good man. Carson's approach to the sergeants was completely different from that of most officers. I made up my mind that when the time finally came to return to England, I'd visit his grave or the RAF memorial in Runnymede which carried Tommy's name. As it turned out, I went to Runnymede three times.'

Poor Tom Carson, a good man with a wry sense of humour. I was told it was a very calm day when he died, which would have been unusual for the North Sea. Tom may have misjudged his height and simply gone into the water, or at least that's what some people thought. Carson seems to have just gone into the drink. When you're flying at fifty feet, it only takes a slight mistake and you go in, especially when there are no waves to remind you what you've got just beneath you. Whatever happened, it was tough on Bill, because he and Tommy had been close. Carson had been more outgoing than me, and he'd liked nothing better than to go out for a beer with the boys. Now he was gone at the age of twenty-five. The war just wouldn't go away, not entirely.

I don't remember a specific day when we realised the Japanese weren't going to come at all. We would probably have been moved from the island to somewhere more dangerous had Churchill been totally confident of it. The tide was to turn against Japan at the end of 1943 and beginning of 1944. But some trace Japan's reluctance to invade Ceylon right back to the Doolittle Raid of 18 April, 1942, when the Americans bombed Tokyo. That gave the Japanese something fresh to think about in terms of the distribution of their resources.

If mainland Japan and all her outlying islands were going to require robust defence, then perhaps a move as draining on resources as the occupation of Ceylon didn't seem like such a very good idea after all, despite her strategic importance. So we were there for an attack which wasn't forthcoming. And I, for one, began to realise that, initial illness aside, there were much worse places to be waiting for nothing to happen.

After I'd recovered from the first bout of dengue fever, they gave me a week's leave and I went to Mount Lavinia to do a bit of swimming. That's when I began to realise we were in paradise. Even though Mount Lavinia is near Colombo, it was wonderful. Funny how they called it Mount Lavinia; there wasn't a mountain, more like a promontory, with a pub and hotel restaurant, where we used to go with friends. To the right of the pub was where I bathed; the water was lovely and warm. There was a beautiful reef, but it was also a bit dangerous. If you went there with a girl – and there were girls in Ceylon – you might have to hold her hand and help get her back to shore again . . . then take her for a meal. It could be a tough life.

Could I have asked for much more? The British women mainly worked for the VAD (Voluntary Aid Department) and there were also the daughters of men who lived and worked on Ceylon's rubber plantations. It wouldn't be gentlemanly to mention any names, but I became quite close to a couple of girls at different times during my long stay in Ceylon. And, if you were near Colombo, there wasn't a better place to spend time with a companion than Mount Lavinia. My crew enjoyed it, too; Bill also liked a bit of swimming – when he wasn't in a bar somewhere:

'After the war they shot some scenes for the famous film, *The Bridge on the River Kwai* at the Mount Lavinia Hotel. The sea was beautiful there. If you swam out twenty-five to thirty yards, you came to a coral reef. Let a wave go by and you could walk over the reef; it was probably only about eighteen inches deep. Once you went out past the reef you reached deeper water, and that's where you'd take a body-board to pick up the waves coming in. You could come in on the first wave, go swishing up and over the coral reef, then catch a second wave on the other side. It was fantastic. As for Arthur, we could tell he was popular with the ladies. He was straight-backed, a gentleman, and he was an officer with gongs . . . girls liked that kind of thing.'

You may be thinking that someone like me could never be truly happy anywhere without my beloved music . . . but we had that, too! While we were in Ceylon they put on a concert in a hall. It was just a disc, there were no musicians, but I still couldn't wait to hear the sound of it. They put on a piano concerto by the composer Schumann. I lapped it up. We hadn't heard any music since Egypt, and to me it was wonderful . . . When I heard it again after the war, I realised it is the worst piece of music ever written; quite pathetically pedestrian! But at the time it was some music and that's what mattered; it made my island paradise complete.

Gradually the likelihood of Japanese invasion receded, until we heard they were on the retreat, at which point the prospect of them invading Ceylon seemed remote indeed. I knew I was lucky to be where I was. If I'd stayed in Europe for the rest of the war I probably wouldn't have survived – not flying Beauforts, with those losses of one in three for every single sortie.

Instead, I was in beautiful Ceylon with good people who had all done our bit, and we were left alone to enjoy our flying and our tennis. And there were plenty of tennis courts, though when we played tennis in Ceylon, we didn't have competitive tournaments like in West Malling. It would have been too much like hard work to try to beat each other. We just played friendly games for the enjoyment of it.

Ceylon was like a tennis club and a flying club combined. We flew around enjoying the sweet sensation of carving through warm air without danger, and you couldn't help but love flying aeroplanes in those conditions. I had two years of that pleasure, sheer bliss, at the expense of the RAF. I saved up quite a bit of money during the war, while enjoying this extended holiday. A year earlier people on all sides had been trying to do their best to kill me, or so it seemed. Now I was in heaven, or rather the Ceylon Flying and Tennis Club.

The locals were so lovely to us; they only enhanced the experience. They were always cheerful and laughing; I liked them very much. They served us beautifully in their restaurants, but it was more than that. You didn't treat them like servants, you treated them like friends. They were always fun and so nice, which makes all the difference. If they had any resentment about 'the white men' in their aircraft taking over the island, they certainly didn't show it to me.

They didn't ask us about what we'd been through earlier in the war, and we didn't have any particular desire to tell them. Malta and Ceylon were islands and that's all they had in common. They could hardly have been more different in terms of what was required of us, and what was on offer. Ceylon was so peaceful; there was no hint of the civil war which came later with the Tamil Tigers. Back then, it was just a paradise. The Singhalese were in a completely different situation to the Maltese; you could go walking with them and they would offer you something sweet, such as a piece of chocolate, which was bliss after the very basic rations of Malta.

I was as happy in Ceylon as I'd been at Oxford University! This haven of peace on a troubled earth gave me the best two years of my life. It wasn't all flying and tennis – the hills offered stunning, glorious views over jungle and plantations, right down to the sparkling sea below. You could almost pick a beautiful, deserted beach from on high – and then head for it.

I came to know another Beaufort pilot from Malta, Des Fenton, much better in Ceylon. Bill had flown with him in the Med, so I'd already been told that Des was very good company. How right Bill was! As with Hutch and Ron Harrison, I became even closer friends with Des than I'd been with Mark Lee in the months before Mark was shot down. Des and I went off to climb some of the hills in Ceylon together when we had a bit of leave. It was lovely to be able to get up to a cool place where we could actually wear our battledress, because we rather liked our tunics. I took a photo of Des at the top of Mount Pedro in Ceylon. We climbed that mountain together and it was hard to imagine how life could be much better.

I don't think Bill Carroll and Vince Aspinall enjoyed Ceylon quite as much as I did. When we were in the air, they had no targets to find and shoot at, which probably meant their more passive experience of flying couldn't in itself be as satisfying as it was for me as the pilot. They didn't play tennis either; so that aspect of Ceylon – very much enjoyed by many of the officers – wasn't going to enhance their experience of the island.

None of these things really mattered, of course, when more intense events were still so fresh in our minds; life-or-death moments when we'd depended on one another so much. We were still a crew, along with the latecomer, Ken Eades. Asp had been through everything with me in the war; and Bill had been through the same with Tommy Carson before joining me in Malta. You don't forget that – ever. Seven decades later, I still hadn't forgotten that. It's just that Ceylon didn't feel like war, and so for Bill and Asp life was a little boring in comparison to what had gone before.

As it turned out, we only had one last job to do as a crew together. The last time I flew with Asp and Bill, in about April 1943, was a strange one, because we were involved in a completely unnecessary exercise. Some idiot suggested we go to the Maldives in our Beaufort, just for the sake of it.

For a start, there were sharks in the sea if we'd had to ditch, and shark-infested waters wouldn't have been any fun. And then we ran into some danger in the air, because we went into some cloud. I never liked being stuck in cloud; and these clouds turned into a bit of a storm.

Bill Carroll was surprised at the storm's ferocity, and the rebellious streak it brought out in me:

'We'd taken off and headed out west into the Indian Ocean, only to be greeted by heavy rain from the ocean up to about

30,000 feet. Arthur decided that the best way to deal with this was not to go through it but under the worst of it. Even flying underneath this terrible storm, we were getting thrown all around the place – and it was night time. Then finally we were just coming out of all this, back into daylight and beautiful weather, when we received the message from base to return the same way! This was the only time I remember Artie not doing what he was told to do.'

I think the leader gave the order to turn back, and at that very moment I came out of the cloud and it was all clear in front of me. Well, I wasn't going to go back into that cloud and try to climb over Ceylon, where there were mountains and hills, with no visibility. So I went on; I disobeyed orders. There was a string of islands going from north to south and I made a landfall at the northern point of the Maldives and flew south to Gan, where there was a remote airfield on Addu Atoll.

I landed on this beautiful spot, not much more than a strip of coral, just about forty minutes south of the equator. We found a signals regiment there and they were extremely pleased to have news of the outside world after being cut off for eighteen months. We took the chance to have a nice swim, too. There was a causeway from one island to the other, and of course there's no tide on the equator; but the current is 8 knots east and then back the other way, and there is no way you can swim against that kind of current. So they had ropes tied from half-way along the causeway to the coral, otherwise you'd be swept out into the Indian Ocean.

We had a very pleasant time and spent the night there. At the evening meal I sat next to the English Group Captain, and we were treated almost like guests of honour. We were in high spirits the next morning because it had been a wonderful stay. So I 'shot up' the place to say goodbye – dipping my wings so sud-denly on my low fly-past that Bill said he was almost thrown out of the plane.

We flew back to Colombo, where I was summoned into the CO's office, and I thought I was going to be ticked off. Instead he said this:

'You're going to be a controller in Colombo.'

'I don't want to be a controller,' I protested.

'I'm afraid you are going to have to be,' he said. 'You need to take a rest.'

'I don't want a rest. I love flying.'

'Sorry. Rules are rules and there it is.'

No other crew had been through this as far as I knew; so I thought maybe there was some way of bending the rule before it started applying to everybody.

'I want to stay here. I don't want a rest, sir. I want to continue on the squadron and keep flying.'

'I'm afraid you've got to have a rest,' he said, remaining calmer than I was.

I had no option but to comply with orders. The policy was to give pilots a rest after a certain amount of operational flying. Crews had to take their turn to be given a break and we were first in line; it was nothing to do with having disobeyed orders. Sadly, the result was that our crew was split up from that point on, and we were never put back together again.

Carroll managed to thrive in an office environment, showing just how versatile he was. He became a junior navigator and worked his way up to Warrant Officer. He could have become an officer, too, had he wanted to put up with taking a fresh round of orders. But deep down he was a man of action, and preferred to take a crack at the Japanese:

'I went out to the Far East to fly a tour of operations in Liberators. They're big four-engine bombers with a much bigger turret. I went on bombing runs to Sumatra, to give the Japanese a bit of what they'd given so many others.'

Bill survived those skirmishes and remained a friend for life. Asp would probably have done the same, had he lived long enough. He did survive the war, though, in one navigating job or another.

Meanwhile I became an Assistant Controller at Colombo, in the Naval Air Operations Room, which didn't involve doing very much at all. Then I was posted to Ratmalana and became a Senior Controller, which involved doing even less. It was thoroughly boring, not even air traffic control work – which unsurprisingly was done by air traffic control. All I did was oversee a few operational aircraft as their crews carried out tests. That way I was promoted to the rank of Acting Squadron Leader in time to be posted back to my squadron as a Flight Commander.

It had been quite a journey through the ranks since the start of the war. I'd started off as an Officer Cadet before being made a Pilot Officer. Then I'd become a Flying Officer, before arriving on Malta as a Flight Lieutenant. Here in Ceylon, the promotions had kept coming, even though we hadn't seen any action. In truth, the latest promotion didn't matter as much as the fact that I was going to be given the chance to fly again.

23

Last Push for Peace

I've never felt more alive than on my return to the cockpit. It was the happiest half hour of my life. I had a new plane; not a Beaufort, but a Beaufighter. The Beaufort was becoming obsolete, and you could see why. The difference between a Beaufort and a Beaufighter was extraordinary, though they were both twin-engine aircraft. Beaufighters were wonderful, absolutely wonderful – much better than Beauforts. They were a sheer delight, so much more manoeuvrable and just a joy to fly compared to stodgy old Beauforts, which were almost lumbering in comparison.

Beaufighters weren't perfect, though. They had a tendency to swing to the right on take-off, so you had to advance the throttle for the starboard engine slightly ahead of the throttle for the port engine. That wasn't a problem, though, you just did it. A chap took me up, showed me the controls, and then I went up on my own.

When I flew a Beaufighter solo, something was unleashed inside me. I'd always wanted to become a fighter pilot; we'd all wanted to be one. Now I could take a Beaufighter up into the skies above Ceylon and I could imagine I really was a fighter pilot. I could pretend to take evasive action, which was exciting. I could almost pretend I was flying in the Battle of Britain.

In a Beaufighter you have one additional crew member instead of the three you have in a Beaufort. He sits half-way down the plane and acts as an observer. Mine was called Chapman, but not even he came with me when I did my most daring aerobatics. So there was no one sitting nervously behind me when I set out to do what that crazy South African, Flight Lieutenant Finch, had almost killed us both trying to teach me more than two years earlier – flying on one engine.

In spite of that experience with Finch, I climbed quickly and then deliberately switched off my port engine. I feathered the prop, then swooped low over Ratmalana airfield to illustrate that a Beaufighter could fly on one engine. Not only that, it could climb on one engine, too, because I did it!

I turned and flew back up to several thousand feet on one engine. I wanted to show those watching on the ground what a Beaufighter could do. And, having shown them, I switched on the engine again and de-feathered the prop. The feeling was one of sheer joy. It was an absolute wonder to fly a Beaufighter after a Beaufort. Now I may not like the word thrill, but that moment really was a thrill. To fly a Beaufighter was like being in heaven. I had the time of my life.

My commanding officer saw me coming in to land. In a Beaufort, you come in downwind and turn for a long approach to land upwind. I suddenly thought, 'This is a Beaufighter, not a Beaufort.' By its very nature it's a fighter and therefore more manoeuvrable. So I turned in to land from a much shorter approach, and did so successfully. That's when it happened. Something I'd been hoping to achieve since my very first hours of learning to fly at Watchfield; something that had eluded me at Cranwell, at Chivenor and all the other places I'd tried to impress people – the instructor took my log-book and wrote: 'Above Average'. Two little words that meant so much to me; I wasn't just average any more.

These were glorious days and I loved flying solo, but there was also an opportunity to give a little something back to a person who made such enjoyment possible – one of my ground crew. Attached to the station flight at Ratmalana was a Tiger Moth. So I invited one of my ground crew to come flying, made sure he was strapped in, and took him up to about 4,000 feet over the sea to do a few loops and side-slips. You could tell by his face when we came back down and landed that he had enjoyed it.

But all good things come to an end and the mood certainly changed when Wing Commander John Lingard, DFC, took charge of 217 Squadron in August 1944. We'd always known in theory that our peace and joy could be shattered at any time but life in Ceylon had become so pleasant that I hadn't really given the possibility of fresh fighting much thought. Lingard seemed hell-bent on making this happen, even when geography wasn't on his side. In early 1945 I began to hear rumours that he was planning an attack on the Japanese battle fleet in Singapore. Then I got to know Lingard and was able to verify the rumours – Lingard was definitely planning something to that effect.

I thought he was talking rubbish, because the Japanese were out of our range. Ceylon to Singapore was 2,300 miles; so we wouldn't even have had the fuel to reach Singapore in our Beaufighters, let alone return. Make an attack on the Japs? I thought it was completely insane. Apparently he was hoping to use the Cocos Islands as his stepping stone. They were 1,760 miles south-east of Ceylon but still more than a thousand miles from Singapore. Even if we'd reached the Japanese, it would have been a suicide mission – rather like the one-way trip they'd almost sent us on from Sumburgh to Norway, to try to sink the *Tirpitz*. Lingard seemed to want us to become kamikaze even before the Japanese unleashed their own kamikaze.

I became quite friendly with the man, so in theory I could have gone up and warned him that he was going to get us all killed for nothing. I didn't say it, though – it wasn't my place to do so. He was a commanding officer and I was a Flight Commander; I wasn't going to be insubordinate. Had he sent me back into action, I'd have had to go, there's no doubt about it. But I never was sent to the Cocos Islands, or indeed to Singapore. Officers higher up the chain of command clearly didn't consider such heroics to be practicable or even necessary; after all, the Japanese were on the back foot in 1945.

I think Lingard hatched yet another plan to hit the Japs, but even that one didn't quite come to fruition ... mercifully. While 217 Squadron had almost been destroyed on Malta, its members were much luckier in Ceylon. But that didn't mean everyone who'd recently converted from Beauforts to Beaufighters was so fortunate.

Some of the pilots I'd flown and had fun with in equal turns in Ceylon were suddenly back in the thick of the action because 22 Squadron was posted up to the border with Burma. I can't imagine what it must have felt like after experiencing two years of relative peace. I didn't particularly want to go looking for the war again; I was happy where I was. Des Fenton, with whom I'd climbed the mountains of Ceylon only months earlier, had joined 22 Squadron and so he was posted up to the Burmese border. I don't think he had much choice about it. He was shot down in a Beaufighter on 5 March, 1945. Dear Des, the man who had become such a good friend to both Bill Carroll and me, survived his crash-landing in the River Thazetayo Henzada area. Eventually he was taken by the Japanese, and that's when events took a really terrible turn.

Des was still in his flying kit on 28 April when he became part of a forced march out of Rangoon jail. A new detachment of Japanese guards were attempting to take 400 prisoners with them as they retreated from the advancing Allies. During a rest period, an air raid siren was heard. Des was apparently slow to his feet when the general command was given by a guard. He may have been injured in his crash-landing, or perhaps he just didn't understand the Japanese command. Anyway, a wild-eyed Japanese guard went up to him and bayoneted him through the stomach.

Others were threatened with the same as they tried to react; the guard was going berserk. He murdered Des. I had that from an eye-witness who was repatriated after the war. As it turned out, the very next morning the marchers woke up to find that the Japanese had disappeared, so Des was denied the rest of his life by a matter of hours. It was murder, and I use the word advisedly; it was a cold-blooded murder. He was a prisoner of war. In fact, I can never forgive the Japanese, because they murdered my best friend.

We were posted to Vavuniya in the north of Ceylon, and there was talk of being given a role in the invasion of Malaya. But the Japanese were on their way out and were increasingly reluctant to face us. Unfortunately, they were equally reluctant to surrender.

It was in the sea around Okinawa that the world was finally introduced to the dreadful concept of the kamikaze, or 'Divine Wind'. They could call it whatever they wanted but deliberately flying into enemy ships to blow them up, killing yourself in the process, was pretty shocking stuff – even to someone like me. I'd flown into an enemy ship and sliced my wing-tip off, but I regarded that as a mistake, not the objective. Yes, I'd accepted near-suicidal orders in the recent past, such as the planned raid on the *Tirpitz,* but I don't think I could have been a kamikaze, strange as that may seem. To be a kamikaze pilot meant absolute certainty of death.

I could feel resigned to my fate, and accept orders that would surely have brought death; I could fly on strikes so dangerous that they should have killed me, and did just that to dear friends; but these things I endured without specifically going out to end my own life. There is a subtle difference, and that subtle difference must be the presence of a hope, however slim, suppressed or unjustified. This is why we remained one step short of the kamikaze in doing what we did, and why I find the comparisons unsound, though I can understand why those comparisons are drawn.

Fortunately for me, I was spared the horrific job of trying to dislodge the Japanese and destroy their resistance at bloodbaths like Okinawa. Though I heard about it, I never saw how a truly suicidal pilot behaved; only how truly brave pilots, men who still secretly hoped for life, gave up that precious gift while protecting their country.

Right at the end of the war in August 1945, the Americans dropped an atom bomb on the Japanese at Hiroshima, and still the Japanese didn't give up straight away. So the Americans had to drop another bomb, this time on Nagasaki. Should they have dropped the second one? I don't know. But my feeling is that we needed to drop at least one, because if we'd tried to invade Japan, it would have been well nigh impossible. The Japanese would have fought to the last man, and there was no adequate base from which to launch a full-scale invasion – not like the Normandy landings.

After all, about a quarter of a million people died on Okinawa alone. The Kamikaze were deliberately flying their planes into American ships. They weren't like us; we wanted to live, whereas the Japanese pilots seemed to embrace death. The entire nation would have fought, probably women and children, too, in the event of a full land invasion. It would have been a massacre.

You can debate various aspects of a horrible war, and the RAF had done some terrible things by then, too. The blanket bombing of Dresden, Germany, in February 1945 was not necessary, in my opinion. What happened in Dresden was a war crime, and at least 25,000 civilians were killed in those bombings. It was completely unnecessary. There were no troops in Dresden at all. We were trying to please the Russians – at least, I assume that was the case. But there was a lot of suffering on the Allied side before and after that. Bill Carroll lost another good friend when the end of the war was in sight:

'Jack Featherstone, with whom I'd done all my training and a lot of flying when Tommy Carson was our pilot, had done well all through the war. He'd been awarded the Distinguished Flying Medal in November 1942, and had become a Flight Lieutenant by 1945. On 10 April he was in a Halifax that went down in the Kattegat, an area of sea between Denmark and Sweden. They never recovered his body. Poor old Jack, if he'd survived another month he would have seen out the war in Northern Europe, because the Germans surrendered on 7 May. I haven't forgotten the good times we had together all those years ago. In fact, I haven't forgotten any of the boys.'

There were many more sacrifices to be made before we finally won the war. I'd seen how terrible the fighting could be from my own experiences during 1941 and 1942. After that I'd been a virtual spectator. That's the way it happened for me, and I'm not sorry it did. I was incredibly lucky and I was about to be given a further reminder of that luck. Towards the end of my time in Ceylon, a familiar face approached me. It was Anthony Gray, the youngest brother of my tennis partner back in West Malling, Sally Gray. He'd joined the RAF and his squadron was just passing through on its way east. Small world! When I saw him, he was holding a package.

'I hear you're going home, Arthur,' he said with a smile. 'Would you take these clothes back to Sally for me, please?'

'Of course I will,' I assured him. He gave me some of the latest news from our part of Kent, and then we went our separate ways.

Anthony never made it home. He died in a flying accident right there in Ceylon. It could have been engine failure, or perhaps something else, we'll never know. Sally had another brother, whose name escapes me, but he'd been killed in a flying accident during the war too, back in Britain.

I was repatriated towards the end of the English summer of 1945. You might think after all the fun I'd had in Ceylon that I was sorry to leave the island. But I'd been away from home a long time by then – since the start of June 1942. So I was delighted to set foot on British soil again, if the truth be told. So many of my fellow countrymen had been lost, people I knew and remembered fondly. But when you're young, life is for living and you try to enjoy it, whatever has happened to others around you. So I immersed myself in the beauty of English life again and cherished the things I'd always held dear.

I even caught the end of the English cricket season and saw the imperious Denis Compton score 142 for Middlesex against

Kent at Canterbury, one of the most beautiful grounds in the country with its famous lime tree inside the boundary. Middlesex won by an innings and 104 runs. And, although I felt lucky to have witnessed the masterful Compton in a setting that made me feel so very much at home again, I did think Kent might have put up a slightly better show after all my years away!

At least the peaceful Kent countryside didn't seem to have changed very much, for all the chaos her airfields and skies had seen during the war. Not that there was any real time to spend with my family back home, because I was summoned straight to Coastal Command Headquarters. They had some kind of job or posting in mind for me, but I never did find out what it was.

I went into the office of the Air Commodore and saluted smartly. When he began the conversation, it emerged that, since inviting me to HQ, he'd taken a closer look at my file, and realised I was in the middle of my course at Oxford.

'Well, you'll want to get back to Oxford, won't you, to finish your course?'

'I'd like that, sir, yes.'

'I'll fix it,' he said.

There was a fast demob system and a slow demob system. He put me in the fast one. Lo and behold, I was demobbed in the space of about a week in October, just in time to begin my second year at Oxford in the autumn term. Still Principal of St Edmund Hall, it appeared that The ABE didn't object to me coming back as much as he had objected to me leaving. He even invited me to sit at the top table for a college dinner, which was quite a privilege at the time, I can tell you.

A rather pretty girl called Beryl Jones was starting her second year at the same time as me. We were both studying modern languages and we both went to the same reading room at the Taylorian Institute Library in Oxford. We both had to translate our passages of poetry into French and we were both using the same dictionary on the table there. She was even sitting next to me as we shared that dictionary; and then, by pure chance, we happened to leave together.

I made some sort of casual remark on the way out.

'Bit stuffy in there.'

It wasn't the most romantic line a young man could come up with, but she seemed absolutely delighted.

'Yes, wasn't it!' she replied.

I soon found out that by some miracle she'd fallen for me! I hadn't fallen for her at that stage, but there would be many more visits to the library ... and that's how it got started. She had a wonderful French accent – better than mine. I think mine was OK, but hers was really perfect.

Beryl was half English and half Welsh. I told her that meant she was only half civilised – the English part, of course. She even let me get away with that, so I knew she must have liked me.

Whereas before the war I'd gone punting alone, after the war I let Beryl come with me sometimes. She was jolly good at punting, too, which I considered to be a terrific advantage in a girl. She didn't ask too much about what I'd done in the war, either, which was rather nice. I never talked about it because I didn't particularly want to. I could have talked about it; I wasn't one of those people who found it all so painful that the subject was taboo; it's just that there didn't seem to be any reason to go on about it, and she seemed to understand that in an unspoken way.

*

Everything was so enjoyable when I went back to Oxford again; my mind was being stimulated at every turn. I could laugh out loud at Molière again, and continue to wonder why anybody could possibly think Shakespeare's comedies were actually funny (apart from *Twelfth Night*). I developed a great love for Racine and wrote a manuscript called, 'The Language of Racine'. Someone even wanted to publish it at one stage, so I must have been talking some sense.

I thoroughly enjoyed getting back to my studies. People talk about post-traumatic stress disorder, but I didn't really get any of that. Only one thing happened that could be remotely related, and that was a recurring dream. I was in a car and the car went backwards, I wasn't in control. It kept taking me backwards, out of control. To me this was the expression of an anxiety I'd suffered many times during the war, when you haven't quite brought your plane under control as you land, and you think you might go over the edge of the runway. So to me, this dream was my mind belatedly compensating for that by firing me into reverse, albeit equally uncontrollably, to avoid going off the edge. Who knows? It didn't really trouble me as such.

It was once suggested to me that the dream may have represented my desire to push all those memories from the war back into the past. There's only one thing wrong with that theory. I didn't want to push my memories of the war back into the past! I enjoyed myself in the war, despite some of the harder things that happened along the way. I think the love I had for flying aeroplanes helped me cope with some of the horrors I'd seen. I enjoyed my five years in the RAF, flying around at the government's expense. What a privilege to have the experience! What wonderful people I met!

Equally, I had no problem adapting back to civilian life either.

I suddenly found myself busy and happy enough to be living in the present as a student in England, not haunted in any sense by the recent past. Even when it wasn't term time at Oxford, there were always the tennis parties at West Malling, and Sally Gray to play with in mixed doubles. We couldn't pretend nothing had happened in the last five years; not when poor Sally had lost her brothers. But sometimes the best way to console someone is to carry on as normal, and that's what we tried to do.

I don't know whether my mother still secretly wanted me to marry Sally, but it wasn't going to happen – I had Beryl now. Sally and I were united by tennis and tennis only – and one day we decided to play against each other in a singles challenge. I could have surrendered the match in sympathy for the losses she'd suffered. But Sally would have known immediately what I was doing and she'd have hated it. So we played a genuine match, just as she wanted. It was a keen contest, much more competitive than any friendly knockabout I'd had with my male colleagues in Ceylon. I'm not ashamed to say that I won – just. At the end she shook hands, smiled and said, 'That determination you have, Arthur, that's why you won the DFC.'

The formal medal ceremony was still to come, and I could hardly have asked for more. In 1946 I went to Buckingham Palace in my RAF uniform to have my DFCs pinned on by King George VI. I was actually going to meet our inspirational king, the man we were so lucky to have on the throne! I drove to the palace in a state of great anticipation, as you can imagine. My mother was next to me because she was to be in the audience, looking on.

Once inside the palace, those of us receiving medals were ushered into a side room, leaving those who had come with us to take their places in the appropriate hall. Then we recipients were shown in to meet His Majesty. It was quite a moment, I can tell you! I bowed slightly before the king and he began to speak. There was no sign of the stutter when he spoke to me.

'How long were you out there?' he asked.

I assumed he was talking about Ceylon. 'Two years, sir.'

And he pinned something on my chest, a hook or bar or something, and then he pinned the medal on. I can't even remember if it was one or two, but I think it was two.

I bowed again, turned smartly to my right and marched off. And once I was out of His Majesty's sight, the medals were whipped off me by one of the Buckingham Palace aides. I don't quite know why – I don't think it was to give them straight to someone else! It was probably to wrap them up. Anyway, I got them back, and there you are. It was a wonderful experience; he was a wonderful king.

But looking back it was rather amusing that he asked me about my two-year holiday in Ceylon, rather than my time in Malta. Or had he been asking me about Malta? In which case, I should have said 'two months' instead of 'two years'? We will never know, and it hardly seems to matter. George VI also decorated Malta, making it the 'George Cross Island'. How its people deserved that recognition of their bravery!

After my moment with the king, my mother and I met up with my father. You could only invite one person into the ceremony, so he'd waited elsewhere; now we could all go for a meal together to celebrate. Good memories, those, always treasured. When King George VI died much later, Churchill put a wreath on his tomb with the words 'For Valour'. And those are the words that are used as the motto for the Victoria Cross, the highest medal for bravery. That's what Churchill thought of the king.

So I had a DFC and Bar. Sergeants Vince Aspinall, Bill Carroll and Alan Still went through the same dangers as me and in my opinion they should have been decorated accordingly. Yet none among them was ever awarded any medal for bravery. Some NCOs got Distinguished Flying Medals – DFMs – but not Asp, Bill or Alan. They didn't fly planes; they weren't the 'drivers', as Bill put it; so somehow they were overlooked. At the time of writing Bill Carroll is still alive, so maybe there's time for someone somewhere to do something about his lack of a medal.

A special king gave me mine, and then I did two more years at Oxford to complete the course. What more could I have asked for? But I was greedy. I enjoyed punting on the river so much that I wanted another summer term to do it all again. That's the main reason I stayed on to do a Diploma of Education course for a further year. This condemned me to teach for the rest of my life! No way had I wanted to teach before I saw it as a way to get more punting! But the more I thought about it, the more it made sense. Teaching foreign languages couldn't do any harm to anyone. Who knows, it might even do a bit of good. Helping people from different countries to have a good chat and a good time before they fell out and decided to kill each other . . . that seemed like a reasonable way forward.

24

A Different Life

I never piloted an aircraft again. It never crossed my mind to do so; I just forgot about it. That may sound unlikely, but it's the way things can happen when you're young. I could've gone to a flying club and paid through the nose to take an aircraft up. But the war was over, I had Oxford, I had Beryl, and then I just wanted to get on with my teaching.

From that moment on, I was never going to have enough money to fly anyway. A teacher doesn't teach for the salary – he teaches for the wonderfully long holidays ... Oh, and because we love teaching children, of course!

Funnily enough, teaching did take me back to the war in one sense, because I had a chance to return to Germany and find out what had happened to some people I'd thought about from time to time for the previous eight years. I had a Goldsmiths scholarship for teaching and that gave me a sabbatical term. The first two weeks I was to spend in Germany on my own, and then the rest of the time, four months, I'd spend in France with my family.

So I went to Frankfurt to try to find the Külenthals, the Jewish couple who'd been so generous to me before the war. I went to their old address in the city but they didn't live there any more. That made me afraid for them, worried that they might have been killed in the Holocaust. I didn't feel I had anyone to turn to, because I wasn't getting on with the German teacher who was overseeing my trip. On the face of it, he seemed friendly enough, because I'd ridden side-car on his motorbike. For all that, I felt inhibited in his presence. 'You haven't made much progress in your German, have you?' That's what he said towards the end of the trip. It felt like a low blow.

All the time I was wondering about the Külenthals; but then I had a good idea. I went to the local police station to find out if they had a new address . . . and they did! It still didn't mean for sure that they'd survived, but I'd soon find out.

Within minutes I was knocking on an apartment door, feeling a little anxious. The door opened . . . and I saw the gentle face of Frau Külenthal. What a relief! She was the one I'd feared for most, because Hitler had refused to guarantee her safety in that ominous pre-war letter. Yet here she was, living proof that some Jews had been lucky enough to survive the mass murder. She remembered me well, and she seemed equally delighted that I, too, was safe. When Herr Külenthal saw me, he gave me a big smile. We sat down at their kitchen table and began to chat, and something wonderful happened – I broke into such fluent German that even the Külenthals were astounded. '*Ausgezeichnet!*' they said happily. It was just like old times – except that I could speak much better German and I didn't have to give a Nazi salute out on the street any more.

No one in Britain was under any obligation to give a Nazi salute either. We were free to do as we pleased, or at least that was the theory. When Bill Carroll finally made it back, things weren't quite as he'd left them or hoped for, though. The fact that he didn't even manage to make it back in the year the war ended couldn't have helped. One rule for the officers . . . another rule for the NCOs. But Bill is Bill and he decided to embrace what he saw as the best of England and leave behind the things that didn't feel right:

'I finally got back to Britain from India on 10 January, 1946. We arrived by boat at Greenock in Glasgow, took a train down to the RAF station in Liverpool, were issued with a replacement UK uniform and given leave to continue on down to London.

'Things weren't the same in England any more, though. My best friend, Alan Johnson, had been shot down over Hamburg in a Lancaster. He's buried over there. To this day, I still can't quite believe it. The first place I went after the war was to see his parents, who'd always been really nice to me. There was this young lady there and Alan's two sisters. Mrs Johnson said, "Why don't you stay for lunch?" I said, "Thanks very much."

'They laid an extra place at table. And this young girl was talking to this empty chair. Mrs Johnson looks at me as if to tell me, "Don't say a word." This young girl's talking to this chair as if it was normal, and it was unbelievable, it really scared me. Alan had been shot down near the end of the war, so the grief was still fresh. But it was weird hearing her talk to him like that; really sad. That really worried me, it was about the only time I was really troubled about the war. The young woman became an air stewardess with Air Canada in the end – just so she could fly back and forth to Germany, to tend to his grave.

'Things were different in other ways, too; Britain was in bad shape. A guy had got half his face shot off at Dunkirk, came back and got a building job when he was finally fit enough to take one. But he got in trouble with the unions for working too hard. They beat him up and left him in hospital.

'I was a trained engineer and I went back to work, too. The steel worker on this one job was even younger than I was and wouldn't do a thing unless I told him to. But he was getting paid thirty quid per week and I was getting nine, because I'd been away at the war and didn't know the right people. I thought that was ridiculous. A deserter at work started talking about how tough he'd had it in prison during the war – and I jumped on him.

'Britain didn't feel right any more. Was this the kind of set-up Alan Johnson and Tommy Carson had died for? Or my good friends and former crew mates Mickey McGrath – who'd been killed when his ship was torpedoed off Gibraltar as he headed home towards the end of 1942 – and Jack Featherstone? I didn't think so. Then I went down to the hardware store to buy a spring for a door at my mother's house. They said I couldn't buy one – I needed a certificate first. "To hell with all this," I said.

'In 1947 my future fell into place when a young WAAF happened to fall at my feet in the ice rink in Streatham – not deliberately, either. I picked her up, which was probably the best thing I ever did in my life. Her name was Brenda and we were married six months later. Two days after that, we set off for a new life in Canada. We've been on our honeymoon for sixty-five years.

'Sadly I'd never see my drinking pal Vince Aspinall again – and neither would Arthur.'

Vince Aspinall died in 1948 in a polio epidemic. That was a terrible disaster. To survive the entire war, and then die of polio! It was such an awful thing to happen to a nice fellow like Aspinall, a great tragedy. I didn't even get to go to the funeral. He lived in Manchester and I didn't hear about his death until later. I'll always remember him with fondness and great respect. Poor

Asp passed away in the same year I married my fellow Oxford student, Beryl Jones.

I used to joke that the trouble with Oxford University is that you can get into bad company there! Personally, I blame the Air Commodore. If he hadn't fast-tracked me, I would never have met Beryl! Seriously, we had sixty-three happy years together, so I was very fortunate to have met her as a student and then shared my life with her. Sadly, she died in her sleep in December 2011 after a long illness.

Alan Still didn't live long enough to see the twenty-first century, though he enjoyed a longer life than Asp. On his return from three years as a POW, he became a teacher, just like me, and stayed with Beryl and me in Malvern once. Bill Carroll was the one who saw him last:

'He came to see me at my sister's place in London, when I brought my family back to England for Prince Charles' wedding to Lady Diana. We talked for hours. It was the last time I saw him. Alan had a heart attack shortly after that. He was sixty-five when he died. What a fine man he was.'

We had Beaufort reunions every year in October, at the RAF Club in Piccadilly. At one stage I was made the wine steward! It must have been someone's idea of a joke because I knew nothing about wines at all. At a Beaufort reunion one year, I met a survivor from the Swordfish squadron which had attacked and been shot down by the German fleet during the Channel Dash. This man had been picked up by the Germans and taken prisoner. I told him, 'You should all have got the Victoria Cross like Esmonde did.'

On another occasion, a big German turned up and was well received! He'd been invited and the reason became clear. He said he'd been a gunner on the *Scharnhorst* during the Channel Dash.

And over the years people grew increasingly confident that it had been the *Scharnhorst* I'd tried to torpedo on that terrible day, 12 February, 1942. The German seemed a fine fellow and we had a good chat about the situation. We could have spoken in German but he chose English. It wasn't a complicated exchange ... he'd been shooting at me and I'd been dropping a torpedo at him! Did I apologise? Certainly not! But I liked him, so I said, 'You should have been on our side.' At the end of our conversation he gave me such a great big bear hug that he almost lifted me off the floor. Wonderful chap!

I didn't visit Italy again for about ten years but when I finally did, I told my cousins what I'd had to do in Malta. I explained, 'If Mussolini had been overthrown earlier, I wouldn't have had to torpedo the *Trento*.' They accepted it, and no more was said. I'm not ashamed of what I did, far from it; but I'm sorry it was necessary. I still love Italy. The war just forced me to suspend that love.

Not even the war and its harrowing aftermath could entirely remove Bill Carroll's sense of humour, which shone long into the twenty-first century. When asked to reflect on his survival and the war in general, he could still make you smile:

'I'm glad it's over. I never was so sure I was going to die during World War Two. Now I'm convinced I'm not going to die during World War Two!

'Life's been good to me since the war, and after I emigrated. I built my own engineering company in Vancouver, which was a bit like being a Warrant Officer – no one could tell me what to do. I had four kids of my own, eight grandchildren ... and at the time of writing eight great-grandchildren. Not bad for someone who could have died quite a few times as a twenty- or twenty-one-year-old.

'Near on seventy years have passed since the end of World War Two and thankfully, at the time of writing, there hasn't been another World War since. As for bringing about a true and lasting peace worldwide, we can only continue to work towards it.'

To teach people to communicate better, that will help prevent a few wars. I hope I've done my bit, having taught French and German to British children for more than thirty years.

My first assignment was in Scotland, at the Glasgow Academy.

'Good morning, Mr Aldridge,' the pupils said politely when I walked in to take my first class.

Not Squadron Leader or Flight Lieutenant or Pilot Officer . . . plain old Mr Aldridge. That suited me just fine.

Epilogue

Summer 2012

'Stay off the booze, Bill! Hope you're leaving it alone, are you?'

'Have you stopped driving yet, Artie? Are the people of Malvern safe now?'

As they've done for seven decades, two torpedo flyers, men from very different backgrounds, are teasing each other. This time they're using recorded messages. Long before they reached old age, Bermondsey-born Bill complained that he couldn't read Oxford-educated Arthur's spidery handwriting.

The situation wasn't going to get any better after they turned ninety; and by then they were feeling too fragile to hop on a plane and visit each other in the UK or Canada, as they'd done in middle age. Recorded messages were the answer, and the odd phone call. Either way, there'd always be a little teasing. That was compulsory.

When Artie turned ninety-two in August 2012, Bill called him from Canada and celebrated too. Why wouldn't he, when

Artie's landmark offered further proof that Air Gunner Carroll was younger? To be a mere ninety-one for a few more months gave Bill all the ammunition he needed for their latest round of banter.

It was my privilege to be able to pass on the odd message while hearing all about their wartime exploits. 'Mr Aldridge' had taught me French at King's School, Worcester, back in the 1970s. Now here we were writing a book together – with Carroll's help.

'Tell Bill I've finally had a haircut,' Artie said one day.

'Tell him it's about time,' Bill replied from Canada.

As the book took shape, ex-teacher and pupil shared the odd bit of banter too. When Arthur invited me out for meals and I wanted to pay, he'd say, 'Put that money away or I'll never have lunch with you again.'

'Is that an order, sir?'

'Yes it is,' he insisted.

We looked forward to this book coming out but he worried he might not be around to enjoy it. 'Dying before publication isn't an option,' I told him. 'Stick around.'

'Is that an order?' he asked.

'Yes it is,' I replied. We laughed and we hoped.

The survivors of 217 Squadron are rare men, indeed; and they deserve our respect. Their Beauforts became obsolete when Beaufighters took over. You won't find any around now – not of the type that Arthur and Bill crewed into battle. As for the last of the torpedo flyers, they're a dwindling band of brothers. The reunions stopped long ago, they couldn't carry on indefinitely. Everyone was getting too old.

Arthur missed the last Beaufort reunion because of a pre-booked holiday to Italy. Many men who did attend had tears in their eyes as they said farewell, knowing they'd probably never see each other again.

These great characters deserve our thanks and their place in history. The Beaufort boys should never be forgotten.

Mark Ryan
November 2012

Acknowledgements

My biggest thanks go to Bill Carroll, my gunner and good friend of more than seventy years, for his tremendous help in piecing together the events we lived through during World War Two. The book wouldn't have been as lively without you, Bill. Your wife, Brenda, and sons, Pip and Paul, also provided valuable assistance in so many ways, which doesn't surprise me because they are such a credit to you.

Bill will understand better than most why I find it hard to mention him without paying tribute one last time to our fellow crew members, Vince Aspinall and Alan Still. How I'd have loved to call upon their memories and expertise, too, but sadly they and so many others are long gone. We haven't forgotten our old friends, Bill and I.

The main purpose of the book is to try to explain what they went through and why. If we've succeeded in this aim, then I hope they'll be remembered in the right way.

Thanks to Mark Ryan, who helped put my words on the printed page; he tried for some months to persuade me to tell my story, and now I'm glad he did so.

The agent who helped us approach prospective publishers was

Robert Smith, who has been clear, fair and professional in his dealings with me and Mark.

Kerri Sharp, the commissioning editor at Simon and Schuster, made the project a reality – and took great interest in the story from the start. Her observations on early manuscripts were vital in shaping the book as it appears here. Jo Roberts-Miller was the next editor to work her magic on the raw material. Mark calls her 'Genius Jo', which is a compliment indeed. We've been so lucky to have Kerri and Jo on board.

Modern-day pilot Stephen Cathcart cast an expert eye over some aspects of the material to ensure that I hadn't remembered wrongly the technicalities behind the art of flying. Steve highlighted several important points which were consequently made clearer or corrected, and he did so in the no-nonsense way that is the trademark of the best pilots.

The Imperial War Museum and the RAF Museum at Hendon were as helpful as you'd expect of such important centres of military history. RAF Cranwell furnished me with my service records; and we were equally lucky that the National Archive in Kew, London, preserved 217 Squadron's operational record book among other gems.

There were many more, I don't doubt, who helped to complete the picture I was trying to paint; people who should really have been named here along with the rest. Please put such omissions down to an oversight, not a lack of gratitude, because I'm grateful to anyone and everyone who assisted.

Finally, thanks to you, the reader, for sticking with me, which you must have done if you've reached this point! I ask you only to take a little piece of what you've read here and pass it on, so that future generations can know a little of what we lived through, and what so many died for.

I don't suppose the latest generation know very much about World War Two. After all, what did I know about the Boer War as a youngster? But some young people may be interested to hear a bit about our war all the same. And if they do show an interest, you might be able to give them a sense of how ordinary young people like us approached the war. Who knows, an anecdote or two from these pages might help.

As for me, I echo Bill's hope that there will never be another World War. We can all play our own little part in making sure of that, don't you think? Thanks again for reading my story.

Arthur Aldridge
March 2013

Arthur Aldridge DFC and Bar,
circa 1945

Index of Ships

HMS *Acasta* (A-class destroyer sunk on 8 June 1940 in action against the *Scharnhorst* and the *Gneisenau*)

Admiral Hipper (German heavy cruiser)

HMS *Ardent* (escorted the *Glorious* with the *Acasta* and was sunk)

HMS *Ark Royal* (aircraft carrier involved in the sinking of the *Bismarck* and the Malta Convoys)

SS *Autolycus* (steamship sunk by heavy cruisers *Suzuya* and *Kumano* and destroyer *Shirakumo*)

Bismarck (one of two *Bismarck*-class battleships built for the German *Kriegsmarine*. Sister ship of the Tirpitz. 55,000 tons. Was damaged by HMS Rodney, torpedoed by HMS Dorsetshire and sunk on 29 May 1941)

HMS *Cornwall* (county-class heavy cruiser of the *Kent* subclass – in early April 1942 she was detached from the fleet to escort the aircraft carrier *Hermes* with the *Dorsetshire* to Trincomalee on Ceylon. Sunk in an engagement known as the Easter Sunday Raid)

HMS *Dorsetshire* (heavy cruiser that torpedoed the *Bismarck* – HMS *Maori* was with her. She was sunk in an engagement known as the Easter Sunday Raid)

HMS *Glorious* (aircraft carrier escorted by the *Acasta* and the *Ardent* and sunk in the North Sea by the *Scharnhorst* and the *Gneisenau*)

Gneisenau (battlecruiser)

Gorizia (Italian cruiser)

HMS *Hector* (armed merchant cruiser sunk in a Japanese air attack in 1942 in Colombo harbour – part of the Easter Sunday Raid)

HMS *Hermes* (aircraft carrier sunk by the Japanese during Easter Sunday Raid)

HMS *Hood* (battlecruiser sunk by the *Bismarck* with the *Prince of Wales*)

HMS *King George V* (battleship which severely damaged the *Bismarck* with the *Rodney* and also spent some time in operations against the Japanese in the Pacific)

Littorio (*Littorio*-class battleship, 35,000 tons)

SS *Madrid* (8,000 tons – sunk by Aldridge and Finch, December 1941)

SS *Malda* (British steamship sunk with *Autolycus*)

HMS *Maori* (Tribal-class destroyer involved in pursuit and destruction of *Bismarck* but was sunk at her moorings in Malta on 12 February 1942)

Nicoloso da Recco (*Navigatori*-class destroyer – shot down two Beaufort bombers while escorting a two-freighter convoy on 21 June 1942 off Tunisia)

HMS *Norfolk* (County-class heavy cruiser, sister ship to the *Dorsetshire,* involved in the chase for the *Gneisenau* and the *Scharnhorst*, and was part of the force to sink the *Bismarck*)

SS *Orari* (part of the convoy to Malta)

HMS *Prince of Wales* (*King George V*-class battleship with the *Hood* during the attack on the *Bismarck* – landed three hits)

Exciting footage of Beaufort torpedo bombers and Beaufighters in action is viewable online in this short piece of German film from 1942, which shows how close to their targets pilots such as Arthur had to fly:

http://www.military.com/video/operations-and-strategy/second-world-war/ww2-raf-bristol-beaufort-torpedo-bombers/660940710001/

Index